VOLUME 25   NUMBER 1   2019

GLQ at Twenty-Five

JENNIFER DEVERE BRODY AND MARCIA OCHOA

Introduction: On the Twenty-Fifth Anniversary of *GLQ*

1

CAROLYN DINSHAW

Afterlives

5

DAVID M. HALPERIN

The Fulfilled and Unfulfilled Promises of *GLQ*

7

ALLEN DURGIN

Baby with the Bathwater:
The Queer Performativity of Eve Kosofsky Sedgwick

11

RACHEL WALERSTEIN

On Enduring Eve Sedgwick

17

GABBY BENAVENTE AND JULIAN GILL-PETERSON

The Promise of Trans Critique:
Susan Stryker's Queer Theory

23

MARY ZABORSKIS

Eve Sedgwick's Queer Children

29

HEATHER LOVE

Beginning with *Stigma*

33

SUSAN STRYKER

More Words about "My Words to Victor Frankenstein"

39

V VARUN CHAUDHRY

Centering the "Evil Twin":
Rethinking Transgender in Queer Theory

45

KAREN TONGSON AND SCOTT HERRING

The Sexual Imaginarium: A Reappraisal

51

RACHEL CORBMAN

Does Queer Studies Have
an Anti-Empiricism Problem?

57

RICHARD T. RODRÍGUEZ

Undead White

63

JOHN PETRUS

Discussing the Undiscussable:

Reflecting on the "End" of AIDS

67

SALVADOR VIDAL-ORTIZ

"Borders Are Both Real and Imagined": Rejoicing on

Lionel Cantú's *"De Ambiente*: Queer Tourism and the

Shifting Boundaries of Mexican Male Sexualities"

73

JOHN S. GARRISON

On Friendship

79

ANDY CAMPBELL

Still Working: On Richard Meyer and David Román's

Art Works, Parts 1 & 2

85

ELIZABETH FREEMAN

The Queer Temporalities of *Queer Temporalities*

91

WHITNEY MONAGHAN

On Time

97

CHASE GREGORY

Critics on Critics: Queer Bonds

101

JAFARI SINCLAIRE ALLEN AND OMISE'EKE NATASHA TINSLEY

After the Love: Remembering *Black/Queer/Diaspora*

107

DANA LUCIANO AND MEL Y. CHEN

Queer Inhumanisms

113

STEPHANIE ANNE SHELTON

The Influence of Barad's "Transmaterialities"
on Queer Theories and Methodologies

119

RAGINI THAROOR SRINIVASAN

Possible Impossibles between Area and Queer

125

OLIVER COATES

Collateral Damage: Warfare, Death, and Queer Theory
in the Global South

131

GLQ Forum / Twenty Years of Punks

NIC JOHN RAMOS

Introduction

137

CATHY COHEN

The Radical Potential of Queer? Twenty Years Later

140

CHRISTINA B. HANHARDT

The Radical Potential of Queer Political History?

145

CHANDAN REDDY

Neoliberalism Then and Now:
Race, Sexuality, and the Black Radical Tradition

150

L. H. STALLINGS

Cathy Cohen: The Quiet Storm Scholar
That Queer Theory Needed

156

C. RILEY SNORTON

The Temporality of Radical Potential?

159

MARLON M. BAILEY

Black Gay Sex, Homosex-normativity, and Cathy
Cohen's Queer of Color Theory of Cultural Politics

162

JIH-FEI CHENG

AIDS, Black Feminisms, and the Institutionalization
of Queer Politics

169

SARAH HALEY

The Radical Potential of Black Feminist Evaluation

178

NAYAN SHAH

Putting One's Body on the Line

183

ELLIOTT H. POWELL

Coalitional Auralities: Notes on a Soundtrack to Punks,
Bulldaggers, and Welfare Queens

188

Books in Brief

ERIN GRAY

Blackinesis

195

COLE RIZKI

Hemispheric Translations

199

MERIDITH KRUSE

Realizing a Different Lacan?

202

DAVID S. BYERS

A Queer Ethic of Conflict and the Challenge
of Friendship

205

About the Contributors

209

INTRODUCTION

On the Twenty-Fifth Anniversary of *GLQ*

Jennifer DeVere Brody and Marcia Ochoa

*A*t twenty-five years, most marriages are dying a slow death, if they have made it that long. Luckily for us (and you, Dear Reader), gay marriage was not legal when this journal was founded: indeed, *GLQ* began promiscuously and without fidelity to any discipline. In doing so, it charted perverse intellectual paths, marrying no one. *GLQ* was created in a heady moment fostered through the queer love and friendship of our fierce founding editors, Carolyn Dinshaw and David Halperin.

In their first editorial, Carolyn and David proclaimed it was "time for a new journal" (Dinshaw and Halperin 1993: iv). Even then, they voiced concerns about lesbian and gay studies "losing its edge and narrowing its desires" with the institutionalization that founding a journal signifies (ibid.). Certainly, formalization has meant that queer studies has not necessarily kept up with the pace of queer desire, queer media, and cultural production, or the changing dynamics of queer and trans lifeworlds. We know that there is no purely queer space, yet we seek survival in queer forms. In the pages of this special issue we see artful critical research inspired by these aesthetics, unbound by the intervening interests of multiple spheres.

Even now, at twenty-five, *GLQ* is just getting started.

Although we have faced marginalization as a field and institutionalization in the "academic-industrial complex," things here are not settled: we seem always to be vacillating between possibility and precarity. What we call queer theory, or "lesbian and gay studies" (to quote our increasingly problematic subtitle), has changed over time as a result of the radical essays produced in our pages. We have transformed from an emergent field defining its contours through the exposition of lesbian and gay subjects into an interdisciplinary area of critique that seeks to produce epistemological and ontological interventions. The constitutive "outside"— once signified by trans studies, disability studies, and queer of color critique—has

GLQ 25:1
DOI 10.1215/10642684-7275152
© 2019 by Duke University Press

been incorporated into the journal's pages. Meanwhile, there's always a hot new thing hanging outside the club.

David, Carolyn, and our dedicated editors throughout the years have envisioned a future for gay, lesbian, and queer studies that may not have come to be. This is the familiar heartbreak of things as we imagine them rubbing up against what is possible. This desire to harness radical potential may be voiced best by Susan Stryker in her 2004 essay "Transgender Studies: Queer Theory's Evil Twin," in which she writes: "The queer vision that animated my life, and the lives of so many others in the brief historical moment of the early 1990s, held out the dazzling prospect of a compensatory, utopian reconfiguration of community. It seemed an anti-oedipal ecstatic leap into a postmodern space of possibility in which the foundational containers of desire could be ruptured to release a raw erotic power that could be harnessed to a radical social agenda. That vision still takes my breath away" (213).

Unfulfilled promise notwithstanding, we are still here, still queer, mediating conversations that could not be imagined in 1993. And so, in anticipation of this unimagined moment, we put out a broad call for submissions from our former editors, editorial board, subeditors, readers, and other constituents. Our call read:

> On the occasion of the 25th anniversary of the journal, we wish to commemorate the impact of *GLQ* on the field of queer theory. This anniversary issue will reconsider key works from the journal that have resonated in their moment and beyond.
>
> We solicit short thought-pieces . . . on an article or special issue published by *GLQ* that has shaped the field of queer theory. These mini-essays should discuss the significance of the essay or issue in question. We encourage creative engagements with those works that have been most important to our readers. This call is open to all readers of *GLQ*, and we welcome your responses both individually and collectively. Finally, we hope that this process will recognize those contributions to the journal that have both sparked debate and transformed the field.

We were lucky to have received a good number of responses, many of which are published here. And we hope that the many more folks we missed in this issue will participate in future conversations (online, at conferences, and beyond) that focus on the role that the journal has played in our intellectual lives. In this issue are detailed readings of and responses to many of the essays and special issues that have moved us as a field. We are pleased to publish a collection of presentations that focus on the twentieth anniversary of one of our most cited articles, Cathy Cohen's landmark 1997 essay, "Punks, Bulldaggers, and Welfare Queens: The Radical Potential of Queer Politics?" We thank Nic John Ramos and all the participants in a number of forums for their contributions to this issue.

Another focus of submissions was the emergence of transgender studies, and *GLQ*'s sometimes fraught relationship to this field. In particular, we wanted to reflect the deep respect for Stryker's work that stood out in the submissions, both for her key essays that have appeared in this journal and for her work in establishing transgender studies and its journal of record, *Transgender Studies Quarterly*.

We received many submissions reflecting on the special issues we have published over the years, from "The Work of Friendship: In Memoriam Alan Bray" to "Black/Queer/Diasporas" to "Queer Inhumanisms." Two figures we lost too soon loomed large in the submissions: Eve Kosofsky Sedgwick and José Muñoz. Since 1993, we have lost many more, and we acknowledge those who were not able to witness or participate more in the flourishing of this field. Many people, touchstone ideas, and special issues are missing from this extended forum. Thus, what appears here is not in the least bit definitive; still, we hope that it is generative and gives a sense of some key concepts, contributors, and contours of the field.

The special issue begins with short reflections from Dinshaw and Halperin; from there, we set out contributions in loose chronological order, starting with the first issue. We clustered essays on works or topics that made sense to go together, and we dedicated the last third of the table of contents to special issues. All in all, we have forty-one scholars contributing thirty-six short essays. As an aggregate, the authors showcase the too-numerous-to-name shifts in the field. Nevertheless, one can chart changes in the authors over the years the journal has been in play.

The field's diversity is reflected even by the fact that we are the first queer women of color team responsible for editing *GLQ*. Notably, we also reside on the West Coast, far from the journal's formative years centered in NYC and the East Coast corridor. Our vision for the journal includes using a diversity of languages, an attention to different artistic forms and formats (poetry, film, dance, performance, exhibition), and ultimately a greater inclusivity for underrepresented voices.

In her contribution to this special anniversary issue, Dinshaw uses the word *generativity* to characterize *GLQ*. This term, unlike *generation*, which suggests procreation and propagation, instead suggests activity, queer world-making . . . and most of all, what we see as its cognate: generosity. As Margo Crawford (2017) reminds us, anticipation holds the idea of the future. It is with all these active terms in mind that we anticipate your pleasure. *Bienvenidas/os/x a GLQ 25.1.* We hope it tickles your fancy . . . or as Janelle Monáe would say, your PYNK.

References

Cohen, Cathy J. 1997. "Punks, Bulldaggers, and Welfare Queens: The Radical Potential of Queer Politics?" *GLQ* 3, no. 4: 437–65.

Crawford, Margo. 2017. *Black Post-Blackness: The Black Arts Movement and Twenty-First Century Aesthetics.* Urbana: University of Illinois Press.

Dinshaw, Carolyn, and David M. Halperin. 1993. "From the Editors." *GLQ* 1, no. 1: iii–iv.

Stryker, Susan. 2004. "Transgender Studies: Queer Theory's Evil Twin." *GLQ* 10, no. 2: 212–15.

AFTERLIVES

Carolyn Dinshaw, Founding Editor, *GLQ*

$\mathcal{A}$s *GLQ* turns twenty-five, I rummage through my mental archive of editing the journal and come across The *GLQ* Archive itself. This was a feature David Halperin and I created to highlight research on unknown primary materials, promote the extension of queer studies' archive, and make obscure materials available to a new readership. The classicist and the medievalist were eager to include in *GLQ* materials from the distant past in particular, to extend the growing field's emphasis on modern and contemporary materials. This was before the "archival turn" in queer studies, instantiated by works that expand the very concept of the archive (like Ann Cvetkovich's *An Archive of Feelings*); I guess you could say we were preparing for that moment.

One of the first items in the Archive appeared in volume 1, number 4 (1995), a special issue on premodern sexualities in Europe, guest-edited by L. O. Aranye Fradenburg Joy (then Louise O. Fradenburg) and Carla Freccero. It was a fascinating short piece from late medieval England, a unique deposition in Latin from a municipal court edited, translated, and annotated by David Lorenzo Boyd and Ruth Mazo Karras. The name of the piece alone tells a story of time past: "The Interrogation of a Male Transvestite Prostitute in Fourteenth-Century London." Not only the medieval past, but also the early days of queer studies: even as, in 1995, we were incessantly worrying about terminology (*sodomite* and *homosexual*, for example, and *queer* above all), some terms we still didn't question; now *transvestite* and *prostitute* are routinely critiqued as pathologizing and criminalizing, and we can't take for granted a solid, identifiable place—in a binary anatomical scheme—that *male* assumes. Karras (with a coauthor, Tom Linkinen) has recently looked back and reevaluated that early analysis and some of its terms, arguing that *transgender*—or *transgender-like*—is more apt for the subject of the deposition, John Rykener, who goes by the name Eleanor, "having been detected in women's clothing" (Boyd and Karras 1995: 462; Karras and Linkinen 2016).

GLQ 25:1
DOI 10.1215/10642684-7275166
© 2019 by Duke University Press

Back in 1995 we had no idea that the document would be so widely discussed, that less than twenty years later two medieval historians would refer to Rykener as "medieval London's most famous cross-dresser"! Karras and Boyd went on immediately to publish an article with their English translation in a volume Fradenburg and Freccero expanded out of their *GLQ* special issue. But what really allowed dissemination was the Internet (not publicly accessible when we started the journal): an image of the actual document—which was recorded on a parchment roll—along with a fresh translation into English were put up on the web, which has made Rykener's story available globally. In scholarly publications as well as popular forms, in a historical novel and "medieval noir" genre fiction, in a puppet show, in a "dance/theater attraction" staged by a former Cockette, it has been taken up as a gay story, a queer story, a trans story.

Indeed, what interests me most about this archival document's afterlife is the way it limns a contested intellectual-political-aesthetic terrain that includes identity-oriented sexuality (Rykener is depicted as gay in works like *The Demon's Parchment*, by Jeri Westerson), queerness (Rykener is a figure of undefinable desire, as in my own *Getting Medieval*), and transness (Rykener is a character whose gender shifts and changes, as in Bruce Holsinger's *A Burnable Book*). This range of analyses, interpretations, and appropriations is exactly what we could have wished for at *GLQ* in 1995. It's temporally extensive and imaginative; it's interdisciplinary; it shows the journal's uptake outside the confines of scholarly discourse. Most strikingly, to my mind, this range of responses demonstrates the limitations or liabilities of queer analysis: it shows in particular the need for more precision and suppleness regarding gender and embodiment. This document in The *GLQ* Archive is contested, riddled with holes, still up for grabs. For *GLQ* to have provided material such as this for new theories, counterarguments, and pushback is one of the best indexes of its generativity. May *GLQ* continue in its next quarter century to open up space for productive contestation.

References

Boyd, David Lorenzo, and Ruth Mazo Karras. 1995. "The Interrogation of a Male Transvestite Prostitute in Fourteenth-Century London." *GLQ* 1, no. 4: 459–65.

Karras, Ruth Mazo, and Tom Linkinen. 2016. "John/Eleanor Rykener Revisited." In *Founding Feminisms in Medieval Studies: Essays in Honor of E. Jane Burns*, edited by Laine E. Doggett and Daniel E. O'Sullivan, 111–21. Cambridge: D. S. Brewer.

THE FULFILLED AND UNFULFILLED PROMISES OF *GLQ*

David M. Halperin

*L*ike every good idea I have ever had, the idea of founding *GLQ* did not originate with me. It was proposed to me early in 1991 by Philip Rappaport, who was
working at the time as an acquisitions editor at Gordon and Breach and who was
looking for ways to make his job more interesting—specifically by taking account
of emerging work in lesbian and gay studies. Philip approached me about the possibility of starting an academic journal, and although I thought it was a terrific
idea, I didn't feel that I could take on such an ambitious project. But I did mention
Philip's proposal, some time later, to Carolyn Dinshaw, whom I had recently met,
and she expressed immediate enthusiasm for it. I told her that if she would be willing to do it with me, I would gladly agree to it. She accepted. I got back in touch
with Philip. The rest is history.

   Carolyn and I worked together intimately on *GLQ* for another fifteen years.
We had similar instincts and values, and we tended to take the same view of many
things. We also shared a number of fantasies, some of them more realistic than
others, about what a scholarly journal should be as well as what a queer journal
should be. At the same time, Carolyn had very strong feelings and highly original
perceptions about a number of matters—aesthetic, critical, political—to which
I often deferred. In what follows, I want to emphasize that I intend to speak only
for myself, not for Carolyn (whom I have not consulted about this statement), even
though I will be speaking about an undertaking on which she and I collaborated
and about the product of our joint efforts.

   LGBTQ studies did not come about because universities felt the lack of
such a field and set out to cultivate it. It came about because participants in various insurgent social movements had produced brilliant new research in the subject
area and because a number of academics, tenured on other grounds, decided to join

GLQ 25:1
DOI 10.1215/10642684-7275180
© 2019 by Duke University Press

in, and universities were powerless to stop them. At the same time, the most important and innovative work in queer studies that was being carried out when *GLQ* was founded did not derive from senior scholars, with some exceptions, but from graduate students and a few assistant professors. These were the people—most of them ABD or untenured at the time, most of them legendary now—who composed the original Editorial Board, the core of *GLQ*, which went on to surround them, for protection, with an Advisory Board of established, prominent figures who vouched for the journal's legitimacy and provided it with authoritative referees.

GLQ undertook a deliberate balancing act, weighing the scandal of queerness against the need for academic legitimation. The editorial statement in the first issue, still worth reading, was forthright and explicit: "We make no bones about the fact that with this journal we seek a broader, wider niche for lesbian and gay studies in the academy and in cultural life. Such institutional and cultural acknowledgment brings money, curricular space, and jobs, and such support increases our capacity to do new work. At the same time, and as everyone is aware, with growing institutional recognition, lesbian and gay studies runs the risk of losing its edge and narrowing its desires. *GLQ* locates itself in this tension, seeks to play it out."

GLQ's great ambition was to walk that line between institution and revolution. Recently tenured and promoted to full professor, I wanted to use the security that the academy had, wisely or not, given me to advance scholarly and political goals that it had never bargained for. In particular, I wanted to promote the work of more talented, emerging scholars, to give them a platform and to enhance their authority, and to put them in a position to rise in the profession (which is not to say that everyone always appreciated the experience of being edited by me). At the same time, I wanted to prevent queer studies from becoming an academic discipline. Part of the struggle of *GLQ*—at a time before queer theory had had the effect of reconsolidating the boundaries between the disciplines—was to maintain and to defend the interdisciplinary design of the field, combining (on the model of women's studies) the full range of the humanities and social sciences, art and law, activism and critique, formal and informal writing, primary source material and commentary. Part of the struggle was also to de-discipline queer studies, to impede it from settling comfortably into academic business as usual with its canons, its hierarchies, and its tedium, its inability to startle, surprise, upset, or transform.

GLQ's editorial policy was driven by some such notion of permanent revolution. It was intended to keep the field constantly off-balance; to promote whatever topics seemed to be neglected or excluded; to refuse work that was located in a single discipline or that simply engaged with some influential article published the previous year that everyone was talking about; to feature traditional scholarship in arcane subject areas alongside edgy experiments in critical theory; and to represent queer research and politics from outside North America and Western Europe (Carolyn and I briefly considered the possibility of publishing work composed in languages other than English). *GLQ* pursued the kinds of diversity that exceeded the usual definitions of diversity (not that it was indifferent to the usual kinds: white gay men, for example, constituted a mere fifth of its original Editorial Board)—namely, diversity of discipline, of methodology, of gendered subjectivity, of historical period, aesthetic form, scholarly archive, geographic and institutional location, personal voice, political attitude, linguistic source material, and national context. An abiding goal, clearly stated in the opening editorial, was to preserve the relation of lesbian and gay studies to sex, specifically to queer sex—interracial sex, intergenerational sex, sex expressive of female, trans, crip, and various nonstandard subjectivities.

In 1991, when Philip Rappaport approached me about starting a journal, a year after Teresa de Lauretis's landmark conference "Queer Theory" (which I attended) at the University of California, Santa Cruz, new work in lesbian and gay studies did not have anywhere obvious to go. The *Journal of Homosexuality* was already an established and respected institution, but it was oriented—though not at all exclusively—to the hard social sciences, and it did not seem an immediate venue of choice for new work in theory and criticism or for scholarship in the humanities. New queer work was appearing in *Representations*, *Screen*, *Yale Journal of Criticism*, *Qui Parle*, *Raritan*, *diacritics*, *Textual Practice*, *differences*, and of course *Signs* as well as in more specialist journals. But it did not always have an easy time getting in. A friend of mine had recently told me, whether truthfully or not I can't say, that he had just submitted an article to a new hotshot feminist publication and got a letter back saying, "Your essay is too homosexual for our journal." By the time *GLQ* began publishing in 1993, queer work was in vogue and every journal wanted it. So *GLQ* could not pick and choose among the available offerings and determine its own content at will. It was limited from the start in what it could achieve.

It will be obvious now, as it was abundantly obvious to Carolyn and me at the time, that the *GLQ* we created was unable to realize all its ambitions. It may be that some of them were impossible, or misplaced, or unwise; in retrospect, some of the aspirations for the journal and the field outlined here may look old-fashioned, out of date, or incomplete. But I have not given them up. I'm aware that my time has passed: *GLQ* has moved on, as it should and as it must. Still, if I were to find myself leading the editorial team of *GLQ* today, I would do everything I could to realize the values and the ideals I nurtured for the journal when Carolyn Dinshaw and I founded it.

BABY WITH THE BATHWATER

The Queer Performativity of Eve Kosofsky Sedgwick

Allen Durgin

"Queer Performativity: Henry James's The Art of the Novel,"
by Eve Kosofsky Sedgwick. GLQ 1.1 (1993).

$\mathscr{I}$n 2003, I abandoned my first love, acting in New York's downtown queer theater scene, to study queer performativity at the Graduate Center, City University
of New York, with Eve Kosofsky Sedgwick. Arriving on Sedgwick's doorstep a
howling beast, another drama queen depending on the kindness of strangers, I
eventually became one of Eve's people, the beneficiary of her depressive habit of
"scattering sequins over" all those she loved (Sedgwick 1999: 108). In her presence, I felt "glamorous and numinous" (ibid.). Versed in medical TV shows (a side
effect of suffering the long emergencies of AIDS and breast cancer), she said that I
reminded her of George Clooney from his *ER* days.

The appearance of Sedgwick's "Queer Performativity: Henry James's *The
Art of the Novel*" in *GLQ*'s debut issue was momentous. As David Halperin and
Valerie Traub (2009: 7) have noted, it "proved to be widely influential as well
as highly controversial. She succeeded in putting shame on the agenda of queer
studies throughout the latter half of the 1990s without, however, securing for that
notion any generally acknowledged solidity, clarity, or coherence." Sedgwick herself kept revisiting and republishing the essay, in various parts and guises, as late
as 2003. But unlike critics who tended to excise James from her sexy neologism,
queer performativity—when Halperin gently mocks the essay title as "unpromising" (ibid.: 42), he's undoubtedly targeting its subtitle—in her ten years of revising
the essay, Sedgwick never did. Looking back now at the essay's first incarnation in
GLQ, what I find most instructive, most tonic, most full of unexplored possibility
is Sedgwick's (1993b: 3) "visceral near-identification with the writing [she] cared

GLQ 25:1
DOI 10.1215/10642684-7275194
© 2019 by Duke University Press

for, at the level of sentence structure, metrical pattern, rhyme"—namely, that of Henry James.

Her take on James spotlighted not his closeted sexuality but the explicit queerness of his writing style. Sedgwick (1993a: 11) explains in the *GLQ* essay, "When I attempt to do some justice to the specificity, the richness, above all the explicitness of James's particular erotics, it is not with an eye to making him an exemplar of 'homosexuality' or even of one 'kind' of 'homosexuality,' though I certainly don't want, either, to make him sound as if he *isn't* gay." Sedgwick turns to James's *writing* for its "*queerness*, or queer performativity." What Sedgwick is looking for is "a strategy for the production of meaning and being, in relation to the affect shame and to the later and related fact of stigma" (ibid.). She returns to the writing of "dead white men" not to rescue James from himself but to rescue Sedgwick, the writer, from herself. She wants "to appropriate what seemed [his] numinous and resistant power" (Sedgwick 1993b: 3) and finds that numinous power, not in the "closeted" James of "The Beast in the Jungle" or the *fisting-as*-écriture James of *The Wings of the Dove*, but in the "unpromising" James of the prefaces.

James composed the prefaces to the New York Edition (a collection of his revised earlier works) "at the end of a relatively blissful period of literary production ('the major phase')" (Sedgwick 1993a: 6). It does not escape Sedgwick that this blissful period was "poised, however, between two devastating bouts of melancholia. . . . The first of these scouring depressions was precipitated in 1895 by what James experienced as the obliterative failure of his ambitions as a playwright, being howled off the stage at the premiere of *Guy Domville*" (ibid.). In near-identification with his writing, Sedgwick writes her *GLQ* essay on his writing at the end of an incredibly productive period in her own writing—one that witnesses the birth of *Between Men* and *Epistemology of the Closet*, not to mention queer theory. And like James, this "major phase" in Sedgwick's oeuvre sits poised between two bouts of depression. The first of her own scouring depressions occurred when she found herself nearly howled out of grad school for failing her orals, an obliterative failure she experienced as the "violent hemorrhage / of the stuff of self" (Sedgwick 1999: 64).

Sedgwick's close engagement with James's prefaces promises to stanch the bleeding. According to Sedgwick (1993a: 6–7), "When we read *The Art of the Novel* . . . we read a text that is in the most active imaginable relation to shame." What impresses Sedgwick is that James neither fully repudiates his past failures nor fully recuperates them: "The speaking self of the Prefaces does not attempt to merge with the potentially shaming or shamed figurations of its younger self, younger fictions, younger heroes; its attempt is to love them. That love is shown to occur both in spite of shame and, more remarkably, through it" (ibid.: 8). James's visceral near-identification with his younger self and what he considers his juvenilia—those small but perceptible gaps between his unmerged and unrepudiated selves—is what gives him enough internal space to cast sequins over them, enough space to think and write. In scattering her own sequins, Eve would later rescue her graduate students from the "mild interest and profound depression" (Sedgwick, Barber, and Clark 2002: 243) that had plagued her dissertation writing.

The second of Sedgwick's (1999: 65) major depressions was precipitated not by a violent hemorrhaging of self but by an excruciating blockage: "Poetry both my first love, I guess, and first self—always with the most excruciating blockages—gone now for years. . . . I don't know if it was depression that drove this muse away or if it was the long rocky strand of her loss that made depression." While Sedgwick's poetic muse abandons her during her eventual rise onto the academic stage, it was during those "chilling" (Sedgwick, Barber, and Clark 2002: 244) doctoral years, between 1971 and 1975, that she found early recognition as a poet. But the intervening years between her poetry prizes and later academic accolades would witness a series of failed recognitions reminiscent of James's "terminal failure to evoke any recognition from any readership" for his New York Edition (Sedgwick 1993a: 6). Unable to find a publisher for her collected work, *Traceable, Salient, Thirsty: Poems, 1973–1977*, despite many revisions and submissions over several years, Sedgwick ultimately abandoned the project (H. A. Sedgwick 2011: 453).

But the source of Sedgwick's most enduring shame was the abandonment of *The Warm Decembers*, "[her] problem child, a half-written novel-length narrative poem with a Victorian setting, and . . . *its* problem child, its heroine Beatrix. . . . the nude child seen by coal-light in the cold bath" (Sedgwick 1993b: 178). Begun in 1978, "*The Warm Decembers* was less than half its intended length when, between 1984 and 1986, [Sedgwick] stopped being able to write it" (Sedgwick 1994: 153). As if in response to her essay "A Poem Is Being Written," "it took [her] three or four more years of punishing incredulity to understand that this poem was not being written. In fact, it was nine years from the time [she] left Beatrix in the bath before [she] seemed to be able to write poetry of any kind" (ibid.: 159). During those nine years, too many of the friends she'd scattered sequins over died of AIDS, the activist Michael Lynch and the writer Gary Fisher among them. In 1991 she received a fatal diagnosis of her own and underwent chemotherapy. Sedgwick plunged into deep depression. It is in this moment she writes "Queer Performativity: Henry James's *The Art of the Novel*." The essay is borne of loss, failure, and sickness. So when we read her essay, we read a text that is in the most active imaginable relation to shame.

Three weeks before she died, Eve called me because she was worried about how I was doing. Eve always worried about those she would leave behind: "I have an intense wish to be assured that the people and communities I'm leaving behind can take care of themselves—that they don't need 'me,' my thought, my labor of regenerating a first person to keep them going" (Sedgwick, Barber, and Clark 2002: 250). When she died, I felt ashamed. I'd run from my failed acting career into her arms, and she'd made academe feel like a warm embrace. But Eve left me with my hand raised, questions unanswered. Without her, I too struggled to complete my dissertation. It took me three or four more years of punishing incredulity after her death to understand that my dissertation was not being written. One by one, the sequins fell.

Speaking of her abandoned child *The Warm Decembers*, Sedgwick (1994: 159) claimed that "the 1984 line 'I see it in the body of Beatrix in the bath,' in the middle of ch. 8, was the last one destined to have been written out of a relatively seamless sense of the integrity and momentum of this writing process." Fitting, then, that the longest passage from the prefaces that Sedgwick quotes is an elaborate set piece in which James figures his revision process as tending to a child in the bath. As Sedgwick (1993a: 10) writes, "In the place where the eye of parental care had threatened to be withheld, there is now a bath where even the nurse's attention is supplemented by the overhearing ear of inquiring and interested visitors." Sedgwick learns from James how to hold her problem child in a different light—not the stark Dickensian cast of deprivation and abjection but the warm chiaroscuro of blushing imperfection. That warm light is what will allow her a year later to publish her first book of poems, including *The Warm Decembers*.

In her essay "The 1001 Seances" (first written in 1976, but published posthumously in 2011 in a special section of *GLQ* dedicated to her), Sedgwick recounts how James Merrill's poem "The Book of Ephraim" is haunted by "the absent presence" of not only the summoned spirit Ephraim but also Merrill's lost novel, "literally lost," Sedgwick (2011: 460) tells us, "in a taxi." A year after Eve died, I lost my dissertation, my laptop left with all my research and writing on a Bronx-bound D train. When I told a friend what happened, he quipped, "It could have been worse; it could have been your baby."

Merrill never recovers his baby; instead, Sedgwick (2011: 461) observes, "the novel has been removed entirely and the poem put in its place. And within the poem, the lost novel has recurred, this time in reported fragments." Sedgwick wanted to be in more interesting relation to past losses—neither repudiate them nor merge with them. I realize now that Sedgwick wrote that *GLQ* essay on James's *The Art of the Novel* for those of us left behind as we struggle to stay interested in this world and write. Close reading Sedgwick's essay has been my way of scattering sequins over Eve, not because she needs me to, but because I do, to rescue myself through near-identification with her work. Only through such visceral near-identification with the writing we care for can we hold and be held by the dead.

References

Halperin, David M., and Valerie Traub, eds. 2009. *Gay Shame*. Chicago: University of Chicago Press.

Sedgwick, Eve Kosofsky. 1993a. "Queer Performativity: Henry James's *The Art of the Novel*." *GLQ* 1, no. 1: 1–15.

———. 1993b. *Tendencies*. Durham, NC: Duke University Press.

———. 1994. *Fat Art, Thin Art*. Durham, NC: Duke University Press.

———. 1999. *A Dialogue on Love*. Boston: Beacon.

———. 2011. "The 1001 Seances." *GLQ* 17, no. 4: 457–81.

Sedgwick, Eve Kosofsky, Stephen M. Barber, and David L. Clark. 2002. "This Piercing Bouquet: An Interview with Eve Kosofsky Sedgwick." In *Regarding Sedgwick: Essays on Queer Culture and Critical Theory*, edited by Stephen M. Barber and David L. Clark, 243–62. New York: Routledge.

Sedgwick, H. A. 2011. "A Note on 'The 1001 Seances.'" *GLQ* 17, no. 4: 451–55.

ON ENDURING EVE SEDGWICK

Rachel Walerstein

"Queer Performativity: Henry James's The Art of the Novel,"
by Eve Kosofsky Sedgwick. GLQ 1.1 (1993).

The first time I encountered the work of Eve Kosofsky Sedgwick, I was reading Silvan Tomkins for my honor's thesis. The text was Sedgwick and Adam Frank's impressive condensation of Tomkins's four volumes into one: *Shame and Its Sisters*. I felt many affects in this first read-through: despair (How do I write my thesis, let alone apply to graduate school, which I was also trying to do); interest (I intended to cruise it, hoping to get the lay of the critical landscape); and shame (I didn't understand the opening essay; how could I possibly enter a conversation whose terms were beyond my reach?). To read *Shame and Its Sisters* felt, and still feels, collaborative, and not just because Tomkins's own writing, they note, "excited and calmed, inspired and contented" while "listing the possible" and "embrac[ing] multiple overlapping voices" even as those voices threaten to take over (Sedgwick and Frank 1995: 2–3). But, because one cannot ignore while reading the presence of Sedgwick and Frank as the caretakers of the ideas therein, my first encounter with Sedgwick as a scholar was as someone who carefully crafted the story to be told, who inspired and contented while asking the reader to endure the terrifying until their fear response was "burned out."

The next time I read Sedgwick's work was during revisions for an article on a portion of my thesis. My interest in shame had brought me back around again to her work in *Touching Feeling*. A friend had directed my attention to the text, which had the same effect on me as her other work that I had by then engaged: illuminating yet simultaneously mystifying. The essays found there are themselves important interventions in the fields of queer theory and affect studies. Sedgwick's trenchant critique of suspicious reading practices in "Paranoid Reading and Reparative Reading, or, You're So Paranoid, You Probably Think This Essay Is

GLQ 25:1
DOI 10.1215/10642684-7275208
© 2019 by Duke University Press

about You" has, on its own, transformed the way scholars of all stripes think about criticism and its functions. Similarly, the version of "Shame, Theatricality, and Queer Performativity" included there resonates across literary studies and studies of sexuality. *Touching Feeling* remains a cornerstone of my own work as well; every return encompasses those same, early feelings of despair (Do I actually understand this book?); interest (I never thought of "x" that way before . . .); and shame (My poor mimicry of Sedgwick has revealed me as an imposter). Yet again and again I find myself brought back into the neighborhood of Sedgwick's core ideas.

Recently, I returned to Sedgwick because my adviser told me to take all the hard copies he had of *GLQ* to my office. Having never read a hard copy of the journal, I didn't know that both Sedgwick and Judith Butler opened the inaugural issue with their respective takes on the work done by the term *queer*. But what impressed me even more than my lack of historical knowledge was the way in which Sedgwick's ideas not only endure but in that enduring perform the very concepts they seek to unpack. Indeed, her endurance seems to stem from the way in which her writing plays out the tension between the figurative and the lived, formally taking up the challenge of performing in the "structural position," as Lee Edelman (2004: 24) writes, of queerness as an "imperative of figuration." Although part of my claim here is, at first glance, that I've (re)read Sedgwick (as one does), my other claim is that her essay "Queer Performativity: Henry James's *The Art of the Novel*" is significant not just for the theory of shame it puts forward but for the way in which Sedgwick's careful crafting of the piece makes it possible for scholars of sex and sexuality to revisit the *figure* of the queer in their work.

Take, for example, her central claim in the opening pages about the speech act that J. L. Austin leaves out of his discussion. "'Shame on you,' she writes, "is performatively efficacious because its grammar—admittedly somewhat enigmatic—*is* a transformational grammar: both at the level of pronoun positioning . . . and at the level of the relational grammar of the affect shame itself" (Sedgwick 1993: 4). In this description, shame becomes a structural position as well as a structuring one; to paraphrase Pierre Bourdieu (1977: 72), shame functions as a kind of habit between a you and an us whose "durable, transposable dispositions" are precisely what enable shame to shift the subject between introversion and extroversion. Or, to quote Sedgwick (1993: 6) again, "Shame is the affect that mantles the threshold between introversion and extroversion, between absorption and theatricality, between performativity and—performativity." As a principle of estrangement, then, shame, Sedgwick (2003: 37) elaborates in the later essay, "is the place where the *question* of identity arises most originarily and most relationally." This question raised by shame is precisely why I continue to return to her essay—both the early and late versions. Not because she asserts that such is the case, but because the question of identity emerges as a question of *style* in the "intergenerational flirtation" staged between the versions of the piece every time I (re)turn to them.

To describe the construction of identity as a matter of style does indeed seem to be what Sedgwick's (1993: 11) definition of queer performativity posits when she writes that it is "the name of a strategy *for the production of meaning* and being, in relation to the affect shame and to the later and related fact of stigma" (emphasis added). In many ways, her definition of queer performativity here is not only contemporaneous with the description of lesbian and gay studies by *The Lesbian and Gay Studies Reader* but nearly the same. As the introduction explains: "Lesbian and Gay studies attempts to *decipher* the sexual meanings *inscribed* in many different forms of cultural expression while also attempting to decipher the cultural meanings inscribed in the *discourses and practices of sex*" (Abelove, Barale, and Halperin 1993: xvi; emphasis added). On the one hand, the terms emphasized here highlight a focus on the discourses producing and disseminating a meaning (or *the* meaning for particular historical moments) of sex, elucidating the task of lesbian and gay studies as the investigation of bodies as they act on and react to those technologies aimed at delimiting the possible meanings of sex and sexuality. On the other hand, Sedgwick's definition reintroduces the body as messy, inarticulate, but nonetheless communicative. The style of the body is not taken for granted as necessarily volitional or even just as a social construction. Style, in other words, emerges in Sedgwick (1993: 12) as a figural effect, as a consequence of shame precisely because "the structure 'identity,' marked by shame's threshold between sociability and introversion, may be established and naturalized in the first instance *through shame*."

I want to conclude by suggesting that in "Queer Performativity," Sedgwick makes it possible to read queer theory as a genre engaged in the figuration of the queer. Looking beyond the development of Sedgwick's own flavor of writerly style to the question of queer theory as a genre inherently concerned with the style of identity construction, it becomes possible to start thinking about how its formalist concerns, concerns about the form of the queer in literature especially, interact with and inform concerns with the not so formally delimitable. Or, it becomes possible to think about the relationship between the formed and unformed, how the two *in*form each other as they coalesce within or on an object. In her own estimation, shame is equally a heuristic:

> Like other affects, [shame] is not a discrete intrapsychic structure, but a kind of free radical that (in different people and also in different cultures) attaches to and permanently intensifies or alters the meaning of—of almost anything: a zone of the body, a sensory system, a prohibited or indeed a permitted behavior, another affect such as anger or arousal, a named identity, a script for interpreting other people's behavior toward oneself. Thus, one of the things that anyone's character or personality *is*, is a record of the highly individual histories by which the fleeting emotion of shame has instituted far more durable, structural changes in one's relational and interpretive strategies toward both self and others. (ibid.: 12–13)

One's durability is thus more than the circulation of meaning "inscribed in the discourses and practices of sex"; it is an effect of shame's having deformed and reformed, and at times altered completely, the story one has for understanding being in relation to both one's self and others. And it is this dynamic that "Queer Performativity" helped illuminate. At the very moment when the queer is hailed, it is also constituted as such, culled from an eclectic array of sources and presumably pinned down. Such movement is perhaps what Heather Love (2007) aims to describe as the backward turn of feeling out the past. More specifically, such movement may be *the* movement of figuration that scholars such as Tim Dean (2000) and Michael Snediker (2008) name personification (that *figuration* sounds like "figure-eight" when enunciated is rather telling for this point, especially if one turns the figure of the eight on its side, turning the specificity of the numerical into the possibilities of the infinite). And yet, queer theory's conceit is that to pin down the queer is an impossible task; one can only ever approach it, be affected toward queerness but never of it. And as one begins to recognize this fundamental dissatisfaction that queer theory remains ambivalent toward yet narcissistically invested in, so does one begin the difficult process of reconciling the sense that "we" are both social and antisocial, introverted and extroverted. The trick is acknowledging that at the moment we mark ourselves as one or the other, we are engaging in a process of being both. What queer theory does, then, for readers and writers is offer us the option of forgetting we are either *or* both, the option of *knowing otherwise*. To that end, what Sedgwick has helped illuminate regarding queer theory, for me at least, is its interrogation of the duration—in the sense of one's self in time, but also the time-lapse of an emotion or an affective response—of the desire to figure, to be intelligible, to endure.

References

Abelove, Henry, Michèle Aina Barale, and David M. Halperin, eds. 1993. *The Lesbian and Gay Studies Reader.* New York: Routledge.

Bourdieu, Pierre. 1977. *Outline of a Theory of Practice.* Translated by Richard Nice. Cambridge: Cambridge University Press.

Dean, Tim. 2000. *Beyond Sexuality.* Chicago: University of Chicago Press.

Edelman, Lee. 2004. *No Future: Queer Theory and the Death Drive.* Durham, NC: Duke University Press.

Love, Heather. 2007. *Feeling Backward: Loss and the Politics of Queer History.* Cambridge, MA: Harvard University Press.

Sedgwick, Eve Kosofsky. 1993. "Queer Performativity: Henry James's *The Art of the Novel.*" *GLQ* 1, no. 1: 1–16.

———. 2003. *Touching Feeling: Affect, Pedagogy, Performativity.* Durham, NC: Duke University Press.

Sedgwick, Eve Kosofsky, and Adam Frank, eds. 1995. *Shame and Its Sisters: A Silvan Tomkins Reader.* Durham, NC: Duke University Press.

Snediker, Michael D. 2008. *Queer Optimism: Lyric Personhood and Other Felicitous Persuasions.* Minneapolis: University of Minnesota Press.

THE PROMISE OF TRANS CRITIQUE

Susan Stryker's Queer Theory

Gabby Benavente and Julian Gill-Peterson

"Transgender Studies: Queer Theory's Evil Twin,"
by Susan Stryker. GLQ 10.2 (2004).

$\mathcal{I}$n "Transgender Studies: Queer Theory's Evil Twin," part of the 2004 forum "Thinking Sex/Thinking Gender," Susan Stryker reflects on the role of trans studies within queer theory, which involves a return to the beginning of *GLQ*. Stryker's essay "My Words to Victor Frankenstein above the Village Chamounix: Performing Transgender Rage" was published in the third issue of the inaugural volume of this journal, in 1994. Along with "The Transgender Issue" that she edited in 1998, the essay marks the foundational position of Stryker's work, and trans studies, to queer theory. Yet as the evocative subtitle "Queer Theory's Evil Twin" also suggests, Stryker's earlier investments in a queer bent to trans inquiry had not been realized more broadly in the field in 2004.

"My Words to Victor Frankenstein," much like Sandy Stone's pathbreaking piece "The Empire Strikes Back: A Posttranssexual Manifesto" (1987), indexes how trans studies moved into and found a home in academic venues like *GLQ* through an indispensable, political merger of self-knowledge and activism as the engines of theory. Drawn and adapted from a performance that Stryker gave at the "Rage Across the Disciplines" conference in 1993, the essay moves in four parts, from "Monologue" to "Criticism" to "Journal" and, to conclude, "Theory." Across these multiple registers Stryker brings queer and trans studies into close relation through her own self, staging from "Rage Across the Disciplines" into *GLQ* how to "perform a queer gender rather than simply talk about it, thus embodying and enacting the concept simultaneously under discussion" (ibid.: 237).

GLQ 25:1
DOI 10.1215/10642684-7275222
© 2019 by Duke University Press

It is this careful attention to making imaginative and rigorous theoretical and analytic interventions through the material experience of the embodied self that, in 2004, had been neglected by queer theory's uptake of the category transgender. "Most disturbingly," Stryker observes in "Queer Theory's Evil Twin," "'transgender' increasingly functions as the site in which to contain all gender trouble, thereby helping secure both homosexuality and heterosexuality as stable and normative categories of personhood" (214). While the historical, conceptual, and lived relationships between what is conventionally named as "gender" and "sexuality" are many in the "Thinking Sex/Thinking Gender" forum, Stryker underlined a critical way in which trans people in particular had become exceptionalized by a certain strand of queer theory, serving as *figures* for a kind of anti-binary subversion of gender that left sexual subjectivity off the hook for accounting for itself as a default cis category. This abstraction into figuration was, precisely, a turning away from how Stryker had theorized the queerness of gender and transness through the lens of her embodied knowledge and affect.

To be sure, this figurative move is symptomatic of a much broader form of trans abstraction and confinement that spans medical, cultural, and theoretical domains, with disproportionate effects on the representation of trans women and trans women of color—this strand of queer theory is not responsible for inventing it. Emma Heaney (2017: 6) argues that the "assumption that trans women's very existence means something outside itself, something about the gender of a putatively cis general subject," was first an allegorical effect of early twentieth-century sexology, before it was picked up as a motif of modernist literature. Many decades later, Heaney shows in *The New Woman: Literary Modernism, Queer Theory, and the Trans Feminine Allegory*, queer theory's "commitment to semiotic critical methodologies" incurred "the reproduction of the form of trans feminine allegory from its literary foundation," so that the field "installed the trans woman as the proof of the social construction of the gender binary" (14), as Stryker pointed out in 2004. This allegorical form, which Heaney traces out of Judith Butler's early 1990s writing, as well as its version of Michel Foucault's history of sexuality (221–41), "imposes a representational disjuncture between trans self-knowledge and trans meaning" (6), so that queer theory's figure of trans femininity remains abstract in the specific sense of being divorced from long traditions of trans women's situated knowledge of gender, all while still claiming transness as radically subversive of the ontology of gender.

This strand of queer theory is not alone, or necessarily unique, then, in reducing trans people and, especially, women to a figuration that places a question mark over their material being and its power as a so-often erased source of knowledge. But considering the foundational position of Stryker's work in *GLQ* from the early to mid-1990s, her critique in 2004 carries a particular weight that invites follow up. Reading Stryker's piece today, we are struck by how persistent this theoretical figuration of trans people has remained, as Heaney's very recent book explores, even if it is not *the* dominant paradigm of the field around gender and transness. The critique of queer theory's allegorization of trans people as the exceptional locus of gender trouble, with its attendant separation of queer and trans categories, still feels as relevant to us today as it was over a decade ago.

Yet why it feels so cannot be disentangled from a different question about trans studies *outside*, or *alongside*, queer theory. While Stryker notes in 2004 that "transgender studies has taken shape . . . in the shadow of queer theory" (214), that relationship has nothing short of dramatically changed over the past decade and a half, and much of that transformation is indebted to Stryker herself. Transgender studies is negotiating a complex and precarious moment of partial institutionalization, with more stand-alone curriculum, monographs, and conferences than ever before while still being overwhelmingly made up of underemployed, marginalized scholars and trans practitioners who face systematic barriers to entering higher education and the academy, as well as facing a dearth of support, not to mention discrimination, once inside its institutions. In 2014 Stryker, with fellow general editor Paisley Currah (2014: 14) and an editorial board composed of nearly two dozen scholars, launched *Transgender Studies Quarterly*, the first nonmedical, interdisciplinary journal of record for transgender studies. While *GLQ* has been an important venue for trans studies work, and *TSQ* shares a similarity in its title, there is now a dynamic and evolving relationship between these two journals, which do share some convergences in content and contributors yet take quite different thematic and structural forms (*TSQ*, for instance, publishes special issues only). *GLQ* and *TSQ* serve differing ends in supporting the flourishing of queer theory and trans studies, respectively. Reflecting what might amount to a kind of generational shift that extends well beyond these two journals, we write as a junior scholar and graduate student who are both able to claim trans studies as a home field without necessarily needing to first make our home inside queer theory to do so, though we are nonetheless enthusiastically invested in both fields.

Why, then, do we insist on the promise of Stryker's critique *of* queer theory at a moment when its relations with trans studies take so many other forms? Will trans studies someday branch off and declare independence from the situation of 2004, moving from being the "evil twin" to something like a "step-sibling"? We hope not, and we want to stay with Stryker's essay because we are inspired by its connections to a broader tradition, carried by trans women and trans women of color, of calling on queer movements that have left trans people behind, as well as histories of trans resistance that have long reminded queer movements of their trans-exclusionary, trans-antagonistic, and marginalizing outcomes.

Reina Gossett's (2013) vital (and too frequently uncredited) historical recovery work of black trans and trans women of color has preserved Sylvia Rivera's foundational 1973 speech "Y'all Better Quiet Down." Shouting at a crowd of predominantly cis gay and lesbian people gathered at the Christopher Street Parade in New York City, Rivera begins with detailing her experiences in the prison system: "I have been to jail. I have been raped. And beaten. Many times! By men, heterosexual men that do not belong in the homosexual shelter."[1] Rivera's words continue to resonate with the experiences of many trans women subject to dangerous and prejudicial overincarceration today. Rivera expressed righteous anger in 1973 over these experiences, frustrated by a nascent queer rights movement that was building momentum from the activism of black trans and trans women of color but did not actually fight for their lives, particularly in these most violent circumstances. Rivera called out the crowd for throwing trans women under the bus, continuing: "But, do you do anything for me? No. You tell me to go and hide my tail between my legs. I will not put up with this shit. I have been beaten. I have had my nose broken. I have been thrown in jail. I have lost my job. I have lost my apartment for gay liberation and you all treat me this way? What the fuck's wrong with you all? Think about that!" Although many queer theorists, such as Judith Butler (2004: 214), have spoken out on the violence trans people experience, noting that to be trans can lead to "losing one's job, home, the prospects for desire, or for life," queer theory also holds a history of abstracting trans experiences and their material livelihoods to which Rivera's words still speak. Queer theory's history of abstraction, which has also been critiqued from the founding of transgender studies not just by Stryker but in foundational texts by Jay Prosser (1998) and Viviane K. Namaste (2000), cannot and does not exist outside a broader world that treats trans women as objects and, as Rivera experienced while fighting her way on stage to speak, as Others rarely permitted to shape their own stories. More recently, Gayle Salamon (2018) maps in *The Life and Death of Latisha King* how the convergence of transphobia and antiblackness effected a complete erasure of fourteen-year-old Latisha King's transness and blackness in the trial of a classmate for her murder. King was deliberately, violently misread as a gay boy to enable a panic defense and in the course of the trial her voice, not to mention her name and image, was expunged from the public record, leaving anger as much as grief behind for anyone seeking to honor her life.

Despite a dismissive and hostile audience in 1973, Rivera continued to speak out and used anger as a tool to hold her community accountable. In 1973, many of the people assembled at the Christopher Street Parade ignored Rivera and her message, but she did reach out to the most vulnerable within the LGBTQ community, many who subsequently found a home through her activism. Her uses of anger presage many later political interventions, including for Stryker, whose rage in organizing a Transgender Nation action around the American Psychiatric Association's 1993 annual meeting is the central motivation and engine of theorizing in "My Words to Victor Frankenstein" (249). Rivera shows us that utilizing anger as a tool for action is not exclusive to the cis woman of color feminisms of our contemporary moment, but that anger has a home in the long-standing activism of trans women of color. Rivera's anger has also inspired trans people who live at other marginalized intersections to remain vocal in the struggle for collective liberation. We can look more recently, for example, to Jennicet Gutiérrez, who like Rivera was booed by a crowd of largely cis white gay and lesbians after interrupting a speech by President Barack Obama in 2015. Gutiérrez echoes Rivera in a contemporary context, fighting for the liberation of undocumented transgender women in the prison system precisely in the moment that forms of partial trans-normalization and biopolitical incorporation of gay and lesbian lives by the state make their lives more invisible than ever.

We do not mean to abstractly invoke Rivera or Gutiérrez as the "source" or inspiration of trans studies, Stryker, *GLQ*, or ourselves, as that would render them yet again as figures rather than acknowledge the specifically activist location of their critiques. Rather, since trans studies, like queer theory, is marked by a major absence of prominent trans of color women in its most visible ranks and domains (see Ellison et al. 2017), we mean to affirm the utility of rage as a vehicle of critique that takes the specific form of Stryker's commitment to knowledge production directly out of the material, embodied livelihood of trans people. This, we offer, is Stryker's queer theory. The recognition and affirmation of self-knowledge and feeling *as* theory inspires us, as two trans scholars of color, to mobilize rage as a concrete affiliation between queer theory and trans studies that continues to hold immense value for reflexive critique and political knowledge production about race, gender, and sexuality.

Note

1. Gossett recovered the video recording of Rivera's 1973 speech during archival research and made a digital version of it available online on *Vimeo* before it was removed under spurious circumstances by the platform, erasing her labor in making trans women of color's history publicly accessible, as more public attention has turned to Rivera and Marsha P. Johnson in recent years (see Gossett 2013; and Rivera 2013). Copies of the video, rightfully crediting Gossett, have been uploaded on alternative platforms, including *Videoactivism 2.0* (see Tedjiasukmana 2018).

References

Butler, Judith. 2004. *Undoing Gender.* New York: Routledge.

Ellison, Treva, Kai M. Green, Matt Richardson, and C. Riley Snorton. 2017. "We Got Issues: Toward a Black/Trans* Studies." *Transgender Studies Quarterly* 4, no. 2: 162–69.

Gossett, Reina. 2013. "On Untorelli's 'New' Book." Reinagossett.com, March 13. www .reinagossett.com/on-untorellis-new-book/.

Heaney, Emma. 2017. *The New Woman: Literary Modernism, Queer Theory, and the Trans Feminine Allegory.* Evanston IL: Northwestern University Press.

Namaste, Viviane K. 2000. *Invisible Lives: The Erasure of Transsexual and Transgendered People.* Chicago: University of Chicago Press.

Prosser, Jay. 1998. *Second Skins: The Body Narratives of Transsexuality.* New York: Columbia University Press.

Rivera, Sylvia. 1973. "Y'all Better Quiet Down." Archive.org. archive.org/details /SylviaRiveraYallBetterQuietDown1973.

———. 2013. "Y'all Better Quiet Down." Posted by Reina Gossett (but later removed by *Vimeo*). Vimeo.com/45479858.

Salamon, Gayle. 2018. *The Life and Death of Latisha King: A Critical Phenomenology of Transphobia.* New York: New York University Press.

Stone, Sandy. 1987. "The Empire Strikes Back: A Posttranssexual Manifesto." sandystone.com/empire-strikes-back.html.

Stryker, Susan. 1994. "My Words to Victor Frankenstein above the Village of Chamounix: Performing Transgender Rage." *GLQ* 1, no. 3: 237–54.

———. 2004. "Transgender Studies: Queer Theory's Evil Twin." *GLQ* 10, no. 2: 212–15.

———, ed. 1998. "The Transgender Issue." *GLQ* 4, no. 2.

Stryker, Susan, and Paisley Currah, eds. 2014. "Introduction." *Transgender Studies Quarterly* 1, nos. 1–2: 1–18.

Tedjiasukmana, Chris. 2018. "Y'all Better Quiet Down." *Videoactivism 2.0*, February. videoactivism.net/en/yall-better-quiet/.

EVE SEDGWICK'S QUEER CHILDREN

Mary Zaborskis

"Queer Performativity: Henry James's The Art of the Novel,"
by Eve Kosofsky Sedgwick. GLQ 1.1 (1993).

*C*hildren animate the field of queer studies. Children—literal and figural, dead and alive, queer and nonqueer—have been a focal point for queer thought since long before Lee Edelman asked queer folks to fuck the Child and the discriminatory present the deployment of this figure enables. The very first issue of *GLQ* reveals why the child was and has remained an enduring figure for the field to generate its theories and worry over its futures—and asks us to interrogate if the field's focus on the child is actually about children at all.

In the inaugural issue, Eve Kosofsky Sedgwick's invocation of figural children sets the stage for generational divides that have come to characterize the field. From the beginning, Sedgwick was already exasperated with the children of this newly institutionalized queer theory: graduate students. The piece opens with Sedgwick (1993a: 1) lamenting how "hundreds of graduate students" were using Judith Butler's *Gender Trouble* to examine acts of possible gender subversion. Sedgwick (1993a: 15) returned in her final paragraph to this graduate work emerging in the field, from which she famously concluded, "The bottom line is generally the same: [all acts are] kinda subversive, kinda hegemonic. I see this as a sadly premature domestication of a conceptual tool whose powers we really have barely yet begun to explore." Sedgwick expressed anxiety over how the younger generation was foreclosing its own future—and the future of the field—through a narrow focus that did not mine the possibilities of the "conceptual tool[s]" Butler's work provided. Fear of how the children were already shaping the field for the worse frames the piece: queer theory could be over just as it is beginning.

GLQ 25:1
DOI 10.1215/10642684-7275236
© 2019 by Duke University Press

In the same article, Sedgwick's own critical practice reveals why she was anxious over the work of the children of the field. In her analysis of Henry James, she remarked on the "startling metaphor . . . of the 'inner child': the metaphor that presents one's relation to one's own past as a relation*ship*, intersubjective as it is intergenerational" (ibid.: 8). Graduate students of the 1990s were the "inner child" of Sedgwick and a generation of academics building a field out of loss, pain, shame, stigma, and opposition. The earlier generation's own self-reflection emerged from care and concern that then manifested as critiques against this new generation entering the field.

Sedgwick understood the reparative work the formative practitioners of queer theory were doing in her opening of *Tendencies*. She provocatively began the text claiming that the deaths of queer youth are the "motive" for "everyone who does gay and lesbian studies" (Sedgwick 1993b: 1). Reflecting on her colleagues, she continued, "I think many adults . . . are trying, in our work, to keep faith with vividly remembered promises made to ourselves in childhood . . . with the relative freedom of adulthood" (ibid.: 3). Published in the same year as her *GLQ* contribution, here Sedgwick turns to both queer children and the "inner child[ren]" of queer theorists to understand field formation. In this formulation, all queer theory is an act of care: it is a fulfillment of childhood promises of the "inner child," and these childhood promises are projected onto all queer youth. The "relative freedom" afforded by adulthood inspires this desire to rescue both past selves and youth who will not grow up. Queer adults who have made it want to create futures for those who have been denied that future; creating that future depends on an elision of the past child self and a generation of queer youth. Literal children get conflated with figural inner children in order to monitor those entering and shaping the field. A reparative move has paranoid effects: an attempt to open up the future for a younger queer generation actually delimits that generation's ability to enter the field at all. The child is deployed to maintain adults' control of the present of the field.

Children recur as threats to the future in metaphorical forms throughout queer work. Children animate queer studies insofar as they risk destroying it. As a queer scholar whose work focuses on literal children, I am fascinated by the figural child who haunts the field and manifests in kinship metaphors deployed to understand field formation. The field of queer studies emerged out of minoritarian fields, and it has been in an oppositional relationship with these fields since its institutionalization, a moment that the first issue of *GLQ* materializes. A generational divide emerged between scholars doing queer theory and those doing feminist critique, women's studies, and lesbian and gay studies, the latter fields critiqued as backward, too invested in identities, and not invested enough in sexuality. In her meditation on the relationship between queer theory and feminist critique, Heather Love (2007: 302) notes that at queer theory's inaugural moment, "many wondered whether such legitimacy could be achieved only at the cost of significant exclusions." In queer theory's commitment to "examining the process by which the norm and the margin were created" (ibid.), it created its own norms for the field that excluded and marginalized other sites and productions of knowledge. Love notes the tense "relationship between feminist 'mothers' and queer 'daughters'" (ibid.) that resulted from this generational divide, a tension that remains very much alive. The institutionalization of queer studies queers children: potential practitioners are excluded from the field ostensibly to ensure its future. This is a discipline that disciplines. Queer theory generates its own queered children.

Queer theory does not need to kill its children, just the generational logic that keeps them queered. Sedgwick's (2003: 8) call in *Touching Feeling* to explore the capacity of the preposition *beside* might offer a way to think of queer work outside the generational mode: "*Beside* permits a spacious agnosticism about several of the linear logics that enforce dualistic thinking." What if the child was invoked "beside" adults as opposed to behind or before them? What if children were not an origin, a future, or a past but co-present? Sedgwick herself explores what possibilities for relationality emerge when age as a factor that separates subjects into different generations collapses. In her afterword to *Gary in Your Pocket*, Sedgwick (1996: 280) writes that after her own diagnosis of cancer, "I finally felt we [Gary and I] were finding our feet with each other, and some ground to put them on. At least, the particular awe or shyness that can separate the healthy from the ill no longer kept us apart." Fisher was a graduate student of Sedgwick's who passed away from AIDS complications before completing his degree. Sedgwick explains that both hers and Gary's illnesses forged their relation in a new way; illness disrupted both of their presents and altered their relationship to the future, aligning them alongside each other temporally in a way that was previously unimaginable. The collapse of and alteration of their relation to time are reflected in the material text. Sedgwick was originally slated to write the book's introduction, which Gary would publish; his untimely death resulted in a posthumous publication that Sedgwick completed, and her textual contribution shifted from introduction to afterword. Illness necessitated a reversal of the usual unfolding of roles according to a normative timeline—the mentee passed before the mentor, and the mentor completed the work of the mentee; instead of opening the text, positioned before what was to come, she drew it to a close. For Sedgwick and Fisher, illness illuminated the illusory stability of age, relation to time, and how subjects in different times should interact. Generations can be reconceptualized "beside" one another, and this proximity can enable community and relations that would otherwise be fore-closed when only conceptualized in temporal language.

The field's reliance on the child has worked to secure its—the child's and the field's—future. It is the current children of queer theory who may have no future if the logic of the generational mode continues to follow normative patterns of distrust and paranoia.

References

Love, Heather. 2007. "Feminist Criticism and Queer Theory." In *A History of Feminist Literary Criticism*, edited by G. Plain and S. Sellers, 301–21. Cambridge, UK: Cambridge University Press.

Sedgwick, Eve Kosofsky. 1993a. "Queer Performativity: Henry James's *The Art of the Novel.*" *GLQ* 1, no. 1: 1–16.

———. 1993b. *Tendencies.* Durham, NC: Duke University Press.

———. 1996. *Gary in Your Pocket: Stories and Notebooks of Gary Fisher.* Durham, NC: Duke University Press.

———. 2003. *Touching Feeling: Affect, Pedagogy, Performativity.* Durham, NC: Duke University Press.

BEGINNING WITH *STIGMA*

Heather Love

"Queer Performativity: Henry James's The Art of the Novel,"
by Eve Kosofsky Sedgwick. GLQ 1.1 (1993).

*I*n her essay "Queer Performativity: Henry James's *The Art of the Novel*," Eve Kosofsky Sedgwick (1993: 4) proposes replacing the ordinary-language philosopher J. L. Austin's example of a statement that does rather than describes ("I do") with the phrase "Shame on you." By shifting from the marriage ceremony to a scene of childhood shame, Sedgwick questions the heteronormativity of Austin's account. What would it mean, she asks, to "begin with stigma" (ibid.), that is, to understand performativity in the context of unauthorized or debased social experience—for instance, in the context of "gender-dissonant or otherwise stigmatized childhood" (ibid.)? Sedgwick, too, knows how to choose her moments: in the lead article in that inaugural issue of *GLQ*, she takes the opportunity to respond not only to Austin but also to Judith Butler, the author of what was then the most influential account of performativity in queer studies: *Gender Trouble* (1990). Sedgwick declares that, for her, "the deepest interest of any notion of performativity . . . is not finally in the challenge it makes to essentialism," thus citing, negatively, Butler's central argument. Sedgwick (1993: 14) points to the limits of parody as a framework for reading queer culture: "I'd also—if parenthetically—want to suggest that shame/performativity may get us a lot further with the cluster of phenomena generally called 'camp' than the notion of parody will."

Gender Trouble ends by articulating the possibility that the proliferation of genders will "expose [the] fundamental unnaturalness" of gender, and so weaken the violent hold of the sex-gender system (Butler [1990] 1999: 190). Sedgwick pursued a similar approach in her 1990 book *Epistemology of the Closet*, using the tools of critical genealogy to denaturalize sexual orientation and thus to "render less dangerously presumable 'homosexuality as we know it today'" (48). But "Queer

GLQ 25:1
DOI 10.1215/10642684-7275250
© 2019 by Duke University Press

Performativity" marks the beginning of a transition in Sedgwick's work, away from the strategy of denaturalization to an emphasis on affect and embodiment. Focusing on the significance of shame in forging identity, Sedgwick redefines performativity as a social scene, and a form of attunement; rather than rely on exposure as the basis for social change, she imagines a queer collective of "those whose sense of identity is for some reason tuned most durably to the note of shame" (ibid.: 14).

Sedgwick's attempt to reorient queer studies away from its post-structural antecedents and toward that bio-psycho-social hybrid now known as "affect studies" was remarkably successful. I was deeply influenced by the "affective turn," and especially by Sedgwick's assertion of the political value of negative affect. Like many others, I was moved by the moral seriousness of this account of queer life, which dignified experiences otherwise deemed simply abject. At the same time, I struggled to reconcile Sedgwick's pronouncements about queer feeling with more pedestrian accounts of gay, lesbian, and transgender identity. Would the focus on feeling, particularly childhood feelings, displace rather than supplement attention to sexual practices and communities? "Some of the infants, children, and adults in whom shame remains the most available mediator of identity," Sedgwick (1990: 13) writes, "are the ones called (in a related word) shy. ('Remember the fifties?' Lily Tomlin asks. 'No one was gay in the fifties; they were just shy.')." Riffing on Tomlin's joke about the closet, and the recoding of homosexuality as shyness in the McCarthy era, Sedgwick goes on to suggest that shyness—but not homosexuality— might *define* queerness: "Everyone knows that there are some lesbians and gay men who could never count as queer, and other people who vibrate to the chord of queer without having much same-sex eroticism, or without routing their same-sex eroticism through the identity labels lesbian or gay" (ibid.).

The sentence is a master class in performativity. The locution "everyone knows" alludes to the emerging distinction between homosexuality and queerness as if it were self-evident, and creates desire to be "in the know," part of an emerging consensus. Redefining queerness as an affective disposition makes space for people who do not identify as gay or lesbian; at the same time, it institutes other exclusions. I read these words as a young—but not particularly shy—lesbian, wondering whether I belonged in this new queer world. Sedgwick reconciles queerness with homosexuality by suggesting that shame-based practices emerge from and live near lesbian and gay social worlds. She writes: "Many of the performative identity vernaculars that seem most recognizably 'flushed' . . . with shame-consciousness and shame-creativity cluster intimately around lesbian and gay worldly spaces: to name only a few, butch abjection, femmitude, leather, pride, SM, drag, masculinity, fisting, attitude, zines, histrionicism, asceticism, Snap! Culture, diva worship, florid religiosity, in a word, *flaming*" (ibid.: 13–14). This tribute to queer culture is at once *scenic*, in the sense attributed to Henry James, and *sceney*, in the sense attributed to queer theory. Refusing to define queerness, and flaunting it instead, Sedgwick not only argues with Butler—she upstages her.

"Queer Performativity" was a bold first move in a campaign to seize queer studies by the root—a campaign Sedgwick (2002: 6) later described as stepping "to the side of the deconstructive project of analyzing apparently nonlinguistic phenomena in rigorously linguistic terms." Shifting the terrain of queer studies involved a disciplinary defection and a historical return. Sedgwick turns to psychology in "Queer Performativity," analyzing the work of the figure she calls "the most important recent theorist of affect," Silvan Tomkins (Sedgwick 1993: 7). Sedgwick also turns to the 1940s–1960s, a period that she, along with her collaborator Adam Frank, went on to call "the cybernetic fold" (Sedgwick and Frank 1995). Midcentury psychology and cybernetics were distant from Sedgwick's preoccupations, and those of queer studies in the early 1990s. As it turns out, however, it was Tomkins's difference, and his *indifference* to the "queer/deconstructive legacy," that made him valuable. Tomkins is a key figure for Sedgwick because his work is "sublimely alien": for this reason, he provides "a different place to begin" (ibid.: 503).

But if Sedgwick's turn to Tomkins seems to take her far afield, another citation in the essay suggests that this flanking action may in fact be a return. In "Queer Performativity," Sedgwick cites another midcentury figure, the Canadian American sociologist Erving Goffman. "There's a strong sense," she writes, "in which the subtitle of any truly queer (perhaps as opposed to gay?) politics will be the same as the one Erving Goffman gave to his book *Stigma: Notes on the Management of Spoiled Identity*. But more than its management: its experimental, creative, performative force" (Sedgwick 1993: 4). Goffman appears to be another "sublimely alien" figure. However, in Goffman's case, his influence, though mostly unacknowledged, was there all along. Goffman's work on mental asylums, prisons, impression management, the performance of gender, and the making and breaking of social norms is tied by many threads, both genealogical and conceptual, to the field of queer theory. However, these interventions did not survive what Sedgwick describes as the "subsuming" of "nonverbal aspects of reality firmly under the aegis of the linguistic." Many of Goffman's key insights about the dynamics of social power were taken up in queer studies and translated into terms more congenial to the deconstructive/queer legacy. As Gayle Rubin (2002) has argued, empirical research by scholars of sexuality laid the foundation for the emergence of queer theory as a discipline centered in the humanities around 1990, but these debts were often unacknowledged. Sedgwick's discovery of the new territory of the "cybernetic fold" is better described as a *rediscovery* of a landscape that was less unknown than willfully forgotten. The insights of midcentury social science were always there in canonical queer studies, hiding—like the reference to Goffman in "Queer Performativity"—in plain sight.

When I first read "Queer Performativity," I agreed with Sedgwick about the need to *begin with stigma*. Regarding the "experimental, creative, performative force" of stigma, I was not so sure. Are all forms of stigma useful for politics? What, I wondered, about ongoing experiences of stigma, and recalcitrant feelings of shame? What about the bad feelings that persist into adult life, resist our efforts to transform them, and continue to circulate in queer communities? Some feelings, surely, are not ripe for transformation. As if refusing an extravagant gift, I demurred from Sedgwick's characterization of shame as "a near-inexhaustible source of transformational energy" (Sedgwick 1993: 4). Would it be possible to pursue a form of inquiry that wasn't about *managing* stigma, or *transforming* it, but simply *acknowledging* it? It was, after all, Sedgwick's acknowledgment of the scene of childhood shame, rather than her belief in its transformation, that changed things for me. I explored this possibility in an early article I wrote about Radclyffe Hall's 1928 novel *The Well of Loneliness*. It is hard to generate political energy from the bad feelings represented in this book, I argued. "The novel's subtitle," I wrote, "ought simply to be: 'Spoiled Identity'" (Love 2001: 494).

I can see now that I overstated my difference from Sedgwick, kicking up a fuss in order to be part of the conversation. "Queer Performativity" celebrates shame's transformative potential, but without offering any guarantees. Sedgwick writes, "Therapeutic or political strategies aimed directly at getting rid of individual or group shame, or undoing it, have something preposterous about them: they may 'work'—they certainly have powerful effects—but they can't work in the way they say they work." Underlining the significance of identity in making individual and group identity, she continues: "The forms taken by shame . . . are available for the work of metamorphosis, reframing, refiguration, *trans*figuration, affective and symbolic loading, and deformation: but unavailable for effecting the work of purgation and deontological closure" (Sedgwick 1993: 13). In other words, shame *is* transformative, but we can never be sure *how* it is transformative. One might therefore add, Careful what you wish for. In conjuring such unruly, pervasive, and harmful feelings, it is possible to repeat the violence that you are hoping to ameliorate; antihomophobic inquiry that makes homophobia too central can be complicit with homophobia.

Disagreeing with Sedgwick helped me formulate an approach to queer literary history that centered negative and painful feelings. But if at one time I thought that this was a difference in politics or temperament, I can now see that it emerges from a specific disciplinary history. We might understand Sedgwick's rewrite of the title of Goffman's *Stigma*, away from management toward creative force, as a sign of the times, the updating of a pre-Stonewall text about secret deviants in light of a new wave of queer activism. We can also understand it as an attempt to translate an empirical and descriptive account of the operations of stigma into the terms of an interpretive and prescriptive (or activist) framework. Whether you believe that scholarship's goal is to observe how people respond to the unequal conditions in the world or to contribute to changing them is not necessarily best understood as a matter of courage, resourcefulness, or commitment. Instead, it points to a fundamental difference in the uses of scholarship. Sociology has been critiqued for its static, descriptive view of the world; queer scholarship has been critiqued for its inflated sense of its own power to act on the world. Descriptive scholarship offers a clear portrait of how the world works, but in doing so it risks accommodating itself to social conditions, and treating as permanent a situation that is temporary. Prescriptive scholarship points to potentials that have not yet been realized in the world, and therefore is a source both of resistance and of hope. But scholarship that focuses on the future risks giving an incomplete, distorted, or "hopeful" portrait of the present, including of its own place in the social world.

"Queer Performativity" effectively stages this tension between the descriptive and the prescriptive. "Shame is *performance*," Sedgwick (1993: 5) writes, and later, on the same page, "shame is a form of communication." This account of performativity draws on performance in the work of Henry James, as a translation of the space of the stage into the intimate theater of the novel. But it also draws on the dramaturgical accounts of social life developed in the 1950s and 1960s. It was Sedgwick's essay that first pointed me to this other scene of queer studies, a tradition that has become a kind of obsession for me over the last couple of decades. This process has convinced me that deviance studies is not only a point of origin for queer studies but also a living presence in the field today. The deviance paradigm remains crucial in queer studies because it is the *carrier* of the material and social specificity of gay, lesbian, and trans lives, and of other yet-to-be-specified experiences of stigma.

References

Butler, Judith. [1990] 1999. *Gender Trouble: Feminism and the Subversion of Identity.* New York: Routledge.

Goffman, Erving. 1963. *Stigma: Notes on the Management of Spoiled Identity.* Englewood, NJ: Prentice Hall.

Love, Heather. 2001. "'Spoiled Identity': Stephen Gordon's Loneliness and the Difficulties of Queer History." *GLQ* 7, no. 4: 487–519.

Rubin, Gayle. 2002. "Studying Sexual Subcultures: Excavating the Ethnography of Gay Communities in Urban North America." In *Out in Theory: The Emergence of Lesbian and Gay Anthropology*, edited by Ellen Lewin and William L. Leap, 17–67. Urbana: University of Illinois Press.

Sedgwick, Eve Kosofsky. 1990. *Epistemology of the Closet.* Berkeley: University of California Press.

———. 1993. "Queer Performativity: Henry James's *The Art of the Novel*." *GLQ* 1, no. 1: 1–16.

———. 2002. "Paranoid Reading and Reparative Reading, or, You're So Paranoid You Probably Think This Essay Is about You." In *Touching Feeling: Affect, Pedagogy, Performativity.* Durham, NC: Duke University Press.

Sedgwick, Eve Kosofsky, and Adam Frank. 1995. "Shame in the Cybernetic Fold: Reading Silvan Tomkins." *Critical Inquiry* 21, no. 2: 496–522.

MORE WORDS ABOUT "MY WORDS TO VICTOR FRANKENSTEIN"

Susan Stryker

"My Words to Victor Frankenstein above the Village of Chamounix,"
by Susan Stryker. GLQ 1.3 (1994).

*T*his short essay marks the third time I've commented in *GLQ* on its publication of my 1994 article, "My Words to Victor Frankenstein above the Village of Chamounix," a performative text that riffs on a scene in Mary Shelley's novel, in which the creature talks back to its maker, to stage a transsexual retort to the devaluation of trans lives through attributions of unnaturalness and artificiality. As such, it helps map a particular dimension of queer theory's development over the last twenty-five years.

While it's difficult to assess the importance of one's own work, I can certainly say I'm happy that my Frankenstein article still has a life of its own a quarter-century after I first let it loose in the world, and that it remains one of the most read works in *GLQ*'s history (currently at number two, after Cathy Cohen's magnificent "Punks, Bulldaggers, and Welfare Queens"). I have a Google alert set for it and take great pleasure in seeing mentions of it pop up in my inbox from time to time, like postcards from the Travelocity gnome, that keep me apprised of how and where it moves and of the company it keeps. It's gained a cult following, supplying pull-quotes for innumerable Tumblr and Twitter accounts, and has contributed to wide-ranging scholarly conversations on embodiment, techno-cultural studies, gothic literature and science fiction, affect theory, posthumanism, animal studies, radical veganism, philosophy of the body, and the relationship between queer and trans studies, to name but a few of the contexts in which it has circulated.[1]

GLQ 25:1
DOI 10.1215/10642684-7275264
© 2019 by Duke University Press

Although I didn't conceptualize it this way at the time, my Frankenstein article offered an implicit critique of what, in today's lingo, could be called an unstated cisnormative bias in queer theory. As I was writing it, I was reading the pair of articles on the queer politics of gay shame by Judith Butler (1993) and Eve Sedgwick (1993) that opened the inaugural issue of *GLQ* and served as a point of departure for a new phase in queer studies' institutionalization; they supplied an unacknowledged background to my own thoughts on the affect of rage.

Shame, as I understood it to be articulated in early queer theory, was predicated on the prior consolidation of a gendered subject, and emanated from the subjective perception that one was a "bad" instantiation of something that one recognized and accepted oneself as being. But what if one balked at that gendering interpellation and was thus compelled to confront not bad feelings but the hegemonic materio-discursive practices that produce the meanings of our flesh to render us men or women in the first place? I was not ashamed that in the name of my own psychical life I needed to struggle against the dominant mode of gender's ontologization—I was enraged.

The first opportunity to reflect on "My Words to Victor Frankenstein" came in the tenth anniversary issue of *GLQ* (2004), to which I contributed an essay called "Transgender Studies: Queer Theory's Evil Twin," which made explicit what previously had been unstated in my earlier work. My own involvement in self-styled radical queer networks in the early 1990s had led me to assume that "queer" was a family to which I belonged as a trans person, and guest-editing "The Transgender Issue" of *GLQ* (1998) helped confirm me in that belief. But as the new millennium dawned, it felt increasingly necessary to flag the ways that cisnormative queer theory naturalized the binary gender categories of man and woman as the enabling condition of queer sexuality's intelligibility, and relegated questions about the production of the categories themselves to a marginal status, or treated those questions as altogether extraneous to queer theory. Trans studies, I suggested, like queer of color or queer crip critique, offered a different way to imagine how queerness could be constituted by attending to other registers of difference than sexuality.

By the time I revisited the article yet again, in 2015, for *GLQ*'s special double issue "Queer Inhumanisms," the ground of queer theory had moved in directions that made my old article appear more prescient than marginal in its focus on a mode of embodiment excluded from the status of human and thereby deemed less worthy of life (Muñoz et al. 2015). Reflecting a broader shift in the humanities and social sciences, queer theory increasingly linked a biopolitical framework, which analyzed the segmentation of populations and the hierarchizing of its groups, with assemblage theories that helped conceptualize connections across scales of existence from the subatomic to the cosmic, and an ontological perspective that emphasized the intrinsic fluidity and liveliness of materiality. In this emerging paradigm, questions about the interrelatedness of such categorizations of life as species, race, or sex, and of how those categories materialized in ways that created greater or less capacities for living, came to the foreground. As queer theory turned toward establishing transversal connections between many varieties of life enfleshed in ways that subordinated them to the white heteromasculine able-bodied figure atop Eurocentric modernity's humanist hierarchy of values—Man— it could now look differently on the figure of transsexual monstrosity already nestled within its folds, waiting to be apprehended anew.

Karen Barad's "TransMaterialities: Trans*/Matter/Realities and Queer Political Imaginings," published in the "Queer Inhumanisms" issue of *GLQ*, articulated the affinities between my old Frankenstein article and the so-called new materialisms far more cogently than I ever have while deftly calling needed attention to the fraught relationship I suggested between processes of transsexuation and racialization (Barad 2015). In the original 1994 article, I had written that my "rage colors me" (Stryker 1994: 244). I deliberately played on the polysemic shades of "color" to make space for holding a question that I did not then know how to properly frame, let alone answer, but which I would now pose as follows: to what extent might the affect that emanated from my own enmeshment as a white transgender person in what Alexander Weheliye (2014) has since termed "racializing biopolitical assemblages" share some kinship with affects emanating from others who have been differently racialized than I, differently subordinated in the hierarchies of life than I, yet with whom I could strive toward some commons that better sustains all of our differently enfleshed lives?

Katrina Roen was the first scholar to comment on that phrase about transgender rage and color in her 2001 article "Transgender Theory and Embodiment: The Risk of Racial Marginalisation" and to note, accurately, of me, "That she is coloured by rage is explicit. How she is coloured by race is not" (256). The unstated whiteness norm of academic transgender theorizing is something with which I have been deeply complicit, even in my best efforts to do otherwise. One genealogy of transgender studies traces its root to Sandy Stone's "Posttranssexual Manifesto" (1992), modeled, in part, on Donna Haraway's "Cyborg Manifesto" (1991), and written during Stone's years as Haraway's student in the History of Consciousness program at the University of California, Santa Cruz, in the late 1980s and early 1990s. Haraway explicitly acknowledged that her figuration of the cyborg drew on queer of color feminisms, but Stone, crafting her own manifesto in the heady atmo-

sphere where Gloria Anzaldúa published *Borderlands/La Frontera: The New Mes-*
tiza (1987) and Chela Sandoval (2000) was writing the dissertation that became
Methodology of the Oppressed, did not make the deeper lineage or broader context
of her figuration of the post-transsexual similarly explicit as her mentor had done
for the cyborg, and it's taken a generation of scholarship to recover the ancestors
and kin of color invisibilized within the post-transsexual strand of thinking that I
think of as my home.

In Barad's engagement with my Frankenstein article, which they approach
from the vantage point of quantum field theory, they dwell on the theme I dwelt
on, of Being being a becoming that emerges from a nothingness that nevertheless teems with lively potentials. I still think the greatest strength of my article is
the way it affectively transforms the experience of being abjected from the human
because of one's mode of embodiment into the joyously empowering experience of
embodying a new modality of techno-cultural life, predicated on different prem-
ises than those that subtend Man. And yet I take to heart Barad's critique of the
metaphorics I deployed in the representation of that insight, of being thrown into
"darkness," and emerging from the "blackness" from which "Nature itself spills
forth" (Stryker 1994: 251).

As Barad (2015: 417) notes, however much my language aims at voicing a
condition of unrepresentability or interstitiality, however much it strives to commu-
nicate a sense of the void as "full and fecund, rich and productive, actively creative
and alive"; it also recapitulates "the underlying metaphysics of colonialist claims
such as *terrae nullius*—the alleged void that the white settler claims to encounter
in 'discovering undeveloped lands,' that is, lands allegedly devoid of the marks of
'civilization'—a logic that associates the beginning of space and time, of place and
history, with the arrival of the white man." In other words, I inadvertently perpetuate the racist trope of imagining blackness as the unmarked and unacknowledged
condition on which the existence of whiteness depends. Marquis Bey, in a recent
article "The Trans*-ness of Blackness, the Blackness of Trans*-ness," does a much
better job than I at expressing my ill-formed intent when he says that blackness
and transness "are differently inflected names for an anoriginal lawlessness" that
manifests "in the modern world differently as race and gender fugitivity" (Bey
2017: 275).

I have no idea where "My Words to Victor Frankenstein" will go from here,
or what it might have to do with queer theory in the future, or if it and queer theory
will go anywhere else at all from here; all things come to an end at some point.
But as we celebrate the bicentennial of Mary Shelley's novel, and come to an even
greater appreciation of how that work has always posed a feminist and implicitly

queer, posthuman critique of Eurocentric biopolitical modernity, I'd be delighted for my own words to share in some degree the longevity of the words that inspired them, as they tag along for the ride with that famous literary monster, and hopefully find new ways to have something to say to whatever present moments yet may come.

Note

1. See Barad 2015; Galofre and Misse 2015; *Liberazioni* 2015; Sullivan 2005; Weaver 2013; Zigarovich 2018.

References

Anzaldúa, Gloria. 1987. *Borderlands/La Frontera: The New Mestiza*. San Francisco: Aunt Lute.

Barad, Karen. 2015. "TransMaterialities: Trans*/Matter/Realities and Queer Political Imaginings." *GLQ* 21, nos. 2–3: 387–422.

Bey, Marquis. 2017. "The Trans*-Ness of Blackness, the Blackness of Trans*-Ness." *TSQ* 4, no. 2: 275–95.

Butler, Judith. 1993. "Critically Queer." *GLQ* 1, no. 1: 17–32.

Cohen, Cathy J. 1997. "Punks, Bulldaggers, and Welfare Queens: The Radical Potential of Queer Politics?" *GLQ* 3, no. 4: 437–65.

Galofre, Pol, and Miquel Misse, eds. 2015. *Politicas Trans: Una antología de textos desde los estudios trans norteamericanos*. Barcelona: Editorial Egales.

Haraway, Donna. 1991. "A Cyborg Manifesto: Science, Technology, and Socialist-Feminism in the Late Twentieth Century." In *Simians, Cyborgs, and Women: The Reinvention of Nature*, 149–81. New York: Routledge.

Liberazioni. 2015. "Monstri(e) Queer." *Liberazioni: Rivista di critica antispecista* 21. www.liberazioni.org/liberazioni-n-21/.

Muñoz, José Esteban, Jinthana Haritaworn, Myra Hird, Zakiyyah Iman Jackson, Jasbir K. Puar, Eileen Joy, Uri McMillan, Susan Stryker, Kim TallBear, Jami Weinstein, and Jack Halberstam. 2015. "Dossier: Theorizing Queer Inhumanisms." *GLQ* 21, nos. 2–3: 209–48.

Roen, Katrina. 2001. "Transgender Theory and Embodiment: The Risk of Racial Marginalisation." *Journal of Gender Studies* 10, no. 3: 253–63.

Sandoval, Chela. 2000. *Methodology of the Oppressed*. Minneapolis: University of Minnesota Press.

Sedgwick, Eve Kosofsky. 1993. "Queer Performativity: Henry James's *The Art of the Novel*." *GLQ* 1, no. 1: 1–16.

Stone, Sandy. 1992. "The *Empire* Strikes Back: A Posttranssexual Manifesto." In *Body Guards: The Cultural Politics of Gender Ambiguity*, edited by Julia Epstein and Kristina Straub, 280–304. New York: Routledge.

Stryker, Susan. 1994. "My Words to Victor Frankenstein above the Village of Chamounix: Performing Transgender Rage." *GLQ* 1, no. 3: 237–54.

———. 2004. "Transgender Studies: Queer Theory's Evil Twin." *GLQ* 10, no. 2: 212–15.

Sullivan, Nikki. 2005. "Transmogrification: (Un)Becoming Other(s)." In *The Transgender Studies Reader*, edited by Susan Stryker and Stephen Whittle, 552–64. New York: Routledge.

Weaver, Harlan. 2013. "Monster Trans: Diffracting Affect, Reading Rage." *Somatechnics* 3, no. 2: 287–306.

Weheliye, Alexander. 2014. *Habeas Viscus: Racializing Assemblages, Biopolitics, and Black Feminist Theories of the Human*. Durham, NC: Duke University Press.

Zigarovich, Jolene, ed. 2018. *The TransGothic in Literature and Culture*. New York: Routledge.

CENTERING THE "EVIL TWIN"

Rethinking Transgender in Queer Theory

V Varun Chaudhry

*"Thinking Sex/Thinking Gender," special issue edited
by Annamarie Jagose and Don Kulick. GLQ 10.2 (2004).*

*"The Transgender Issue," special issue edited by Susan Stryker.
GLQ 4.2 (1998).*

*"Punks, Bulldaggers, and Welfare Queens: The Radical Potential
of Queer Politics?," by Cathy J. Cohen. GLQ 3.4 (1997).*

*N*early fifteen years after the publication of *GLQ*'s 2004 forum "Thinking Sex/
Thinking Gender," tensions continue between studies of gender and sexuality. The
ongoing institutionalization of the category transgender, through the codification of
transgender studies as a field of inquiry and increased attention to trans and gender-
nonconforming communities in the nonprofit sector, both clarify and complicate
the ways scholars can and should study "gender" and "sexuality." The 2004 *GLQ*
forum ventured into this terrain positing gender/sex/sexuality as simultaneously
separate and related. The articles in the forum refuse to answer the question of
whether and how "transgender" can fit neatly into what we conceptualize as "queer
theory." While that specific question is beyond the scope of this essay (or any singular project), I am interested in how studies of "sexuality"—particularly queer
studies and queer theory—can address the needs of trans and gender-nonconforming communities, and gender (in)justice more broadly.

Here, I take histories of funding for US-based transgender-focused advocacy as an object of inquiry, focusing specifically on the convergence and diver-
gence between LGB(T)Q and "transgender." Institutional relationships between
categories—which have also persisted in scholarship—reveal the evident and
often necessary interconnections between gender and sexuality. On the flip side,

GLQ 25:1
DOI 10.1215/10642684-7275278
© 2019 by Duke University Press

precarious realities for trans and gender-nonconforming communities and more recent trans-specific funding demonstrate the need for "transgender" to be seen distinctly. Therefore, despite significant gains for LGBTQ studies and communities in both academic and funding arenas, trans and gender-nonconforming people, particularly people of color, have not unequivocally benefited from the convergence of "LGBTQ" and "trans" as institutionally legible categories: these histories together demonstrate the material and discursive significance of separating the "T" from LGB(T)Q.

In perhaps the most famous essay in the 2004 *GLQ* forum, the historian Susan Stryker (2004: 212) positions then-burgeoning transgender studies as queer theory's "evil twin": transgender studies grows out of the "same parentage" but simultaneously "willfully disrupts" narratives of desire where individuals need a stable and coherent notion of their own gender in order to be attracted to members of the same or "opposite" gender. By disrupting the stability and coherence in the realm of what Stryker describes as "that vast apparatus for producing intelligible personhood that we call 'gender'" (ibid.: 214), *trans* throws a wrench into this narrative of desire. At the same time, however, Stryker warns against the dangers of positioning "transgender" as "the site in which to contain all gender trouble": it is this logic, where "transgender" is the site for all nonnormative forms of personhood (and thus desire), Stryker argues, that leads the "T" to be continually neglected from LGB(T)Q politics. Despite this call, scholars throughout the issue position *trans* as a "compelling site" (Love 2004: 260) or "challenge" for the field (Sinfield 2004). Most scholars would indeed agree that *trans*—and its corollaries in transgender studies and transgender advocacy—has queer(ing) potential as a category that exists *over* and *above* existing and mostly fixed gender and sexual categories (i.e., gender, woman, and man).

I worry, however, about the implications for seeing transgender *only* for its queer potential—that is, as a site for scholars to place their anxieties and visions for what was once imagined as a (radical) queer politic (see also Cohen 1997). Any trans scholar can tell you that we are a diverse people: "trans," with or without an asterisk or other attached signifier, represents a myriad of things to people around the world. At the same time, trans and gender-nonconforming people, particularly people of color, face violence, discrimination, ridicule, and misunderstanding worldwide: it is the lack of coherence in our genders that, while certainly ripe with a beautiful queer potential, makes us targets of this discursive and material violence. Trans of color scholars (Snorton and Haritaworn 2013) and women of color feminisms (Spillers 1987; Stallings 2015) have contended with these realities of violence more explicitly and have sought out radical visions for gender justice.

Queer studies, however, continues to invoke transness as a category of potentiality, expansiveness, and diversity (in many ways, a kind of *ultimate* queer): this positioning can not only obscure the often-precarious realities for trans and gender-nonconforming people (especially people of color) but also risk further marginalization through theoretical emphasis on transgender in name and idea alone.

The contradictions within the category of transgender, particularly in relationship to the LGB(T)Q acronym, become exceedingly clear in the realm of funding: trans and gender-nonconforming people have led the charge for various kinds of issue- and needs-based advocacy, but trans-specific funding has, until recently, been hard to come by. The history of funding for LGBTQ causes appears to be one of progress and growth: between the 1970s and today, funding for LGBTQ causes has grown from only a few hundred thousand dollars to over $150 million in total grants (Kan et al. 2017). A closer look at this relatively short history of growth reveals disparities in terms of grants awarded explicitly to work focused on such populations as LGBTQ people and cis- and transgender women of color, as well as trans and gender-nonconforming and intersex communities.

Funding patterns of growth, accompanied by widening disparities, become even more glaring in the most crucial moment in the history of LGBTQ philanthropy, and perhaps in philanthropy generally: the rise of the HIV/AIDS epidemic. During this time, according to data from Funders for LGBQ Issues, funds given to "LGBTQ" causes and organizations doubled between 1980 and 1984, and then grew exponentially, from $1 million in 1984 to $21 million between 1985 and 1993 (Bowen 2012). Increased stigmatization and homophobia as a result of the epidemic also led to more funding for work in the realms of civil rights, visibility, and community building. During this period, potential funders went from seeing the diverse group labeled as "gay" as a small group of marginalized angry voices (i.e., the Gay Liberation Front) to an aggrieved population in need of a specific philanthropic response. On the receiving end of this philanthropic response, however, were primarily white gay men, whose white (gay) male bodies were newly marked as "other" (Triechler 1987): this meant women, people of color, trans and gender-nonconforming populations (and the intersections between them) continued to receive less attention and funding, often with severe consequences (Cohen 1999; Butler 1997).

The philanthropic response to HIV/AIDS was not only about prevention and treatment of the disease but also about battling homophobia and stigma through civil rights advocacy and community-building efforts. Numerous gay and lesbian organizations leveraged the epidemic as a way to receive funds and sustain their organizations. The growth and expansion of lesbian and gay organizations led to the emergence of a transgender-specific funding agenda: some of the largest funders to transgender issues domestically and internationally are HIV/AIDS-focused funders, and many large-scale LGBTQ service agencies in the United States that now serve trans communities grew out of responses to the HIV/AIDS epidemic. In my ethnographic field site of Philadelphia, the organizations that serve trans and gender-nonconforming people were initially funded for HIV/AIDS-focused prevention, education, and advocacy efforts. The Mazzoni Center, for example, which provides necessary health and legal services to thousands of trans-identified clients and hosts the Philadelphia Trans Health Conference (the largest annual trans-focused convening in the world), was founded as Philadelphia Community Health Alternatives (PCHA), expanding tremendously in direct response to the HIV/AIDS epidemic. Most recently, Mazzoni has received sizable grants for trans-focused work from AIDS-focused funders. It is true that trans and gender-nonconforming communities continue to face high rates and risk for HIV/AIDS: it is not the epidemic that is new but, rather, targeted funding and resources that are.

In terms of funding, then, attention to trans communities in relationship to broader LGBTQ institutions functions much like transgender studies in relationship to queer studies, where "queer" is often synonymous for "gay and lesbian" and transgender studies emerged "in the shadow of queer theory" (Stryker 2004: 214). Even outside HIV/AIDS-focused funding, that is, the work of the trans philanthropist Reed Erickson (whose life and institutional relationships are described in detail in the same 2004 issue of *GLQ* that features the "Thinking Sex/Thinking Gender" forum), fraught relationships between "gender" and "sexuality" as funding agendas abound. As Aaron Devor and Nicholas Matte detail in their historically rich article, Erickson, who founded the Erickson Educational Foundation in the 1960s to support transgender research, services, and educational programming, maintained "uneasy" relationships to early gay rights activism and institutions, specifically ONE, Inc. While Erickson's family fortune supported trans causes, including the medical work of Harry Benjamin and John Money, his work at ONE was rife with tension—these difficulties were due not only to Erickson's personal troubles but also to tensions between "gay-" and "transsexual-" focused work. One of the leaders at ONE, Jim Kepner, is quoted in Devor and Matte's article as being "kind of nervous" about whether ONE was primarily a "homophile" organization or a transsexual one. Kepner wondered, "If transsexuals define themselves as gay, well then, they're part of our community; if they define themselves as straight, well, we'll counsel them or help them or so on, but they're not really part of our community, by their own definition" (Devor and Matte 2004: 197). As Kepner's boundary making—unsurprisingly, bereft of attention to the material needs of "transsexuals"—demonstrates, the question of whether trans belongs inside or outside of the "gay community" has long been prevalent in considerations of LGB(T)Q philanthropy. The HIV/AIDS funding imperative and the Erickson example together reveal tensions between "gay" and "trans," desire and identity, and sexuality and gender, as they have been conceived historically through and within institutional contexts, particularly in terms of questions of resource allocation.

This (limited)[1] history of funding for transgender-focused issues demonstrates the ways in which a "queer" or "LGB(T)Q" agenda has historically marginalized the "T," only to attend to it as an afterthought or in deep, complicated relationship to gay and lesbian identities. Throughout this history, transgender and gender-nonconforming folks have always been present and needed funding: this fact is most clearly demonstrated by the historical significance of Erickson's donations, which, though not necessarily remarkable in the grand scheme of funding dollars, stands out as the first iteration of a trans-specific funding agenda. This background helps contextualize and historicize our so-called transgender moment, marked by increased visibility in a number of institutions, including the media, advocacy, and funding, as well as by the publication of the first issue of *Transgender Studies Quarterly* in 2014, ten years after the publication of this *GLQ* forum and sixteen years after the publication of *GLQ*'s "Transgender Issue" in 1998. The "transgender moment" also has an ugly flip side in heightened violence against gender-nonconforming people, particularly people of color, and antitransgender bathroom legislation. By focusing on the numerous iterations of "trans" in a variety of contexts, transgender studies must contend with this complicated historical and present-day reality. To do the same, queer studies must take the lead from transgender studies (and not the other way around): rather than being new, trendy, and theoretically sexy, trans studies has always been there, often lurking in the theoretical shadows, with little attention or resources to back up its importance. To fully contend with the "transgender moment," then, queer studies must thus attend to the full, messy, and institutionally fraught picture of, to draw on the language of David Valentine in his contribution to the *GLQ* 2004 forum, the "category itself."

Notes

Thank you to Shoniqua Roach, for generously providing critical feedback on various drafts of this essay. Portions of the ethnographic research cited in this essay have been generously supported by the Social Science Research Council, the Wenner-Gren Foundation, and the Sexualities Project at Northwestern.

1.   A fuller history of trans-focused institutions would include such moments as the 1990s to early 2000s, where transgender begins to emerge as an institutionally legible category through organizations like the Transgender Law Center and the National Center for Trans Equality. For the purposes of drawing out the relationship and tensions between gender and sexuality in trans-focused funding, however, I have left this piece of the story out.

References

Bowen, Anthony. 2012. "Forty Years of LGBTQ Philanthropy: 1970–2010." *Funders for LGBTQ Issues.* www.lgbtfunders.org/research-item/forty-years-lgbtq-philanthropy.

Butler, Judith. 1997. *The Psychic Life of Power: Theories in Subjection.* Stanford, CA: Stanford University Press.

Cohen, Cathy J. 1997. "Punks, Bulldaggers, and Welfare Queens: The Radical Potential of Queer Politics?" *GLQ* 3, no. 4: 437–65.

———. 1999. *The Boundaries of Blackness: AIDS and the Breakdown of Black Politics.* Chicago: University of Chicago Press.

Devor, Aaron H., and Nicholas Matte. 2004. "ONE INC. and Reed Erickson: The Uneasy Collaboration of Gay and Trans Activism, 1964–2003." *GLQ* 10, no. 2: 179–209.

Kan, Lyle Matthew, Ben Francisco Maulbeck, and Andrew Wallace. 2017. "2015 Tracking Report: LGBTQ Grantmaking by U.S. Foundations." *Funders for LGBTQ Issues.* www.hrfn.org/wp-content/uploads/2017/05/20170530-LGBTQ-Grantmaking-by-US -Foundations.pdf.

Love, Heather K. 2004. "'Oh, the Fun We'll Have': Remembering the Prospects for Sexuality Studies." *GLQ* 10, no. 2: 258–61.

Sinfield, Alan. 2004. "The Challenge of Transgender, the Moment of Stonewall, and Neil Bartlett." *GLQ* 10, no. 2: 267–72.

Snorton, C. Riley, and Jin Haritaworn. 2013. "Trans Necropolitics: A Transnational Reflection on Violence, Death, and the Trans of Color Afterlife." In *The Transgender Studies Reader 2*, edited by Susan Stryker and Aren Aizura, 66–75. New York: Routledge.

Spillers, Hortense J. 1987. "Mama's Baby, Papa's Maybe: An American Grammar Book." *Diacritics* 17, no. 2: 65–81.

Stallings, L. H. 2015. *Funk the Erotic: Transaesthetics and Black Sexual Cultures.* Urbana: University of Illinois Press.

Stryker, Susan. 2004. "Transgender Studies: Queer Theory's Evil Twin." *GLQ* 10, no. 2: 212–15.

Treichler, Paula A. 1987. "AIDS, Homophobia, and Biomedical Discourse: An Epidemic of Signification." *Cultural Studies* 1, no. 3: 263–305.

Valentine, David. 2004. "The Categories Themselves." *GLQ* 10, no. 2: 215–20.

THE SEXUAL IMAGINARIUM

A Reappraisal

Karen Tongson and Scott Herring

"Get Thee to a Big City: Sexual Imaginary and the Great Gay Migration," by Kath Weston. GLQ 2.3 (1995).

Scott Herring: In anticipation of this brief back-and-forth, we had a preliminary exchange about an article useful to our respective research—the anthropologist Kath Weston's foundational essay "Get Thee to a Big City: Sexual Imaginary and the Great Gay Migration" (1995). This piece was first published in the second volume of *GLQ* and later reprinted in Weston's *Long Slow Burn: Sexuality and Social Science* (1998). A member of *GLQ*'s initial Advisory Board, Weston (1995: 255) had interviewed close to one hundred queer women and men to grasp "the part played by urban/rural contrasts in *constituting* lesbian and gay subjects." Focusing largely but not exclusively on small-town migrations to San Francisco, this essay coined the phrase "the Great Gay Migration of the 1970s and early 1980s," an allusion to the Great Migration of African Americans to urban spaces in the twentieth-century United States. Alongside its emphasis on the City by the Bay, however, it also outlined movements to global megalopolises such as New York City and Los Angeles as well as other cities such as Birmingham, Alabama; movements from Caribbean locales such as Puerto Rico; "traveling within a metropolitan area" (ibid.: 268); and treks to Maine. Her ethnographic subjects are a wide-ranging lot, including individuals such as Rose Ellis, an African American lesbian from Virginia, and Simon Suh, a Korean American living in Honolulu. Grounded in cultural anthropology, the piece is also truly interdisciplinary as it announces its findings with aid from social history, the sociology of literature, and media studies. Karen's book, *Relocations: Queer Suburban Imaginaries*, refers to it as a "watershed work," and that strikes me as exactly right (Tongson 2011: 224). I'd like from

GLQ 25:1
DOI 10.1215/10642684-7275292
© 2019 by Duke University Press

my end to just state the case that Weston's piece—perhaps unintentionally— inaugurated the subfield of queer rural/regional studies before it named itself as such. It introduced a framework to think through the critical concept of *metronormativity* that Jack Halberstam later coined, and it has had a rich afterlife (309 Google Scholar citations and counting). What still reads fresh to you, Karen, after its publication almost a quarter century ago? What strikes you as lasting about its contribution?

Karen Tongson: First of all, let me say I'm thrilled to be having this conversation with you directly—finally. Even though our work has spoken to each other, and with each other for many years, we've never really had the opportunity to weave our insights together into a single project, so I appreciate this opportunity. One thing that struck me when I revisited Weston's article was its personal, anecdotal tone, which in my memory I had completely sublimated into the case studies. I bring this up because of the way both *Another Country* and *Relocations* come from that same place of situating and locating the self, of narrating the encounter with the gay "imaginarium," as Weston (1995: 255) so aptly describes it, as the opening gambit for an inquiry into the formation of sexual geographies.

There are several strands of the argument that I feel are central but ultimately lost in "Get Thee to a Big City's" broader incorporation into scholarship about gay geography and sexual cultures. In many respects, the title alone becomes the citational touchstone—the thing that names the desire and trajectory that other works on metronormativity begin with as a premise. But it is truly Weston's notion of the "imaginarium," which she animates throughout her case studies, that became fundamental to scholarship on queer sexual geographies. Weston effectively argues that there is no material formula for "being" urban or rural, but (as you so beautifully expanded on in *Another Country*) the urban/rural binary itself is the seed for a "gay imaginary" that construes these points of origin and destination as the spatial trajectory for coming out and into a broader gay culture and community (Herring 2010: 260).

I also think it becomes clear throughout the article that that binary is more of an urban/elsewhere binary and less strictly urban and rural, which has always been vital to my work on spaces characterized as "sub" urban. Most of the subjects she interviews, as you noted above, model different styles of migration, be it lateral—between cities like Boston and Philadelphia, or Los Angeles and San Francisco, for example—or more constellated, à la Atsuko Ito's story (she moves from Tokyo to a Japanese alpine commune, to "women's land" in Oregon, to the Bay Area) (Weston 1995: 255). Nevertheless, even in my work that strove to leave behind that constitutive binary to seek queer imaginaries elsewhere, I felt compelled to begin with the premise of a compulsory gay migration to "somewhere elses," which is something that I believe this article crystallized for us.

Another influential thread from Weston, which I also see running through both of our projects on queer space, is her discussion of books, movies, TV shows—essentially all *media* objects, or at least the tools for mediation. These media are what forge the Andersonian "imagined community" that Weston transposes into a descriptor for gay life and culture—or the "imagined *gay* community" (ibid.: 257; emphasis added). Her anecdote about nervously checking out Violette Leduc's steamy boarding-school romance *Thérèse et Isabelle* from the library inaugurates her own discovery of this spatial and sexual orientation. As she writes: "This common mode of 'discovering' the gay imaginary depends upon access to print, television and other media. Getting beyond the family dictionary or the television set that projects directly into the privatized realm of the home requires access to facilities such as libraries, bookstores, and movie theaters that disseminate gay-related materials" (ibid.: 259). I credit this part of Weston's essay for leading me to the concept of remote intimacy in *Relocations*, even though my own queer suburban imaginary has to assemble itself through the media one can access from *within* the privatized realm of the home, in addition to the other sites she named (Tongson 2011: 27). Of course those platforms for mediation have changed with shifting technologies, and these historical transformations to media mark many of my own efforts to conceptualize certain queer spatial imaginaries.

I think Weston's account of media and discourse networks also anticipates the richness of your own print and media archive in *Another Country*. Am I purely projecting here? Or did you also find that her descriptors of the "imagined gay community" influenced your own efforts to forge a "paper cut politics" (Herring 2010: 23)? What are some of the other aspects of the essay—some that you may have forgotten, but struck you anew upon rereading—that proved most significant to your own approach to queer geographies?

SH: You've rightly picked up on a latent influence for one of the interventions I hoped to have made in *Another Country*. With "paper cut politics" I meant to describe a resistance to metronormativity that aggravates its self-seriousness through something like death by a thousand paper cuts. Sometimes just the reminder that queers can and do thrive in a nonmetropolitan space can be enough to cause some unrest. For me, this is frequently a strategy that pops up across literature, film, performance, and photography to chip away at the social pressures of queer urbanity. Your comments are a helpful cue that Weston's subjects do more

of the same, as she recorded them piecing together lives that don't fit metronorma-
tive molds. These persons are spatial theorists in their own right as they engage
in what *Relocations* refers to as "an ethos of 'making do'—a special alchemy of
making something out of nothing" (Tongson 2011: 105). Making do and paper-cut
politics strike me as even more urgent to recognize and facilitate now as they have
ever been.

 These strategies are, of course, never stress-free undertakings, and this
acknowledgment brings me to another point about Weston's essay that I see in
hindsight thanks to your nudging. Weston (1995: 255) refers to one of Ito's migrations as "a disillusioning sojourn," and I'm struck again by how bittersweet these
movements often felt, as interviewees grapple with finding their "way to"—and
"away from"—urbanity (ibid.: 268). Weston calls this feeling "a kind of anti-
identification" (ibid.: 269), one that proved extremely productive for queers who
attempted their elsewheres as best they could. Words like *disillusionment* and *dis-
location* course through the article, and I attempted to document some of that sting
in *Another Country*. It's an enduring question for many of us: what happens when
you let go of geographic FOMO? I remind myself that you get at something like this
with the emphasis of *Relocations* on nostalgia within the dyke-aspora.

 Paying tribute to Weston with you has been a real pleasure and a reminder
that *GLQ* has been advancing this work since its earliest years. A parting question prompted by your reference to shifts in new media: in ways that Weston could
not have foreseen, what else has unexpectedly changed (for the better or for the
worse) alongside such innovations since her article's publication in 1995? For me,
one thing that stands out is potentially easier access to queer travel thanks to an
increase in transregional aircraft over the past few decades. I'm a terrible flyer
but truly grateful I can puddle-jump from Indianapolis to the southeastern United
States in less than two hours. Yourself?

KT: I'm so glad you brought up the melancholic elements of "Get Thee," because I
think a lot of us forget that it lands really hard—or better yet, *settles into*—these
feelings of disillusionment and disappointment in a way that anticipates, and makes
possible, letting go of the "geographic FOMO" you mention above. Fear—not only
of missing out as an isolated subject cut off from a queer everyday but also for
one's safety, as many have argued—becomes the implicit precondition for the gay
migratory impulse. As Weston points out, the fundamental whiteness and maleness
of the "gay imaginary" is subsumed by the mere promise of its gayness for many of
the subjects she interviews. I'm struck, in particular, by Simon Suh's and Tyrone

Douglas's case studies. Even in a place like Honolulu, Suh's gay milieu is, in his words, "not-me" (Weston 1995: 272), that is, predominantly white and not Korean American. Douglas, meanwhile, cannot move with ease across the thresholds of racial segregation in Philadelphia, which becomes apparent when he tries to enter his first gay bar, and he's harassed for additional ID, even though his white friends are waved right in.

In hindsight, *Relocations* started from this place of disillusionment, with the premise that queer people of color are acutely alienated from a gay main-stream, or a national gay imaginary. Even the ease with which JJ Chinois moves across the country in Lynne Chan's parodic online narrative is facilitated by a certain naïveté—by his failure to realize he's actually missing out on anything, anywhere. JJ brings the party wherever he goes. His cocksure cluelessness (attrib-utable to his putative "foreignness," and lack of awareness about the decorum of everyday life in the United States) makes it so that he *is* the party. The "where" becomes purely incidental.

It's actually funny to think back on how Chan's JJ Chinois project was a rudimentary, early Internet experiment that was at the same time skewering the utopianism of the "World Wide Web," and the different modalities of mobility it promised to isolated queer subjects. In fact, JJ's narrative is structured like a social media "story," and it anticipates how such self-representation is tremen-dously vulnerable to unreliable narration and fluffing. Weston's books, magazines, movies, and even television shows seem quaint and more reliable by comparison.

To answer your last question, I think "Get Thee" didn't quite anticipate Web 1.0, let alone all the subsequent platforms and apps available not only for LGBT+ *representation* (on networks like OpenTV or on auto-documentation sites like YouTube, etc.) but for the actual mapping, tracking, and enumeration of queer bodies. As everyone knows, wherever you are, you can log into Grindr or any one of a number of apps to reassure yourself that you are "not alone," because your Sub-way sandwich artist, a mere two feet away, is also pulsatingly gay on the same map.

Of course, these technologies and platforms primarily evolved in the ser-vice of gay men, so lesbians and many queer people of color are networked in other ways, some of which still has to transpire off the grid. In this way, our net-worked lives mimic the segregations and spatial privileges that inhere in "meat space," as they call it, even if we ostensibly have access to more people, and other conversations.

By way of parting, I want to acknowledge the remoteness and the intimacy of our exchange here. It's been fun writing back and forth, even though I don't think we've laid eyes on each other in person in at least two or three years. I also want to thank you for the intellectual companionship in the "sexual geographies" universe. Even though we've both turned our focus to other topics, I think our research on spatial imaginaries informs all the work we have since undertaken.

Between 2013 and 2016, there was a premature sense that discussions of queer geographies, regionalisms, and migrations were "over," and that we'd all moved on to other material (or rather, to other materialisms). What has become increasingly apparent in the last two years, especially after the shock of November 2016 to so many in the United States, is how much *more* relevant and salient work on queerness, regionalism, and migration has actually become. As Weston (1995: 275) writes at the end of "Get Thee to a Big City," "homelands can be easier to desire from a distance than once you arrive on their figurative shores."

It's a good thing we still haven't found home yet.

References

Herring, Scott. 2010. *Another Country: Queer Anti-Urbanism*. New York: New York University Press.

Tongson, Karen. 2011. *Relocations: Queer Suburban Imaginaries*. New York: New York University Press.

Weston, Kath. 1995. "Get Thee to a Big City: Sexual Imaginary and the Great Gay Migration." *GLQ* 2, no. 3: 253–77.

Weston, Kath. 1998. *Long Slow Burn: Sexuality and Social Science*. New York: Routledge.

DOES QUEER STUDIES HAVE AN ANTI-EMPIRICISM PROBLEM?

Rachel Corbman

"The Discipline Problem: Queer Theory Meets Lesbian and Gay Studies," by Lisa Duggan. GLQ 2.3 (1995).

$\mathcal{I}$n 1995, early in *GLQ*'s publication run, Lisa Duggan contributed a provocative article on the state of the field. At the time, Duggan was a relatively recent PhD, having completed her degree in history at the University of Pennsylvania in 1992. With a dissertation on the trial of Alice Mitchell, which was later revised into *Sapphic Slashers* (2000), Duggan struggled to find a job in a history department. Bouncing around for three years, Duggan ended up accepting a postdoc in criticism and interpretive theory at the University of Illinois (1992–93), followed by a visiting position in American studies at Brown (1993–95), before securing her current position in American studies at New York University in 1995.

While she was still navigating the job market, Duggan presented an early version of the essay that would become "The Discipline Problem: Queer Theory Meets Lesbian and Gay Studies" (1995) at the 1994 meeting of the American Historical Association. As a conference paper and article, "The Discipline Problem" centered Duggan's plight as a historian of sexuality in order to lodge broader critiques of, on the one hand, the marginalization of historians of sexuality in history departments and, on the other, the disinterest of queer theory in empirical research. "For us," Duggan wrote, "isolation equals cultural and professional death," suggestively riffing on ACT UP's famous mantra of silence=death (ibid.: 189).

In recent years, Duggan's argument from the 1990s has taken on a new resonance in queer studies, as a number of scholars have advanced similar critiques of the field's pervasive anti-empiricism in the current moment. In *Dis-*

GLQ 25:1
DOI 10.1215/10642684-7275306
© 2019 by Duke University Press

turbing Practices (2013), Laura Doan, for example, revisited Duggan's essay to diagnose a continued rift between academic history and queer studies, which she attributes in part to a queer discomfort with the "enduring importance of the empirical" in academic history (27). Published the same year, Valerie Traub's (2013: 78) widely read *PMLA* article "The New Unhistoricism of Queer Studies" eviscerated a distinct cohort of queer early modernists for their shared "apathy to empirical inquiry." While Traub's article left open the question of the general applicability of her analysis, her more recent monograph *Thinking Sex with the Early Moderns* (2015) doubled down by expanding her critique beyond her initial target into a more generalized appraisal of queer studies' proclivity toward "universalizing modes of thought" and attendant doubts about empirical research (278). In a final example of this critical trend, Heather Love's contribution to a much-buzzed-about special issue of *differences* titled "Queer Theory without Antinormativity," "Doing Being Deviant" (2015), similarly polemicized the field's "frequent dismissals of social science methodologies and epistemologies" (77), stemming from a queer skepticism about empirical claims.

Although this recent work ostensibly extends Duggan's earlier argument, I am struck by the comparative lack of attention to the specific institutional practices—such as hiring trends, publications, or conferences—that featured so prominently in Duggan's article. Instead, most of the above-cited work is principally concerned with probing what Traub (2015: 266) terms the "field habitus" of queer studies, which I understand as referring to the field's critical tendencies. In emphasizing discursive debates over material institutional practices, I argue that queer studies scholars often produce stories about queer studies that are strikingly at odds with what the field actually looks like on an institutional level. In this reflection, I make this case by focusing on the discipline problem as it existed in the 1990s and continues to circulate in critical conversations today. I begin by returning to Duggan's essay to historicize the development of queer studies in the early 1990s, especially Duggan's engagement with Jeffrey Escoffier's earlier article. In the second part of this essay, I speculatively question the continued existence of a discipline problem in order to more broadly argue the necessity of grounding arguments about queer studies in relation to the specific institutional histories that shape the field.

The History of Queer Studies

In "The Discipline Problem," Duggan expended a good deal of ink on Jeffrey Escoffier's controversial essay "Inside the Ivory Closet" (1990). Published in the gay periodical *OUT/LOOK*, Escoffier wrote this essay at a moment when gay and lesbian studies was finally developing university-based research centers (such as CLAGS), journals (such as *GLQ*), book series (such as Series Q), and a short-lived but significant national conference series, after two decades of gay and lesbian studies work outside universities. In contemplating this historical shift, Escoffier identified two distinct generational cohorts of gay and lesbian studies scholars, which he termed the Stonewall and post-Stonewall generation. In Escoffier's account, the former included academic and community-based historians, archivists, sociologists, anthropologists, and writers with strong ties to the political movements of the late 1960s and the early 1970s. The post-Stonewall generation, in contrast, consisted of younger scholars trained in the humanities at prestigious universities. Clearly written on behalf of the Stonewall generation, Escoffier bemoaned the predominance of theoretical work while calling for sustained "dialogue with the communities that created the political and social conditions" for the field (116–17).

Five years later, in "The Discipline Problem," Duggan read this essay in terms that are more legible to us today than Escoffier's generational argument. In essence, his essay traced the ascendency of queer theory within the broader field of gay and lesbian studies, which was, by 1995, often referred to as queer studies. In a clarifying footnote to a recent essay, Robyn Wiegman offered a similar distinction between "queer theory" and "queer studies." Queer theory, Wiegman (2015: 67) noted, refers specifically to a "genre of critical analysis that emerged largely in US English departments in the late 1980s"; queer studies refers to a more expansive "interdisciplinary project" that is "increasingly institutionalized in formal terms" through courses, certificate programs, and undergraduate degree programs.

Without question, queer theory profoundly shaped gay and lesbian studies in the early 1990s, as evidenced, for example, in the rebranding of the institutional presence of the field as queer studies. However, as much as I am persuaded by Duggan's account of the discipline problem in the mid-1990s, I am less certain of the persistence of queer studies' disciplinary alignment with theoretical work in the humanities. In fact, I worry that overemphasizing the influence of queer theory in the development of queer studies occludes the strong influence of other intellectual lineages—such as the history of sexuality, feminist sexuality studies, lesbian feminism, sociological studies of sexuality—in the formation of queer studies, a field that arguably bears little resemblance to the field Duggan critiqued in the mid-1990s.

The Discipline Problem Today

If, as Wiegman suggests, queer studies is an internally complex field that is inclusive of a wide range of disciplinary traditions, some of which are an uncomfortable fit with queer theory, why does the discipline problem remain a touchstone in recent writings by Doan, Traub, and Love, among others? To begin to answer this question, I am struck by an observation that Escoffier made in passing. In the late 1980s, when gay and lesbian studies first achieved some measure of institutional presence in the US academy, the field notably privileged its intellectual development (research centers, journals, book series) over curricular development (programs, departments, courses). Not only did this emphasis distinguish gay and lesbian studies from nearly every other interdiscipline that grew out of a late twentieth-century social movement, this institutional history also continues to have significant ramifications for how we understand queer studies today.

Since the 1990s, queer studies course offerings have expanded, and a smattering of US colleges and universities now offer minors, majors, and certificates in the field, most often under the auspices of women's, gender, and sexuality studies departments. But despite this growth, queer studies continues to lack the infrastructure to exist in the same way that nearly every other field exists. In the absence of most credentialing mechanisms, we become queer studies scholars primarily through self-identifying as such and then convincing others we are queer studies scholars by publishing in queer studies journals (especially *GLQ*) and presses associated with queer studies (such as Duke or NYU). Furthermore, precisely because of the amorphous institutional existence of queer studies, claims about what the field does (or does not) do are invariably predicated on very selective constructions of the field. On some level, all claims about fields function in this way. However, the nature of queer studies may explain why arguments about this particular field take on unusual polemic force. Not surprisingly, most arguments about queer studies evidence the continued gravitational force of queer theory in the field's critical imagination. Since the 1990s, for example, queer theory *and* queer studies have routinely been imagined as male dominated and/or oppositional to feminism, despite a preponderance of key scholars who are not male, a thriving body of work on the intersection of feminist and queer thought, and the fact that queer studies is routinely housed in women's, gender, and sexuality studies departments.[1] Similarly, as I have already shown, queer studies' proclivity for theory and/or anti-empiricism has been argued with a comparable strength of conviction stretching back to the 1990s, and continuing today.

More striking still, the above-stated claims about queer studies are now so firmly rooted in critical common sense as to require very little stated proof. The introduction to "Queer Theory without Antinormativity," for example, explains that Love's article challenges queer studies' "long-standing tradition" of privileging "the humanities and their culture-oriented forms of critical practice," a claim more presumed than substantiated in the introduction or Love's longer article (Wiegman and Wilson 2015: 19). I do not intend this as a pointed critique of Wiegman and Elizabeth Wilson as the editors of this special issue, or for that matter Love. On the contrary, as Clare Hemmings (2011: 21) points out, decisions about "which aspects of an article are assumed to need referencing, which ways of telling stories need further explanation or argumentations, are never individual decisions alone." In other words, much like Hemmings's broader critique of the reductive stories feminists tell about the development of feminist (and queer) theory, I am suggesting that queer studies' purported hostility to empirical work might be best understood as a story we tell about the field, even as we know that the field is more complicated than the stories we tell about it.

Queer studies, I would thus wager, no longer has the same discipline problem that Duggan tackled in the fifth issue of *GLQ*. In fact, the new discipline problem might instead be our failure to recognize the field's (inter)disciplinarity, amid concerns that queer studies remains stubbornly tethered to the humanities. To solve this problem, what we might need most—and what this essay has preliminarily worked toward—is a reckoning with the institutional history of queer studies as a way to understand the field in all its underappreciated complexity.

Note

1. As an early example, Suzanna Danuta Walters's "From Here to Queer" (1996) critiques the male bias in queer studies. More recently, Janet Halley's *Split Decisions* (2006) premised her argument on a sharp division between feminism and queer studies.

References

Doan, Laura. 2013. *Disturbing Practices*. Chicago: University of Chicago Press.

Duggan, Lisa. 1995. "The Discipline Problem: Queer Theory Meets Lesbian and Gay Studies." *GLQ* 2, no. 3: 179–91.

Escoffier, Jeffrey. 1990. "Inside the Ivory Closet." *OUT/LOOK* 10: 40–48.

Halley, Janet. 2006. *Split Decisions*. Princeton, NJ: Princeton University Press.

Hemmings, Clare. 2011. *Why Stories Matter*. Durham, NC: Duke University Press.

Love, Heather. 2015. "Doing Being Deviant: Deviance Studies, Description, and the Queer Ordinary." *differences: A Journal of Feminist Cultural Studies* 26, no. 1: 74–95.

Traub, Valerie. 2013. "The New Unhistoricism of Queer Studies." *PMLA* 128, no. 1: 21–39.

———. 2015. *Thinking Sex with the Early Moderns*. Philadelphia: University of Pennsylvania Press.

Walters, Suzanna Danuta. 1996. "From Here to Queer: Radical Feminism, Postmodernism, and the Lesbian Menace (or, Why Can't a Woman Be More like a Fag?)." *Signs* 21, no. 4: 830–69.

Wiegman, Robyn. 2015. "Eve's Triangles, or Queer Studies beside Itself." *differences: A Journal of Feminist Cultural Studies* 26, no. 1: 48–73.

Wiegman, Robyn, and Elizabeth Wilson. 2015. "Antinormativity's Queer Conventions." *differences: A Journal of Feminist Cultural Studies* 26, no. 1: 1–25.

UNDEAD WHITE

Richard T. Rodríguez

"Dead White: Notes on the Whiteness of the New Queer Cinema,"
by José Esteban Muñoz. GLQ 4.1 (1998).

During the first semester of my last year as an undergraduate at the University of California at Berkeley, I enrolled in a course titled Queer(y)ing the Canon, in which we read literary texts like *The Canterbury Tales*, *The Book of Margery Kempe*, and *Sir Gawain and the Green Knight* alongside critical writings of Michel Foucault, Stephen Orgel, Eve Kosofsky Sedgwick, and Derek Jarman. I also clearly remember viewing Gus Van Sant's 1991 film *My Own Private Idaho* in conjunction with reading Shakespeare's *Henry IV*. The instructor of that course was Professor Carolyn Dinshaw, one of the two founding editors of *GLQ: A Gay and Lesbian Quarterly*. Toward the end of the term, Professor Dinshaw distributed postcards to fill out if we wished to receive by mail the inaugural issue of *GLQ*. As a budding bibliophile, academic journal hoarder, and queer studies scholar, I happily complied.

While taking this course, I was also preparing an undergraduate thesis on representations of Latino gay men in literature and visual culture. Given that my nascent academic interests stood at the intersection of Chicano/a studies and the emergent project of queer theory, I searched high and low for critical work that would assist in establishing an interpretive framework for my thesis. By then, Teresa de Lauretis's edited special issue of *differences* titled "Queer Theory: Lesbian and Gay Sexualities" had been out for about a year, and it featured Tomás Almaguer's groundbreaking essay "Chicano Men: A Cartography of Homosexual Identity and Behavior." While Almaguer's piece was enormously insightful and generative, I longed for additional work to help me make sense of Latino gay male identity and sexuality.

GLQ 25:1
DOI 10.1215/10642684-7275474
© 2019 by Duke University Press

Five years after the first issue of *GLQ*, I encountered as a graduate student an essay in the pages of that very journal which I had longed for while writing my thesis: José Esteban Muñoz's "Dead White: Notes on the Whiteness of the New Queer Cinema."[1] Appearing in the first issue of volume 4, Muñoz's short but powerful piece was part of the "Film/Video Review" section. The essay investigates, as he puts it, "three queer films by white men that chronicle the lives of white people" (128). Indeed, by examining *Jeffrey* (dir. Christopher Ashley, 1995), *Frisk* (dir. Todd Verow, 1995), and *Safe* (dir. Todd Haynes, 1995), Muñoz brilliantly elucidates how whiteness and death are intimately intertwined in these films that, he insists, pass the torch of what the feminist film critic B. Ruby Rich in 1992 coined "the New Queer Cinema." Despite some critics' insistence that this film movement had quickly come and gone or should not account for mainstream gay productions (in one of the essay's footnotes, Muñoz (1998: 138) himself concedes that "it is safe now to say that the initial wave has passed; the New Queer Cinema, as it was commonly understood, is over"), he nonetheless holds on to the phrase "not in its strictest sense but instead in an attempt to do [his] own periodizing around the white normativity of queer film." And while the essay's dedication to gay Latino representation was not its sole focus (namely, Muñoz's critique of Wally White's 1995 film *Lay Down with Dogs*), the overall ardent appraisal and takedown of the whiteness seemingly part and parcel of the New Queer Cinema served as a model for my own work in graduate school and currently motivates my recent book project.

That project, titled "Undocumented Desires: Film Fantasies of Latino Male Sexuality," critically assesses an array of representations of Latino sexuality in recent queer cinema while tracking the ways Latino men in particular are cast within the terms of fantasy.[2] In many ways, Muñoz's reading of *Lay Down with Dogs* matches my assessment of many of the films I write about. The film, he maintains, is "a disturbing example of the way in which white fags eroticize difference" whereby "the racist dynamics that are usually somewhat camouflaged are made explicit." Categorizing it as "boring, meandering, and aesthetically weak," Muñoz identifies a "racist aura that envelops the Latino body" within White's film, as well as in Terrence McNally's play *Love! Valor! Compassion!* Avoiding the well-rehearsed charge of fetishism, Muñoz instead reveals how white gay male fantasies materializing as film and theater tend to rely on casting racial difference as an advantageous aberration. Thus it's not simply a problem that the Latino body is the object of white gay male desire; rather, the problem exists in how the Latino body conveniently serves as a conduit for harnessing racial (and class) hierarchies in the articulation of this desire. Using the white actor Randy Becker, who appears as a Latino in both White's film and McNally's play, as an example, Muñoz (1998: 129) maintains that Becker's performances as "a shifty, brainless, oversexed Latino" and "a brainless dancer whose body is traded between white men" ultimately affirm "white-supremacist culture."

Like Muñoz, I am compelled to discuss films like *Testosterone* (dir. David Morton, 2003), *Quinceañera* (dir. Richard Glatzer and Wash Westmoreland, 2006), and *Longhorns* (dir. David Lewis, 2011) not only for the way New Queer Cinema's persistence is predicated on its firm grasp on "white normativity" but also for its clichéd deployment of how the "Latino body, like other racialized bodies, functions as an exotic kink for dominant gay male culture" (Muñoz 1998: 129). While these films, like the ones Muñoz writes about, are also "queer films by white men that chronicle the lives of white people," I also focus on films by Latinos and white women—such as Lane Shefter Bishop's *The Day Laborers* (2003), Carlos Portugal's *East Side Story* (2006), and Peter Bratt's *La Mission* (2009)—that chronicle the lives of both queer white people *and* queer people of color but, in due course, deploy the Latino body—and its attendant exotic sexual kink—in ways that hinge on and normalize whiteness.

Similar to how Muñoz must explain his "expanded use of the 'New Queer Cinema'" to those who "would most object to the inclusion of *Jeffrey*, a film that many serious gay and lesbian critics dismissed as multiplex trash" (ibid.: 138), I have had to clarify why I have elected to write about such "bad" films.[3] In her essay "What's a Good Gay Film?" Rich (2013: 44) writes that she wants—as most likely the answer to the question her title poses—"a post-coming-out, post-get-it-together kind of movie, something full of sex, romance, tragedy and life outside The Relationship." Who doesn't want this? But more often than not the films I'm drawn to—sometimes against my will and other times not—conform to the clichés Rich is clearly over. Without a doubt, the films I find myself committed to for this project are habitually troubling with respect to the politics they tender, just like those films about which Muñoz writes. And while they may have received ample praise for indelibly contributing to the meager offering of films representing queers, Latinos, and queer Latinos just as they've been relegated to the trash bin for their failures from both politicized spectators and those only in search of satisfying entertainment, the films constituting my archive for this study also function as crucial texts for ascertaining the politics of fantasy mirrored from everyday life practices and the ideologies of whiteness that interminably circumscribe them.

The title of Muñoz's essay, he explains, recycles the discarded titled proposed by Mandy Merck, former managing editor of *Screen*, for the British film journal's now famous special issue edited by Isaac Julien and Kobena Mercer titled "The Last Special Issue on Race." For Muñoz, the title's coupling of "dead" and "white" helps signal the rigid join of death and whiteness in the New Queer Cinema. Furthermore, it's also a way to register how the New Queer Cinema is always relentlessly, and insufferably, dead white. Yet, given the persistent multicultural window dressing of this unfolding cinematic genealogy, the violence perpetuated by these films leaves one with no other option—as the title might be said to do—than to call for the death of New Queer Cinema's vampire-like undead whiteness. Following Muñoz's lead, our goal to expose whiteness's incessant ambition to pass as common sense persists. With "Dead White" as our critical compendium, we will continue to throw light (and no doubt shade) on whiteness, exposing its flaws while strategizing how to drive a wooden stake into its callous heart.

Notes

1.   I hope this piece makes clear that Muñoz's essay stands as an enduring model for film and media studies scholars working at the intersection of race, sexuality, and representation. Moreover, the elegance, argumentation, and biting critique of the essay is representative of Muñoz's deep and incisive thinking, crystallized one year later in the publication of his groundbreaking first book, *Disidentifications: Queers of Color and the Performance of Politics* (1999).

2.   I am thankful to Professor Muñoz for his valuable feedback on an early version of one of the chapters, "Gentrify My Love," presented at the symposium "Sexing the Borderlands: From the Midwest Corridor and Beyond" at the University of Texas at Austin (October 12–13, 2012) and for which he was the keynote speaker.

3.   "Dead White" made such an impact on me that after watching Jim Fall's *Trick* (1999) in a Berkeley cinema, I went home and wrote a scathing analysis of the film's overt and covert racism with respect to Latino men (despite the fact that I was in the throes of writing my dissertation). I sent the piece to *GLQ* for consideration in the "Film/Video Review" section, but it was turned down. I was told by the editor that readers of the journal would most likely not be interested in the piece since *Trick* was, at best, "queer-lite."

References

Muñoz, José Esteban. 1998. "Dead White: Notes on the Whiteness of the New Queer Cinema." *GLQ* 4, no. 1: 127–38.

———. 1999. *Disidentifications: Queers of Color and the Performance of Politics*. Minneapolis: University of Minnesota Press.

Rich, B. Ruby. 2013. "What's a Good Gay Film?" In *New Queer Cinema: The Director's Cut*, 40–45. Durham, NC: Duke University Press.

DISCUSSING THE UNDISCUSSABLE

Reflecting on the "End" of AIDS

John Petrus

"Not-about-AIDS," by David Román. GLQ 6.1 (2000).

$\mathcal{L}$et's talk about 1996 as a moment. Before July 1996, before the eleventh International AIDS Conference in Vancouver, a diagnosis with AIDS, or indeed HIV, was a get-your-things-in-order, face-your-mortality, get-ready-to-hop-on-the-rickety-US-healthcare-ride sort of situation. Although AZT and DDI were being used somewhat effectively in certain cases, their effectiveness varied widely among patients and lead almost inevitably to HIV growing resistant to the drugs, higher viral loads, lower CD4 counts, opportunistic infections, and long battles with disease. I was going to write something like "well, you know the rest," but part of this piece is that you might not.

David Román's article "Not-about-AIDS" (2000), from the first issue of volume 6, not only reframed a watershed moment that fundamentally changed gay male culture but also pointed to the importance of performativity and performance and its impact on queer (and hegemonic) culture before and after combination therapy with protease inhibitors. Most importantly, he marks a discursive shift in the national conversation about HIV/AIDS that places the crisis either "over" or "elsewhere" and a shift in gay and lesbian leadership disassociating with the HIV/AIDS.

There is a certain amnesia attached to this time that many intellectuals didn't quite expect. Román highlights how the innovation in treatment created a discursive shift where lack of media interest, lack of public interest, and the call for post AIDS-as-crisis models as a response to HIV triggered radical rearticula-

GLQ 25:1
DOI 10.1215/10642684-7275488
© 2019 by Duke University Press

tion in queer culture. As Román's article points out, the post-1996 moment pinned white queer communities against other minority communities, and it spurred a very nonqueer reinforcement of racialized and class-related boundaries.[1] Access to prevention, to medicine, and to treatment was (and is) significantly affected by race, class, and geographic location. In 1996, while many in mass media were celebrating the "End of AIDS," others knew all too well that, as Mario Cooper stated, "AIDS isn't over. For many in America, it's just beginning" (quoted in Román 2000: 6).

Indeed, the circuit parties and revival of sex clubs that Andrew Sullivan problematically refers to as the "post-AIDS gay life-style" were spaces of exclusion and transmission. Circuit parties and raves reflect a moment in gay culture where body image (including racialized standards of beauty) were tied closely with gay male culture. Sullivan (1996: 55) asserts, "Sexual danger translated into sexual objectification, the unspoken withering of the human body transformed into a reassuring inflation of muscular body mass." Throw into the mix the use of steroids, ecstasy, and ketamine to bulk up, push risk completely from the mind, and facilitate finding beauty in yourself and others, and you have a recipe for terrible morning-afters: depression, exclusion, and the cult of the masc, swoll, straight-acting white guy.

Meanwhile, off the dance floor and into the conference room, Román (2000: 8) signals a decline in monetary donations for AIDS-related services and prevention because of "AIDS burnout, the growth in non-AIDS-related organizations catering to lesbian and gay communities, and the sense that AIDS is over." What's more, 1996 marks the beginning of the legislative push to criminalize HIV transmission.[2] These acts of criminalization have yet to be successfully fought by activists in the United States. In terms of queer radical community formation and freedom from state control of sexuality, these pieces of legislation reveal the legal precarity of poz queers' sexualities. Surely this is of concern to gay and lesbian leadership, right?

Combination therapy and the call for the "end" of AIDS in 1996 allowed for gay conservatism and splintered the poz community and AIDS survivors from mainstream gay culture. The medication that permitted HIV to become "a manageable disease" became controlled by medical and state apparatuses that determined access, price, distribution, and production. In a way, 1996 marks a shift from queer activism operating outside official channels, a return to structural inequalities that disproportionally affect queers of color, and a call to forget the past and embrace the future.

Román (2000: 8), in the face of this call to forget, insists on the importance of performance as "a powerful means on intervening in the public understanding and experience of AIDS and of countering neglect of it by the larger culture." In this way, we can understand performances as a powerful mode of agency to craft discourse to counter hegemony. Consensus can always be swayed, and one of our many weapons is memory. It is key for the HIV/AIDS crisis to be remembered not only as part of the past but also continuing in a different form into our present. Memory entrepreneurs—a lovely name for activism—could potentially critically remember (and solicit remembering) the shift that took place in 1996 in order to show continuity *and* change in queer culture.[3] How come it has been so thoroughly forgotten?

It's not uncommon here in rural Iowa to see faded stickers on trucks proclaiming "Never Forget" with reference to the 9/11 attacks on the Twin Towers. Everyone knows about these victims and mourns them. The Towers' memorial site is a pilgrimage location that ensures the active reproduction of memory. I ask myself, where is the memorial to the approximately 692,789 people who have died of AIDS in the United States (Centers for Disease Control and Prevention 2016: 83)? Surely, this is cause for pause and media attention. Yet the most avid news consumer could tell you much more about the flu. What is alarming is that not only have we lost memory of the lived realities of the AIDS crisis, HIV and AIDS are systematically displaced in discourse as pertaining to the past or pertaining to "elsewhere"—either the Third World or the Third World within the First World.

Román is right to show the embodied theorization present in the dance performances of Neil Greenberg and Bill T. Jones, and their complex contributions to discourse on AIDS. They not only memorialize different moments in the crisis; they draw viewers into affectively charged dialogues with the national conversation on HIV/AIDS. Jones was perhaps one of the most well-known HIV-positive dance performers, whose work dealt directly with AIDS and the discourses surrounding it. Román writes about how Jones casually or accidentally disclosed his HIV status during an interview for the *Advocate* in 1990, and ever since, Román (2000: 20) states, "Jones is always already read in the context of AIDS." While Román does not delve further into this point, it is important to recognize how HIV status could typecast, limit, or censure artists, performers, or activists who intend to contribute to a conversation on HIV/AIDS. Indeed, Jones faced cruel criticism, especially once his real-life sero-status became public knowledge, once he was always already read in the context of AIDS. In many ways, this made him always already read as victim, not just positive or a PWA. Arlene Croce famously refused to review *Still/Here*, but wrote an extensive piece in the *New Yorker*, without having seen the piece, questioning whether it was art. Her piece is perhaps one of the most powerful examples of discursive backlash.

Its title, "Discussing the Undiscussable," poses the question, "When players in a production aren't just acting out death but are really dying—as in Bill T. Jones's *"Still/Here"*—is it really art?" She accuses Jones of "putting himself beyond the reach of criticism," of crossing "the line between theater and reality," and of producing "victim art" (Croce 1994). She claims that Jones's work is "literally undiscussable," but somehow she manages to fill the pages with such gems as: "In quite another category of undiscussability are those dancers I'm *forced* to feel sorry for because of the way they present themselves: as dissed blacks, abused women, or disfranchised homosexuals—as performers, in short, who make out of victimhood victim art. I can live with the flabby, the feeble, the scoliotic. But with the righteous I cannot function at all" (ibid.). Her coup de grâce is to perform a logical 180-degree pivot: she takes a break from attacking the self-absorbed egotism of "victim" art to claim that this popular, philistine faux art is indeed the end of postmodern dance at a turn to "utilitarian art" and "twentieth century collectivism." Indeed, it is at once self-centered and collectivist. Discursively, she dismisses Jones's work for its clarity of message and clear connection to reality, maintaining that any aesthetic value within is "undiscussable." It begs the question: according to Croce, is any art that addresses AIDS discussable?

Lee Edelman (1994), in *Homographesis*, delves deeper into the discursive structures that tie AIDS with the real rather than the fictive or creative—what Croce questions as art. "The most disturbing feature of the Western discourse on 'AIDS' is the way in which the literal is recurrently and tendentiously produced as a figure whose figurality remains strategically occluded—and thus as a figure that can be used to effect the most repressive political ends" (ibid.: 80). He argues that the truth value and the scientific realness of AIDS is seen as literal without any element of the figurative. Indeed, while AIDS is famously a metaphor and conjures up complex imaginaries, it is perceived in terms of absolutes: positive or negative, living with HIV or dying of AIDS. Edelman recognizes that, on the one hand, AIDS carries a discursive charge that links it to absolutes, biomedical, logical, no-nonsense literalness. How very unqueer. On the other hand, activists and intellectuals have been calling for more-nuanced, humanistic discourse to counter the institutional rhetoric that paints us in such unflattering and inaccurate one-dimensional renderings. We are, after all, the queer *humans* affected by AIDS. And we contain multitudes.

Román's article in 2000 echoes the importance of artistic interventions to counter literal, politicized understandings of AIDS as well as anticipating problematic shifts in the crisis and the dynamics of the crisis. He anticipated the question: what do humanistic AIDS discourses look like and how do they escape being co-opted and folded back into the consensus of the hegemony?

This question gets taken up in important platforms like *GLQ*: Lucas Hilderbrand in "Retroactivism" (2006) also criticizes the loss of interest among gay males for the new "at risk" populations while advocating for the maintenance of cultural memory of the ACT UP era. In 2010, Paul Sendziuk revives this debate once again to question how AIDS films from the past allow for contemplating critically the so-called post-AIDS condition. Once again, Julian Gill-Peterson (2013) repeats eloquently the concerns that Román articulated in his "Not-about-AIDS." While mainstream media may still be "Not-about-AIDS," *GLQ* was and continues to be one of the crucial spaces where these important counternarratives and counterdiscourses are circulated and debated.

Notes

1. "While white gay men who argue for the end of AIDS neglect to account for increasing infection rates among racial minorities, leaders in communities of color discount queer people in the AIDS emergency discourse that calls attention to AIDS in their communities. Queers of color do not fare well in these scenarios. In fact, homosexuality and race continue to be imagined as oppositional" (Román 2000: 7).
2. This push still prevails: to date, twenty-four states require people who are aware of their HIV status to disclose it to partners before any risk behavior. What that behavior might be is open to interpretation: some states such as Alabama reserve the right to isolate, quarantine, or civilly commit people living with an STD, including HIV.
3. "Memory entrepreneurs" is a term that Elizabeth Jelin uses in *State Repression and the Labors of Memory* (2003) to describe those who actively seek to alter narratives of the past constructed by "official" state-sanctioned history.

References

Centers for Disease Control and Prevention. 2016. *HIV Surveillance Report, 2016*, vol. 28. www.cdc.gov/hiv/library/reports/hiv-surveillance.html.

Croce, Arlene. 1994. "Discussing the Undiscussable." *New Yorker*, December 26, 54–60.

Edelman, Lee. 1994. *Homographesis: Essays in Gay Literary and Cultural Theory*. New York: Routledge.

Gill-Peterson, Julian. 2013. "Haunting the Queer Spaces of AIDS: Remembering ACT UP/New York and an Ethics for an Endemic." *GLQ* 19, no. 3: 279–300.

Hilderbrand, Lucas. 2006. "Retroactivism." *GLQ* 12, no. 2: 303–17.

Jelin, Elizabeth. 2003. *State Repression and the Labors of Memory.* Translated by Marcial Godoy-Anativia and Judy Rein. Minneapolis: University of Minnesota Press.

Román, David. 2000. "Not-about-AIDS." *GLQ* 6, no. 1: 1–28.

Sendziuk, Paul. 2010. "Moving Pictures: AIDS on Film and Video." *GLQ* 16, no. 3: 429–49.

Sullivan, Andrew. 1996. "When Plagues End." *New York Times Magazine*, November 10, 52–62, 76–78, 84.

"BORDERS ARE BOTH REAL AND IMAGINED"

Rejoicing on Lionel Cantú's "*De Ambiente*: Queer Tourism and the Shifting Boundaries of Mexican Male Sexualities"

Salvador Vidal-Ortiz

"*De Ambiente: Queer Tourism and the Shifting Boundaries of Mexican Male Sexualities*," by Lionel Cantú. GLQ 8.1–2 (2001).

*I*n 1994, having recently moved to Washington, DC, I briefly joined a local group called Gente Latina de Ambiente (GELAAM). We collaborated with the National Latino/a Lesbian and Gay Organization, since they too were housed in DC, and since the local and the national coalesce in critical ways—often hurting the local. GELAAM organized events, conducted social activities, participated in the gay pride parade, often winning the best parade float (but don't celebrate too much, it was the praise of the exotic other at its best), and had a newsletter, which Edgardo Guerrero edited (*guerrero* means "warrior" in English, and boy, is Edgardo that, and more!).[1] GELAAM was instrumental in creating a space for Latina/o gay, lesbian, and bisexual and transgender local folks while attempting to produce a difference between the local needs buried under the politics of national governance and think tanks. And it did, at least for a while. Like GELAAM, other organizations in cities and rural areas of the country, and Puerto Rico, faced the challenge, and tension, between the local aspects and needs, and the overarching politics of representation at a national level.

As I reread "*De Ambiente*: Queer Tourism and the Shifting Boundaries of Mexican Male Sexualities," written by my dear friend Lionel Cantú, I was reminded of the balance between the colonizing and liberating in the tourism processes he documented in his research. *De ambiente* means "in the know," and

GLQ 25:1
DOI 10.1215/10642684-7275502
© 2019 by Duke University Press

implies a shared sense of belonging among peers. To say someone is "de ambiente" is to denote their participation in a gay and lesbian environment including clubs and the bar scene, though not limited to them (sometimes, folks "de ambiente" may not be gay or lesbian—for instance, heterosexually identified parents and siblings who go to gay clubs to accompany their LGBT family). Gente Latina de Ambiente, like hundreds of local groups in the United States and Puerto Rico, gathered thousands of LGBT Latinas/os in political and sociocultural groups and spaces, at times moving forward and resisting political agendas, other times celebrating their lives and existence.[2]

The local and the national, the colonial and the "modern," the racialized and marked as White, are two sides of a not-so-imagined border: they produce an understanding of the other in ways that erases one; even more prominently, it makes them complicit in this arrangement. For Cantú's research on tourism—an economy that drives multiple dynamics in countries around the world—showcased the project of consolidating a sense of nationhood through the development of tourism, and the attention to the gay or lesbian foreigner, to the detriment of the gay, lesbian, or bi local. In the case of gay Mexican men, it was also about the liminal spaces of the "gay caballero" (whether a member of a gay and lesbian community, and/or a sex worker—but often a stereotypically imagined endowed, top Mexican man) who met the "gringo" tourist, and how the desire for the former made him simultaneously conquerable and domineering to the latter. These contact zones produce an imagery and fantasy of consumption of the other abroad:[3] for USAmericans, this occurs in the context of gay resorts and bars that cater and depend on tourism and its related industries; and for Mexicans, it is about the imagined US gay haven, and heaven, devoid of any homophobia. Of course, Mexican gay and bisexual men, like many other sexual minorities who migrate to the United States, face more racism, and still experience homophobia, when moving to the United States. Sometimes, they experience less sexual empowerment and same-sex sexual behavior in this so-called heaven, where they can call themselves "gay" (Reddy and Syed 1999).

Cantú noted in *De Ambiente* that borders are real and imagined. The borders (that serve as barriers) between USAmericans who brought condoms and lube to use, and leave their "friends" what remained once they left México, are illustrative of the power dynamics embedded between these two countries and populations. In the tension in tourism, migration, and these other scenarios (e.g., the subjugation of the local into the global, or the folding of the colonial into empire), what comes out as a result is the idea of complicit subjects—whether they are objectified or not—into this sexual arena, an arena asymmetric at best, and at worst, filled with inequality. Although not explicitly stated in the article, it seems as if for Cantú, privileges accorded to his informants—based, for example, on gendered, migration, and socioeconomic status—allowed for a negotiation between the imperial and the colonial that inevitably sustained both. One side of the border cannot live without the other.

The sexual tourism Cantú described was, for him, an extension of the borders and geopolitical limits between the United States and México. *Zonas de tolerancia* in México began to create these contact zones, and tourism, and gay tourism in particular, pushed an expansion of the repertoire of sexual identification—although Cantú warns that gay identities are not the result of "imported" identities and practices. What Cantú suggests is that the range of cultural, economic, and social factors combine for fostering an ever-evolving sense of Mexican gay sexualities, Mexican gay masculinities, and Mexican sexualities and masculinities.

Cantú was concerned with power and social stratification, and his quest was to try and understand the political economy of "gay" and "queer" settings (terms he often bracketed, as he did with "sexual minorities," as explicitly minoritized and implicitly racialized). Migration and tourism served his project in that the movement of Mexican gay and bisexual men followed migratory patterns abroad depending on their socioeconomic standing and perceived loss of privilege. Clearly, to him, not all migrants were struggling with their sexual identity, not all gay Mexican men needed to migrate, and not all spaces eliminated the possibility of a sense of community (while living in México). Furthermore, his *De Ambiente* article shows how global South sexual minorities may in turn generate a similar tourist power dynamic, not unlike the work on tacit subjects by Carlos Decena (2011). While the global political economy of migration might have shaped some aspects of the contact zones—many, indeed—the spaces of *ambiente* did not exist merely because of such economy, especially given the social transformation of the cultural landscape in México that Cantú notes.

What I gained—as a friend, colleague, and collaborator in publishing Lionel Cantú's work after his untimely death (Cantú 2009)—was to think of queer theory as an explicitly racialized project. To think of borders and boundaries as conduits of a more complex understanding between those so-called extremes. Cantú also made me reconsider assumptions about power and the geopolitical in ways that have become important to think, for instance, about queer theorizing and doing in the Américas (Viteri et al. 2011). But Cantú's *De Ambiente* also reinforced how simultaneous processes may be operating in tandem—for example, how racialized dynamics from the United States may be reproduced, and reinvented, in the very tourist settings in México. And that at the same time as a series of seemingly contradictory readings may be in operation, there are critical economics elements: like queer youth of color who are often pushed and kept out of gay bars because of ID requirements or two-drink reinforced policies in urban centers in the United States; in México, tourist spaces become commodified in ways that demand access to minimal capital in order to participate in those spaces. Borders do operate in real ways to demarcate exclusion and privilege.

I often think about how to discuss Cantú's work and its impact with students who may generalize, or read the global as the local. Not being sure of what location they may use as a referent, and whether (and to what extent) they can compare those two, I bring up DC and national politics. In doing so, I wish to replicate the global-local dynamics often discussed, in order to distinguish them; yet in conversation with students, almost immediately the local is dismissed. The privileging of the global/ized as something that matters more is an inherent curse that will continue to push scholarship—particularly queer theory—not to reproduce such borders, such barriers, but also, not to generalize a global imposition onto the various spheres where queer may do, or may inhabit.

Like *Gente Latina de Ambiente*, multiple Black and Brown organizations manage racialized experiences, seek to build coalitions with Native/Indigenous and Asian/Pacific Islander groups, and denounce the institutional and inherently ingrained cultural racism in "mainstream" White organizations (locally and nationally). In doing so, these groups continue to push back, so as to not remain invisible. That interplay between colonization and liberation in Cantú's research may serve us well in other colonial contexts and other seemingly clear dualities— for a better understanding not just of the erasures, but of the potential resignifications in community responses.

Notes

1. Throughout their years, GELAAM has had incredible leadership including Edgardo Guerrero, José Quiroga, Marisa Demeo, Carmen Chávez, and Orlando Aponte. GELAAM, although an independent group, followed from another group's activism and visibility work in the late 1980s–early 1990s, *Enlace* (or "link" in Spanish)—for more on them, see the personal archives collection owned by Letitia Gomez, and visit the Rainbow History Project website.

2. Please refer to the introduction of *Queer Brown Voices: Personal Narratives of Latina/o LGBT Activism* (Vidal-Ortiz 2015), for a brief historical (and incomplete) illustration of the issues LGBT Latinas/os faced in the 1970s, 1980s, and 1990s.

3.   In *Imperial Eyes: Travel Writing and Transculturation*, by Mary Louise Pratt (1992: 8), she notes: "A 'contact' perspective emphasizes how subjects get constituted in and by their relations to each other. It treats the relations among colonizers and colonized, or travelers and 'travelees,' not in terms of separateness, but in terms of co-presence, interaction, interlocking understandings and practices, and often within radically asymmetrical relations of power."

References

Cantú, Lionel. 2001. "*De Ambiente*: Queer Tourism and the Shifting Boundaries of Mexican Male Sexualities." *GLQ* 8, nos. 1–2: 139–66.

———. 2009. *The Sexuality of Migration: Border Crossings and Mexican Immigrant Men*. Edited by Nancy A. Naples and Salvador Vidal-Ortiz. New York: New York University Press.

Decena, Carlos U. 2011. *Tacit Subjects: Belonging and Same-Sex Desire among Dominican Immigrant Men*. Durham, NC: Duke University Press.

Pratt, Mary Louise. 1992. *Imperial Eyes: Travel Writing and Transculturation*. London: Routledge.

Reddy, Chandan, and Javid Syed. "I Left My Country for This?!" *Trikone Magazine* 14, no. 4 (1999): 8–9.

Vidal-Ortiz, Salvador. 2015. "Introduction: Brown Writing Queer: A Composite of Latina/o LGBT Activism." In *Queer Brown Voices: Personal Narratives of Latina/o LGBT Activism*, edited by Uriel Quesada, Letitia Gomez, and Salvador Vidal-Ortiz, 1–27. Austin: University of Texas Press.

Viteri, María Amelia, José Fernando Serrano, and Salvador Vidal-Ortiz, eds. 2011. "¿Cómo se piensa lo queer en Latinoamérica? / How Is Queer Thought of in Latin America?" *Iconos: Revista de Ciencias Sociales* 39, no. 1: 47–60.

ON FRIENDSHIP

John S. Garrison

*"The Work of Friendship: In Memoriam Alan Bray," special issue
edited by Jody Greene. GLQ 10.3 (2004).*

At the 2018 MLA conference, I attended a session called "Thinking Queer History in Shakespeare: A Conversation on Method." I was a bit late and ended up squeezing in between two people after asking them to move their winter coats. Sitting down, I realized that I knew them—one I had seen regularly at a public pool the summer before (at least I recall seeing him in the showers several times), and the other turned out to be a fellow contributor to a recent anthology (or at least it was someone with the same name). I had missed the introduction to the panel and the start of the first talk, but I quickly realized that the first speaker, Valerie Traub, was anatomizing the methodology of Jeffrey Masten's *Queer Philologies: Sex, Language, and Affect in Shakespeare's Time* (2016). The second speaker, Masten himself, discussed the lines of argument in Traub's *Thinking Sex with the Early Moderns* (2015).

It occurs to me now that I'm not sure Shakespeare was mentioned, but of course he had to have been. I was thrilled to hear reflection on both Traub's and Masten's books, which have broad applicability for queer theory and which suggest pathways into still-unforeseeable scholarship. As Masten took the podium to discuss Traub's book, it struck me how the panel not only pointed to the future but also was deeply rooted in the past. These books—and my own personal sense of the authors as closely connected to each other—can be traced to a special issue of *GLQ* published in 2004. "The Work of Friendship: In Memoriam Alan Bray" collected essays that reflected on (or, in some cases, simply reflected) Bray's interventions into the study of queer social relations, and it contained essays by Traub and Masten that later appeared in updated versions as chapters in these recent books.

GLQ 25:1
DOI 10.1215/10642684-7275516
© 2019 by Duke University Press

There's no such thing as a direct throughline. The path from the panel to the books to the special issue intersects with what has revealed itself to be a vital flashpoint in ongoing debates about the history of sexuality. Traub published the polemical essay "The New Unhistoricism in Queer Studies" in *PMLA* in 2013. The piece sparked strong reactions, both in the sense that it seemed unavoidable in conversations with people at conference hotel bars and also in the sense that subsequent response statements by Carla Freccero (who had also been a contributor to the *GLQ* special issue on Alan Bray) and by Madhavi Menon appeared in *PMLA* (Freccero 2013; Menon 2013). Jack Halberstam (2013) also chimed in, offering an extended comparison of Traub's piece to a season of *Game of Thrones* because the essay actively fueled "skirmishes between queer houses." Traub's (2013: 23) stated aim in *PMLA* was "to advance a more precise collective dialogue" between theorists, but Halberstam interpreted the essay's assessment of current theoretical work to only further territorialize strands of thought.

Traub's contribution to *GLQ*'s memorial issue was titled "Friendship's Loss: Alan Bray's Making of History," and it located Bray's scholarship in a larger constellation of queer work, including that of John Boswell, Mario DiGangi, Jonathan Goldberg, David Halperin, Eve Kosofsky Sedgwick, and Laurie Shannon. I'll stop there. Any list (by Traub or by me) is inevitably incomplete. Her discussion of Bray's work allowed her to pose questions that would become central to her book and to disagreements between the camps of theory that Halberstam likens to HBO's Baratheons, Greyjoys, Lannisters, and Targaryens. Traub (2004: 350) wondered, "How do we *know* when there were no homoerotic desires between historical figures? What is the basis for our knowledge of the eroticism of the past? How *do* we know what (we think) we know?" The questions find articulation in her most recent book that challenges scholars to rethink our "presumptive knowledge" about sex, to reconsider "*how* we know as much as *what* we know" (Traub 2015: 34). At another point in the *GLQ* essay, she posits, "What requires new theorizing is how to stage a dialogue between *one* past and *another*" (Traub 2004: 357).[1] "The Work of Friendship: In Memoriam Alan Bray" did indeed feature essays that discussed different historical periods, and the issue itself had a particular past. The special issue and Traub's contribution to it both stemmed from a session in honor of Bray organized by George Haggerty at the 2002 MLA convention. Jody Greene (2004: 321) appeared on the memorial panel, and her introduction to the special issue suggests that "without [Bray], 'friendship studies'—a field that resolutely and carefully reads the history of friendship and the history of sexuality into, through, and across each other—might well not exist." Bray was not the first person to write a monograph on the queer implications of early modern friend-

ship. Laurie Shannon (another contributor to the special issue) had already published *Sovereign Amity: Figures of Friendship in Shakespearean Contexts* (2002)
before Bray published *The Friend* (2003), but surely her book is indebted to Bray's
Homosexuality in Renaissance England (1982).

Masten's (2004) contribution to the volume, "Toward a Queer Address: The
Taste of Letters and Early Modern Male Friendship," married a foundational practice in literary studies—philology, analysis of the origins and changing meanings
of words—with another practice central to literary and historical work: analysis
of the "republic of letters." That is, he examined how private expressions of affec-
tion using the erotically charged term *sweet* can be found in what was once a very
public forum: letters between same-sex friends that were copied and shared among
small coteries of readers. George Haggerty's essay in the special issue made the
private public as he composed an encomium to his deceased lover. "Love and
Loss: An Elegy" is written in the spirit of Bray's work even as it does not mention
the historian. The essay takes the occasion of the loss of the author of *The Friend*
to reflect on the loss of another friend, and then to tap into "sources of consola-
tion this rich tradition [of the elegy] offers" (Haggerty 2004: 385–86). Nor does
Stephen Orgel's contribution, "Ganymede Agonistes," name Bray, but the historian
had read an early draft of the piece and had urged Orgel to "be more outrageous"
(Greene 2004: 232). So Bray undergirds these pieces even as they spectralize him.

I did not know Alan Bray, and I imagine that some of the contributors to
the special issue were close friends with him and others merely acquaintances or
only just connected by a shared field of interest. Michael Warner (1999: 115–16)
remarks that an "astonishing range of intimacies" emerge when one begins to
unpack the interleaved relationships among a group of queer friends. And I find
that the notion of friendship—with all its possible layers and sense of remaining
connected even when out of touch—speaks to the way the essays are and are not
in dialogue, how some of them went on to be something more and some did not.
For me personally, I feel uniquely connected to the issue, especially in retrospect,
having gotten to know some of the contributors long after having read it and having written my own book on friendship. And that it was in *GLQ* that these essays
appeared also holds special meaning for me. My own budding interest in the intersection between friendship and queer theory was already brimming during my
undergraduate days at UC Berkeley. When I graduated in 1993, it happened to
be the same year that *GLQ* was founded by Carolyn Dinshaw (who was at Berkeley at the time but with whom I never had a class) and David Halperin (whom I
met around that time through a then boyfriend at a lunch that I am sure neither
Halperin nor the ex would recall). It is hard to remember all the details now, but

these early seeds of experience and of scholarship end up proving fruitful in ways I could not have imagined and probably still cannot imagine.

In her introduction to this *GLQ* issue, Greene (2004: 321) stressed the complexity of discussing a founding figure in our field such as Bray because "familial and reproductive language in the vocabulary of memorialization is no accident; in fact, it may explain, at least in part, why scholars in LGBT studies, more than those in other fields, have found the territory of memorialization difficult, troubling, fraught." While I have been tracing lines of connection in this essay, I am avoiding the heterosexual logics of seminality, genealogy, and the notion of the founding (mother or father) figure so often used to describe relations between scholars and ideas. I have been instead, of course, thinking of that more comfortably queer model for relations: the rhizome. As Gilles Deleuze and Felix Guattari (1983: 12) put it, "A rhizome never ceases to connect semiotic chains, organizations of power, and events in the arts, sciences, and social struggles."[2] As we try to make sense of a field of scholarship, we often lose the sense of where things begin and end, of the very order of things. All work so often begins as something else, rhizomatically connecting casual conversations, love affairs, scholarly roundtables, published essays just as people are so often connected by shared friends. Indeed, as many queer people have known for a long time, friendship disrupts simple, vertical, teleological lines of relation. Yet this should not make us hesitate to celebrate certain manifestations of ideas, especially in the study of the history of sexuality, no matter how labyrinthine tracing lines of connection might become. "One of the most important characteristics of the rhizome," Deleuze and Guattari (1983: 26) remind us, "is that it always has multiple entrances." In our own work of coming out as queer and as queer scholars, we create our own histories in terms of previous scholarship that we realize we connect to. I find myself reminded here of a friend who described a medical appointment when the physician, conducting a rectal exam, asked if my friend felt any discomfort. He responded, "Only around the entrance." The doctor responded, "Around here, we call that 'the exit.'"

As queer scholars, we find our own ways in and our own ways out.

Notes

I wish to thank Leah Allen and John Petrus for their helpful suggestions on this essay.

1.   Certainly one answer to this call would have been that posed by Jonathan Goldberg (who also contributed to the *GLQ* special issue) and Madhavi Menon (2005) in "Queering History," *PMLA* 120, no. 5 (2005): 1608–17. Their proposed methodology

of "unhistoricism" or "homohistory" urges us to avoid seeing early texts as precursors to later ones or contemporary sexualities as expressed embryonically in earlier ones.

2. The explanation of the concept is more commonly drawn from Deleuze and Guattari's *A Thousand Plateaus* (1980), but I prefer this edition. I'm certain the book is actually an ex-boyfriend's copy because it has marginal notes in two different handwriting. One is mine and the other must be that of the same ex whom I joined for lunch with Halperin in 1993 (or it may have been 1992).

References

Deleuze, Gilles, and Félix Guattari. 1983. *On the Line*. Translated by John Johnston. New York: Semiotext(e).

Freccero, Carla. 2013. "Forum: Historicism and *Unhistoricism* in Queer Studies." *PMLA* 128, no. 3: 781–82.

Greene, Jody. 2004. "Introduction: The Work of Friendship: In Memoriam Alan Bray." *GLQ* 10, no. 3: 321.

Haggerty, George. 2004. "Love and Loss: An Elegy." *GLQ* 10, no. 3: 385–86.

Halberstam, Jack. 2013. "Game of Thrones: The Queer Season." April 8. bullybloggers .wordpress.com/tag/pmla/.

Masten, Jeffrey. 2004. "Toward a Queer Address: The Taste of Letters and Early Modern Male Friendship." *GLQ* 10, no. 3: 367–84.

———. 2016. *Queer Philologies: Sex, Language, and Affect in Shakespeare's Time*. Philadelphia: University of Pennsylvania Press.

Menon, Madhavi. 2005. "Queering History." *PMLA* 120, no. 5: 1608–17.

———. 2013. "Forum: Historicism and Unhistoricism in Queer Studies." *PMLA* 128, no. 3: 782–84.

Traub, Valerie. 2004. "Friendship's Loss: Alan Bray's Making of History." *GLQ* 10, no. 3: 339–65.

———. 2013. "The New Unhistoricism in Queer Studies." *PMLA* 128, no. 1: 21–39.

———. 2015. *Thinking Sex with the Early Moderns*. Philadelphia: University of Pennsylvania Press.

Warner, Michael. 1999. *The Trouble with Normal: Sex, Politics, and the Ethics of Queer Life*. New York: Free Press.

STILL WORKING

On Richard Meyer and David Román's *Art Works, Parts 1 & 2*

Andy Campbell

"Art Works, Parts 1 & 2," special issue edited by Richard Meyer and David Román. GLQ 12.3 (2006).

"*U*nder my bed. In the studio" (Middleman 2006: 474). This was the answer Glenn Ligon gave when asked about the location of a rarely exhibited series titled *Lest We Forget* (1998). Occasioned by a residency at Artpace in San Antonio, Texas, Ligon produced a set of five metal plaques—the kind most commonly associated with monuments—and placed them around the city, using double-sided tape to attach them to their supports. Each had a title and text of its own, broadly evocative of the "aesthetics of existence" that John Paul Ricco (2016) has called the consummate cruise, "a sense of incommensurability and an equality of inequivalence that is shared between you." Yet Ligon's plaques consistently end in disappointment, or at least a turn toward self-doubt and the quotidian business of living. For example, here is how the plaque titled "Hunky Guy" reads: "Hunky guy wearing sandals that scuff the ground as he walks. Long hair, black, shiny eyes. He looks at me as he's walking by. A little something-something between us, but so brief that I can't be sure if anything really happened beyond what I felt." I find it remarkable that such a text should live under someone's bed—the site of recuperation and sexual encounter, nested within the ostensibly productive space of the artist's studio.

Here is what is under my bed: five pairs of shoes, a twin foam mattress (for nonhunky guy guests), and a small stack of books and journals. To be fair, the books and journals are scattered all over my house and office, stacked two deep on bookshelves, and in random piles on my kitchen table and desk. But one of the journals under my bed is the second of two special issues of *GLQ* edited by Rich-

GLQ 25:1
DOI 10.1215/10642684-7275530
© 2019 by Duke University Press

ard Meyer and David Román (2006: 349) dedicated to unspooling "visual objects and cultural episodes as a queer way of knowing." When I initially bought these issues, over a decade ago, I was a PhD student in art history. I remember purchasing them on a research trip to Los Angeles while I was feeling particularly low—I had recently run up against some institutional barriers concerning what I wanted to study: the visual and material cultures of BDSM communities of the 1970s and 1980s, and the contemporary artists who engaged and renegotiated these historical aesthetics. Was such a thing art history? I thought so, but many others told me no. What I was doing, they said, was cultural studies, or visual studies, or visual cultural studies, but it was not art history. Policing of disciplinary boundaries is a mainstay of academic work, but, of course, these parsings felt personal. Which is why Meyer and Román's issues were a relief—calling in those who didn't quite fit within their disciplinary contexts. To my mind many of the articles in these issues would equally be at home in disciplinary journals—ones dedicated to art history or theater or performance studies. That such work was gathered together, and deserved not only one, but two, specially themed issues, was a symbolic and realpolitik gesture of affirmation and generosity.

In their first joint introduction Meyer and Román (2006: 167) posed two questions that remain relevant: "How have the visual and performing arts reshaped the governing terms of gender and sexuality? How have the arts fashioned a queer world, both in the past and the present?" To answer these questions, the issues' editors and authors turned to archives of various kinds, illuminating the vast methodological map/morass of queer possibility. Looking back now, I see that the issues' foregrounding of questions of the archive, and the dynamic relation of archives to queer thought and performance, captures a particular moment, or turn, in queer studies when archival methods and objects were under a new embrace and scrutiny.[1] The contents of the first of these special issues circled around questions of authenticity, absence, presence, and the seeming illegibility of rural and international queer lives: from the theatrical repositioning and ostensibly mainstream acceptance of the life of Charlotte von Mahlsdorf, "an East German transvestite"; to the censorship surrounding the fin-de-siècle photographer Wilhelm von Gloeden; from the archival findings (now validated by other scholars many times over) suggesting the depth and breadth of the artistic collaboration between French surrealist photographers Claude Cahun and Marcel Moore; to Michael Meads's photographs of Alabaman white men that "suggest and surpass homosocial bonding."

Photography and the circulation of photographic reproductions through periodicals are recurring concerns across the two issues. Photography's truth-claims have long been interrogated, and that line of critique found extensions in

Richard Meyer's article "Gay Power circa 1970," addressing (in part) Fred W. McDarrah's photographs of the exterior and interior of the Stonewall Inn, New York, and Ricardo Montez's read on a description of a Tseng Kwong Chi photograph of the artists Keith Haring and Angel Ortiz (better known as LA2) posing beside each other. Meyer's discussion of McDarrah's photographs and the self-representation of the Gay Liberation Front have been valuable in reassessing the visual cultures of gay liberation. Of particular interest is Meyer's (2006: 459) discussion of a handful of publicity ads published in "Gay Power," in which naked people (mostly, but not exclusively men) read the publication—the upraised newspaper masking their faces and evidencing the tension between "collective power and presence [and . . .] individual liability and restriction." You can see the influence of Meyer's archival findings in the work of the photographer and medieval scholar Leah DeVun, who created a body of work while she was in residence at ONE National Gay and Lesbian Archives in 2012.

In a photograph from the resultant series titled *Latent Images*, two women read a copy of the feminist periodical *Everywoman*. Unlike the publicity ads for "Gay Power" in which every reader grasps a copy of the periodical, the two figures in DeVun's photograph share in the task of reading—their two heads peeking above the top horizon of a single upraised newspaper, leaning on each other. Their closeness seems to contradict the issue of *Everywoman*'s hetero-dyadic headline: "Woman as Masochist / Man as Sadist." Another of DeVun's photographs, this one featuring a single reader, appears elsewhere on the cover of a 2014 special issue of *Radical History Review* dedicated to "queering archives" (Murphy, Marshall, and Tortorici 2014). I notice and read these as critical expansions on Meyer's project, additions, and echoes of his archival findings and readings.

The best inclusions of this special double issue of *GLQ* are the ones where a writer's vulnerability and pizzazz are allowed to break through the sometimes deadening curtain of academic style. The republication of a long blog entry written by Jill Dolan on the Five Lesbian Brothers' play *Oedipus at Palm Springs* is admirable in this regard. In it, she considers the production alongside her own expectations, and in doing so she worries about the Brothers' growing mainstream acceptance. In her writing I find a Brothers' lover, a fan and a friend, and an incisive theater critic not complacent with coasting. Then there is Deborah Bright and Erica Rand's "Queer Plymouth," a collaborative look at the "queer history of Plymouth," a place of mythological pull on the political imaginary of the United States. Reading their accounting of the monuments of Plymouth and their appearance in popular culture, for example, on television reality shows such as *The Real World Philadelphia* and *Colonial House*, the duo's self-described "lovely buzz that ani-

Figure 1. Leah DeVun, *Everywoman* (2012), C-print, 23.5" × 31".
Courtesy of the artist

mates our pal-dom"(Bright and Rand 2006: 259) comes through loud and clear. In sections titled "Booty" and "Clothes Make the White Man," Bright and Rand inhabit the tourist's temporal drag ("We are dykes who found tourist thrills that might not match our personal ads . . .") (2006: 273) to enact a critique of historical sites central to the fictive coherency of nationalist discourse. Both articles end with similar sentiments (Dolan: "Blog on."; Bright and Rand: "Rock on."), and they remain for me exemplary of writing that, in the face of having to decide between rigor and humor, chooses both.

Embedded in the first of these two issues was a special section curated by Meyer and Román (2006: 279) addressing the twenty-fifth anniversary of "living with AIDS." The three articles in this section included Román's rumination on Craig Lucas and Norman René's 1990 film, *Longtime Companion*, analyzing Vito Russo's embrace of the film's portrayal of homosexuals as "white, handsome, and upscale professionals" and instead offering a reading of the film emphasizing AIDS as a "collective social experience." Lucas Hilderbrand (2006: 310) reviews the literature on AIDS activism and enters the fray as a person generationally removed from the inception of ACT-UP, arguing for video as a technology that "presents our most immediate connection to this earlier moment." And, finally, Alexandra Juhasz's article, "Video Remains: Nostalgia, Technology, and Queer Archive Activism," connects Hilderbrand's enframing of activist videos as profoundly necessary texts to the messy media temporalities that make such attachments possible. She writes of video as "both duration and action machine that allows us to embrace responsibility and interactivity in the face of mourning" (Juhasz 2006: 236). In each of these articles the authors grapple with the moving remains of an activist moment that each seems to believe had already passed on. Of course this is a handy fiction, one that puts in abeyance the activist geometries of the present—but then again, reexamination and reevaluation are necessary for projects that seek to redress the present from another angle, one at a historical "remove" from the subject in question.

Like how some things find their way under your bed, so that one day, you might remember them again.

Note

1.   Key texts here would include Diana Taylor, *The Archive and the Repertoire: Performing Cultural Memory in the Americas* (2003); Ann Cvetkovich, *An Archive of Feelings: Trauma, Sexuality, and Lesbian Public Cultures* (2003); and J. Jack Halberstam, *In a Queer Time and Place: Transgender Bodies, Subcultural Lives* (2005). For a critical historiography of this literature, see Kate Eichhorn, *The Archival Turn in Feminism: Outrage in Order* (2013), especially Eichhorn's introduction.

References

Bright, Deborah, and Erica Rand. 2006. "Queer Plymouth." *GLQ* 12, no. 2: 259–77.

Hilderbrand, Lucas. 2006. "Retroactivism." *GLQ* 12, no. 2: 303–17.

Juhasz, Alexandra. 2006. "Video Remains: Nostalgia, Technology, and Queer Archive Activism." *GLQ* 12, no. 2: 319–28.

Meyer, Richard. 2006. "Gay Power circa 1970: Visual Strategies for Sexual Revolution." *GLQ* 12, no. 3: 441–64.

Meyer, Richard, and David Román. 2006. "Introduction: Art Works, Parts 1 & 2." *GLQ* 12, no. 3: 349–50.

Middleman, Rachel. 2006. "History with a Small 'H': A Conversation with Glenn Ligon." *GLQ* 12, no. 3: 465–74.

Murphy, Kevin P., Daniel Marshall, and Zeb Tortorici, eds. 2014. "Queering Archives: Historical Unravellings." Special issue, *Radical History Review*, no. 120.

Ricco, John Paul. 2016. "The Art of the Consummate Cruise and the Essential Risk of the Common (2/2)," *Feedback*, February 46. openhumanitiespress.org/feedback /sexualities/the-consummate-cruise-2.

THE QUEER TEMPORALITIES
OF *QUEER TEMPORALITIES*

Elizabeth Freeman

"Queer Temporalities," special issue edited by Elizabeth Freeman.
GLQ 13.2–3 (2007).

$\mathcal{T}$here's something very odd about being asked to reflect on my special issue of *GLQ*, "Queer Temporalities," for a twenty-fifth anniversary issue. Anniversaries mark births, marriages, graduations, and deaths: they are the stuff of normative timelines and of events that mark the legible contours of a life sanctioned as such. Furthermore, as I sit looking at the special issue and wondering what to say about it a little over a decade later, I'm flooded with temporal clichés: is it still fresh, or has it become obsolete? What might we learn from it now? Were we all just stuck in millennial thinking of a sort that has been superseded by 2018? What if I could go back in time and do it better (why was I so stupid as not to consider Afropessimism, for example)? How have the ideas explored in it—in just the roundtable alone, the affective relation to history and the emotional aspects of becoming-historical; the question of multiple temporalities in the present; the paradoxes of derivation; critiques of rational and progressive time; the possibility of un-becoming; the ways that everyday queer life fosters alternate temporal schemas; and mourning and death—developed in the last decade? Can I just take credit for inventing the roundtable for *GLQ* and run? These all seem beside the point of the temporal thinking that actually took place in the issue.

More than anything, from the vantage point of over a decade later, I'm struck by the capaciousness of what thinking about time allows us to address. The articles are all challenging theoretical works, each of which offers concepts that are still meaningful: Kathleen Biddick's "excessive flesh" that refuses the supercessionary logic of martyrdom, for example, seems especially fruitful for think-

GLQ 25:1
DOI 10.1215/10642684-7275544
© 2019 by Duke University Press

ing about the African American bodies gunned down by police violence. Tom Boellstorff's "coincidence" that works against the apocalyptic futures of straight time and queer radicalism alike seems to have come to fruition with the advent of legalized gay marriage in the United States, which has surely cemented all kinds of relations of mutual care as much as it has rendered non-couple-centered forms of relationality less significant. Similarly, Dana Luciano's careful unfolding of the "open memory" that emerges from melodrama's static, bourgeois-domestic moments seems relevant to the project of not having contempt for domesticity when fewer and fewer people can afford simple shelter. As we enter the eighteenth year of what may be the longest war in US history, the war in Afghanistan, it also seems salutary to recall Geeta Patel's demonstration that the hetero-reproductive order is based less in marriage and the division of labor it engenders than in economies of war that turn dead soldier-spouses into insurance and pension payouts. In light of how last February's shooting at Marjory Stoneman Douglas High School in Park-land, Florida, has brought youth activism against gun control into vivid focus, I am reminded of Kathryn Bond Stockton's understanding that the motiveless activity of murderous children begets unpredictable modes of relationality—though here, it is friends of the murdered rather than the murderer who represent those modes. Kate Thomas's exploration of how two incestuous, intergenerational lesbian lovers of the Victorian era made "being out of their own time" the basis for their passion shows how completely we flatten the erotics of temporal difference under the discourse of pedophilia (a discourse also taken up by the review essay for that issue, in which Jon Davies discusses a series of films about intergenerational love). As to the late José Esteban Muñoz's early articulation of a concept central to his brilliant *Cruising Utopia*, the "no-longer-conscious as the not-yet-here"—that feels like a flame in a darkness that grows ever nearer.

Like poetry, the patience of thought that I see in these pieces and in the roundtable is not a luxury—especially, the patience of thought that it takes to read these complicated theoretical works is not a luxury in a moment in which our "President" speaks in one-word sound bites ("Sad!") alternating with long strings of asyntactic gibberish ("Look, having nuclear—my uncle was a great professor and scientist and engineer, Dr. John Trump at MIT; good genes, very good genes, OK, very smart, the Wharton School of Finance, very good, very smart—you know, if you're a conservative Republican, if I were a liberal, if, like, OK, if I ran as a liberal Democrat, they would say I'm one of the smartest people anywhere in the world—it's true!—but when you're a conservative Republican they try—oh, do they do a number—. . .").[1] Nor is the taking up of a seemingly abstract and immaterial problem such as temporality a luxury. As with the dissident sexual practices and the critical stances that *are* queerness, there can be no advance certainty about what thinking about temporality can yield, politically speaking. Far from being a set of empty containers—minutes, hours, days, weeks, months, years, decades, periods—into which our experience gets poured, time is actively constructed by the powerful such that any number of other, more obviously political aspects of life, seem natural: it is a tool for the naturalization of power relations. Turning the lens onto time, brightening up the "color" of time so that it emerges from the background, as it were, scholarship such as the work in this special issue allows us to think about terrorism, marriage and domesticity, childhood and adolescence, poetry, and revolution, in new ways.

It also allowed me to think about how collective thought might be made across the distances that separate us as academics who often work alone, launching our ideas into a void and waiting for responses in the form of reviews that can take years, and otherwise limited to whatever time we can cobble together from within our departments or at annual conferences. Editing is one way that thought becomes collaborative, if not quite collective, the rhythm of draft-response-revision being quicker than that of the academic review system. So when I agreed to edit a special issue, it was partly out of the purely selfish motive of wanting to be in conversation with people while I was, in real life, mostly trapped at home with a newborn. But another way was the roundtable, whose relationship to time was improvisatory and imperfect, but also different from the usual ways that academics think together. I invented it out of a political conundrum: how do I honor the important extant work in the then-unnamed subfield of queer temporality studies while making room for emerging work? I decided to invite scholars who had already written a book (or in one case, produced a set of videos) touching on or elaborating the topic: Carolyn Dinshaw (*Getting Medieval*, 1999); Lee Edelman (*No Future*, 2004); Roderick A. Ferguson (*Aberrations in Black*, 2003); Carla Freccero (*Queer/Early/Modern*, 2005); J. Jack Halberstam (*In a Queer Time and Place*, 2005); Annamarie Jagose (*Inconsequence*, 2002); Christopher Nealon (*Foundlings*, 2001); and Nguyen Tan Hoang (video work, 1990s–early 2000s). I asked a set of open-ended, fairly simple questions, sent them to the first three, then collated their answers and sent them to the next three, did the same, and sent to the final group, for three rounds. The scholars were unfailingly polite about my nudges and reminders to keep the process moving, and extremely generous about engaging with one another's ideas, even where they disagreed. I had to edit the whole a little bit, breaking up chunks of text so that similar topics appeared near one another, rearranging the order of some responses, and so on—and of course the last person to send in responses got, it seemed, the "last word." So there was an intriguing analog-meets-digital temporal aspect to the project, where I could not fully preserve the analog time in which people responded to one another, and had to cut-and-paste a little bit to make it look as conceptually flowing as I could, and to make it look a bit more like a live roundtable. The resulting piece, it seems, is cited and used in classrooms fairly often, for it offers a density of concepts and a kind of crash course in the field—but what I like best about it is that it was, for a brief couple of months, the closest thing to a scholarly conversation that I could produce out of almost complete isolation.

After I put this special issue to bed, as we say in publishing, I wrote one more document about time for it, titled "How to Edit a Special Issue of *GLQ*." It was my gift to Ann Cvetkovich and Annamarie Jagose, then editors of the journal. They had spent umpteen hours answering my queries, helping me smooth out political problems, and plotting out a timeline for the issue's production. I wanted to put everything I had learned from them into a tool kit, so that they would not have to reinvent the wheel every time a special issue editor came aboard. In short, I wanted to save them some time in the future. I daresay that this attempt to reclaim their time for them, to lay out the process for collating collective thought into a lasting document, has circulated and been used as often as the special issue has.

Note

1. Republican presidential candidate Donald Trump spoke this "sentence" on July 19, 2016, at Sun City's Magnolia Hall in South Carolina, as captured by C-Span at www.c-span.org/video/?c4546796/donald-trump-sentence.

References

Dinshaw, Carolyn. 1999. *Getting Medieval: Sexualities and Communities, Pre- and Post-modern*. Durham, NC: Duke University Press.

Edelman, Lee. 2004. *No Future: Queer Theory and the Death Drive*. Durham, NC: Duke University Press.

Ferguson, Roderick A. 2003. *Aberrations in Black: Toward a Queer of Color Critique*. Minneapolis: University of Minnesota Press.

Freccero, Carla. 2005. *Queer/Early/Modern*. Durham, NC: Duke University Press.

Halberstam, J. Jack. 2005. *In a Queer Time and Place: Transgender Bodies, Subcultural Lives*. New York: New York University Press.

Jagose, Annamarie. 2002. *Inconsequence: Lesbian Representation and the Logic of Sequence*. Ithaca, NY: Cornell University Press.

Nealon, Christopher. 2001. *Foundlings: Historical Emotion before Stonewall*. Durham, NC: Duke University Press.

Appendix A

Table of Contents, "Queer Temporalities," special double issue of *GLQ* (13.2–3), edited by Elizabeth Freeman.

Elizabeth Freeman, Introduction.

Carolyn Dinshaw, Lee Edelman, Roderick A. Ferguson, Carla Freccero, Elizabeth Freeman, Judith Halberstam, Annamarie Jagose, Christopher Nealon, Nguyen Tan Hoang, "Theorizing Queer Temporalities: A Roundtable Discussion."

Kathleen Biddick, "Unbinding the Flesh in the Time That Remains: Crusader Martyrdom Then and Now."

Tom Boellstorff, "When Marriage Falls: Queer Coincidences in Straight Time."

Dana Luciano, "Coming Around Again: The Queer Momentum of *Far from Heaven*."

Geeta Patel, "Time to Tell: How to Tell the Proper Time? Finance and Cinema."

Kathryn Bond Stockton, "Feeling Like Killing? Queer Temporalities of Murderous Motives among Queer Children."

Kate Thomas, "'What Time We Kiss': Michael Field's Queer Temporalities."

José Esteban Muñoz, "Cruising the Toilet: LeRoi Jones / Amiri Baraka, Radical Black Traditions, and Queer Futurity."

Moving Image Review: Jon Davies, "Imagining Intergenerationality: Representation and Rhetoric in the Pedophile Movie."

Book Review: Peter Coviello, "World Enough: Sex and Time in Recent Queer Studies."

ON TIME

Whitney Monaghan

"Queer Temporalities," special issue edited by Elizabeth Freeman.
GLQ 13.2–3 (2007).

*I*t happened in 2007 (volume 13, number 2–3, to be precise); *GLQ: A Journal of Lesbian and Gay Studies* was on time. By this I mean literally on the topic of "time," but also I mean to gesture to the notion of timeliness and arriving on time to the conversation, to the party, to work. In her introduction to this special issue on queer temporalities, Elizabeth Freeman laid out some ideas for incorporating time into queer theory (and queer theory into time), noting correlations and correspondences between the erotic and the temporal. Freeman demonstrated how we might combine queer theory and temporality into a framework to think critically about everything from life narratives to the eight-hour workday, to premature ejaculation, the AIDS crisis, the queer past and future, the lived experience of being an LGBTIQ person, and everything in between. She also elucidated ways to think about temporality, sensation, and affect in and through queer theory, noting in an early comment that "the sensation of asynchrony can be viewed as a queer phenomenon—something felt on, with, or as a body, something experienced as a mode of erotic difference or even as a means to express or enact ways of being and connecting that have not yet arrived or never will" (Freeman 2007: 159). This provocative introduction was followed by a roundtable "theorizing queer temporalities," where Carolyn Dinshaw, Lee Edelman, Roderick A. Ferguson, Carla Freccero, Judith Halberstam, Annamarie Jagose, Christopher Nealon, and Nguyen Tan Hoang ruminated on several key questions and puzzles: How does sex intersect with temporality? How is time part of the history of sexuality and in what ways has it shaped queer studies? What might queer theory's temporal turn open up "conceptually, institutionally, politically, or otherwise?" (Dinshaw et al. 2007: 177).

GLQ 25:1
DOI 10.1215/10642684-7275558
© 2019 by Duke University Press

You don't have to dig very deep to see that temporality is laid in the foundations of our critical project. We encounter this coalition between the erotic and the temporal in every Queer Studies 101. Look back at volume 1 of Michel Foucault's *History of Sexuality*, and you'll find it in his description of the moment that homosexuality and heterosexuality were invented. He describes sexual and bodily norms as constructions motivated by a set of basic concerns: "to ensure population, to reproduce labor capacity, to perpetuate the form of social relations" (Foucault 1990: 37). For Foucault, this process was governed by the desire to constitute a normative sexuality connected to a normative body and "economically useful and politically conservative" (ibid.). To me this reads as evidence of an emergent heterosexual ideology shaping the temporality of labor, social life, and politics. Take a leap to Judith Butler's oeuvre, and you'll also find temporality, especially when she describes gender as the "repeated stylization of the body, a set of repeated acts within a highly rigid regulatory frame that congeal *over time* to produce the appearance of substance, of a natural sort of being" (Butler [1999] 2006: 45; emphasis added). Even the foundational work of Eve Kosofsky Sedgwick drips with time. Her description of queer as "the open mesh of possibilities, gaps, overlaps, dissonances and resonances, lapses and excesses of meaning" (Sedgwick 1993: 8) could very well be about queer temporal experience—it has since been taken up by those scholars interested in the affective possibilities of queer temporality.

What I'm getting at is that queer theory was always in some way inflected by temporality (some may say this relationship is as old as time), but it was the "Queer Temporalities" special issue that marked the field's distinct and deliberate turn toward temporality as a critical frame, a move that aimed to "reimagine 'queer' as a set of possibilities produced out of temporal and historical difference," to illuminate "the manipulation of time as a way to produce both bodies and relationalities (or even non-relationality)" (Freeman 2007: 159) and to think of temporal orientation (whether one is focused on the past, present, or future) as a profoundly political act.

They say that queer time is like being on a fifteen-minute delay, but this special issue of *GLQ* was by no means late. At just the right time it entered into fiercely oppositional debates between optimistic and antisocial queer projects, which sought to frame queer politics through either futurity or negativity (Caserio et al. 2006). In many ways the issue responded to the works that had ignited these debates and that had been published in the years preceding (see Edelman 2004; Halberstam 2005; Caserio et al. 2006), providing these scholars with a way to directly address their positions on the politics of queer temporality. Later that same year came Heather Love's (2007) powerful reflection on backward orientation and queer history, suggesting that *GLQ* was right in the middle of a broader conversation about the political efficacy of one's temporal orientation.

For me, this special issue provided an avenue for thinking about the time of queerness and for thinking through queerness in relation to the temporality of lived experience. For others, this opened up what Freeman (2007: 159) describes as "a more productively porous queer studies" conceived in relation to other disciplines, shaping studies of race, nation and migration through this groundbreaking union of the erotic and the temporal. For scholars such Sara Ahmed (2010) and José Esteban Muñoz (2009), this framework opened up queer theory to the future, the future to queerness, and both to happiness. The issue also inspired works by Lauren Berlant (2011), Freeman (2010), and Kathryn Bond Stockton (2009), all of whom grappled with the question of what a queer alternative to heteronormative linear temporality might look or feel like, or how it might be represented or experienced.

Taking up the questions posed in Freeman's introduction and in the articles that followed, many of us have since asked, can time be queered? What would a queer temporality look like? How might it be experienced? What would its political worth be? Where does queerness stand in relation to futurity? And, perhaps most importantly, is there future for queer theory itself? Rather than provide us with a straightforward means of answering these questions, "Queer Temporalities" reframed our conversations, debates, and polemics on sexuality, politics, and the erotic, enabling us to rethink the very meaning of queer as a concept that is always entangled with temporality. This was perhaps best demonstrated by the late José Esteban Muñoz, a scholar who was profoundly invested in the queer future. Muñoz penned the final article in the special issue. His article concludes with a statement worth remembering: "Queerness should and could be about a desire for another way of being both in the world and in time, a desire that resists mandates to accept that which is not enough" (Muñoz 2007: 365). Given the unprecedented changes in the political landscape in the United States and beyond, the expansion of (some) queer rights that have come at the expense of others, the oppressive violence leveled against queer people on a daily basis, and the precarity of the academy, particularly for young queer academics such as myself, now more than ever we need to remember this.

References

Ahmed, Sara. 2010. *The Promise of Happiness*. Durham, NC: Duke University Press.

Berlant, Lauren. 2011. *Cruel Optimism*. Durham, NC: Duke University Press.

Butler, Judith. [1999] 2006. *Gender Trouble: Tenth Anniversary Edition*. New York: Routledge.

Caserio, Robert L., Lee Edelman, Judith Halberstam, José Esteban Muñoz, and Tim Dean. 2006. "PMLA Conference Debate: The Antisocial Thesis in Queer Theory." *Modern Language Association Annual Conference* 121, no. 3: 819–28.

Dinshaw, Carolyn, Lee Edelman, Roderick A. Ferguson, Carla Freccero, Elizabeth Freeman, Judith Halberstam, Annamarie Jagose, Christopher Nealon, and Nguyen Tan Hoang. 2007. "Theorising Queer Temporalities." *GLQ* 13, nos. 2–3: 177–96.

Edelman, Lee. 2004. *No Future: Queer Theory and the Death Drive*. Durham, NC: Duke University Press.

Foucault, Michel. 1990. *The History of Sexuality*. London: Penguin.

Freeman, Elizabeth. 2007. "Introduction." *GLQ* 13, nos. 2–3: 159–76.

———. 2010. *Time Binds: Queer Temporalities, Queer Histories*. Durham, NC: Duke University Press.

Halberstam, Judith. 2005. *In a Queer Time and Place: Transgender Bodies, Subcultural Lives*. New York: New York University Press.

Love, Heather. 2007. *Feeling Backwards: Loss and the Politics of Queer History*. Cambridge, MA: Harvard University Press.

Muñoz, José Esteban. 2007. "Cruising the Toilet: LeRoi Jones / Amiri Baraka, Radical Black Traditions, and Queer Futurity." *GLQ* 13, nos. 2–3: 353–68.

———. 2009. *Crusing Utopia: The Then and There of Queer Futurity*. New York: New York University Press.

Sedgwick, Eve Kosofsky. 1993. *Tendencies*. Durham, NC: Duke University Press.

Stockton, Kathryn Bond. 2009. *The Queer Child, or Growing Sideways in the Twentieth Century*. Durham, NC: Duke University Press.

CRITICS ON CRITICS

Queer Bonds

Chase Gregory

*"Queer Bonds," special issue edited by Joshua J. Weiner and
Damon Young. GLQ 17.2–3 (2011).*

*E*ight years after *GLQ* published a special issue titled "Queer Bonds," the questions it poses are still unanswered. This is partly by design. Suspending long-standing debates about sociality, utopia, negativity, antinormativity, and identification, guest editors Joshua J. Weiner and Damon Young (2011: 233) "aim less to identify a 'new wave' in queer scholarship than to uncover the ways that alongside its project as a theory of the subject (of 'queer' subjects), queer theory has also always already been a project of theorizing the relations *between* subjects." In 2011 the editors of the second issue of volume 17 used the issue to interrogate a wide range of relations, and the contributors to "Queer Bonds" take its title many different ways, without resolution. Today, the debates persist, sometimes to the point of stagnation. But the charge of this special issue—to think the (im)possibility of queer sociality—continues to be a generative and uneasy challenge.[1]

The subject of queer bonds harks back to queer theory's foundation. At the start of her 1993 collection *Tendencies*, Eve Kosofsky Sedgwick recalls a scene of queer bonds forged across identities: marching with ACT UP activists in 1990, she notices that most of the lesbians sport T-shirts that read "BIG FAG," while the majority of the gay men in the crowd wear shirts emblazed with the words "LICK BUSH" or, more simply, "DYKE." As Sedgwick goes on to explain, the cross-identifications that she observes at the gay pride parade in New York epitomizes an aspect of *queer* she wants to emphasize in her theoretical work. "The word 'queer' itself," she observes, "means *across*" (Sedgwick 1993: xii).

GLQ 25:1
DOI 10.1215/10642684-7275572
© 2019 by Duke University Press

It is no coincidence that this particular understanding of *queer* emerges in 1993, in a climate of relentless right-wing social, economic, and political attacks on women, gay men, and racial minorities. At the time of Sedgwick's writing, state violence blatantly relied on the invocation of certain identities.[2] As such, the term *queer* proved useful for activists in multiple instructive ways: as a reclaimed slur, it sided with perversion and pleasure rather than respectability and assimilation; as a uncertain descriptor, it disavowed identity categories while still invoking specific stigmatized sexualities. As the threat of AIDS in the United States has—at least, in public perception—shifted from immanent death to long-term illness, conceptions of queer have also shifted. Given this shift, the *queer* that Sedgwick invokes in her early work might not be the same *queer* that is often employed today to mean antinormative or radical sexuality. In contrast to this current understanding, *queer* understood in the context of cross-identificatory bonds delinks the antinormative from the anti-identitarian.[3] "Queer Bonds" continues this admirable theoretical work, calling on theorists to attend to socialities that "have won space in the world without being reducible to violent modes of appropriative privilege" (Weiner and Young 2011: 230).

As Weiner and Young point out in their introduction, "academic sociality itself" now constitutes just such a space in the world (ibid.).[4] With this in mind, they spend time performing academic sociality, most notably in a section titled "Critical Bonds," which constitutes about a third of the issue. Nearly all the mini-essays in the "Critical Bonds" section follow a "[critic X] on [critic Y]" formula: Carla Freccero's "Daddy's Girl—on Leo Bersani"; Zakiyyah Iman Jackson's "Waking Nightmares—on David Marriott"; Heather Love's "'His Way'—on D. A. Miller." The titillating prospect of "critic on critic" action gestures toward the erotics of friendship and familiarity that permeate US queer criticism (made all the sexier by the subtitle's valences of bondage play). As the contributors to the special issue would most likely be quick to admit, the world of academic queer theory itself is at times a heady and intoxicating brew of celebrity and exclusivity, what Lauren Berlant and Michael Warner—writing in 1995!—refer to as its "star system" (347). It still feels like this, to me, often, especially at conferences.

As it happens, "Queer Bonds" is the result of a graduate student conference by the same name held at the University of California, Berkeley, in February 2009. I did not go, because in February 2009 I had just started college. In fact, by my calculation, I had read my first queer theory only two months prior. It was Miller's "Anal Rope." I downloaded a grainy photocopy for my first undergraduate English class, Lee Edelman's infamous "Hitchcock" lecture course. I still remember trying to explain to my patient but incredulous roommate the thrill of this initial exposure. Here was close reading, threateningly close; world-shakingly close in a way I could not articulate for many years, after more reading, more queer criticism, more copies of articles and more borrowed theory books.

It was also in 2009 that I first read Sedgwick's (1987) "A Poem Is Being Written" (again for class; this time Joe Litvak's). I found many things in "A Poem Is Being Written" that afforded me the occasion to forge a queer bond of my own with Sedgwick: an adolescence spent composing poems, a long-standing cross-identification with gay men, a shared perverse affinity for both long sentences and anality, and a reflexive narcissism that I hoped others found charming. Again, this story is excruciatingly familiar. The guest editors also describe their own initial "queer bonds" as forged through cross-identificatory encounter—in their introduction, they remember a "straight" female teacher knowingly lending her male student a copy of Leo Bersani's *Homos*. We aren't told if this memory belongs to Weiner or Young, but we are told that "it doesn't matter" (Weiner and Young 2011: 226).

I like reading "Queer Bonds" because it affirms things that I feel but am embarrassed to admit: namely, the power of the bonds that structure this field. Some of these bonds tie us down. Some we might want to break, or even more rigidly define. There are bonds of labor exchange, for example, between professors and their graduate student workers—bonds that the recent graduate union movements across the country continue to bring to light. Here are some of the things these academic and pedagogical bonds can feel like/can be: mentorship, friendship, rivalry, embarrassment, flirtation, celebrity stalking, the family romance, regular romance, acting, spectating, capitalist exploitation, coaching, having a nemesis, having an uncle, awkwardness, debt, networking, pen pal correspondence, hatred, love, uncertainty, failure, anger, exchange, ambivalence. I am only six years out of college, and that means that right now I still negotiate what it means when my academic bonds, now a decade old, shift from mentorship into collegiality.

The bonds produced by the academy are also bonds that bind us to the names with whom we have studied, or under whom we have worked. As young scholars, we are encouraged to commit some light parricide, but not too much; citation, after all, also catalyzes powerful bonds that result in social capital. Though it may make us chafe to admit it, these academic pedigrees often feel like family bonds—and not "queer" family bonds, either; just regular, boring oedipal ones. The introduction to "Queer Bonds" boasts that the special issue comprises "as many as three 'generations' of queer scholarship" (ibid.: 233). But what makes an academic generation? How do you measure it? In book acknowledgments? In tenure granted? (In midnights? In cups of coffee . . . ?)

I was born the year *Epistemology of the Closet* and *Gender Trouble* were published. By my estimation, this makes me a third-generation queer theorist. Miller, in his contribution to "Critical Bonds," writes about the privileged position of the third. Miller notes that his subject, the late, great deconstructionist Barbara Johnson, often found herself mediating between two opposed approaches, claims, or ideas. "In that cognitively enviable third position," he writes, "[Johnson] could give the series a sense of completion, put forward a decisive-seeming last word" (Miller 2011: 368).[5] I question whether Johnson's "third position" always resulted in decisive conclusion. Often, presented with two sides, Johnson argues that they are both true and untrue; she answers, slyly, "Yes and no." In her classic feminist essay, "Apostrophe, Animation, and Abortion," she writes, "It is often said, in literary-theoretical circles, that to focus on undecidability is to be apolitical. . . . on the contrary, the undecidable *is* the political. There is a politics precisely because there is undecidability" (Johnson 1986: 35). In Johnson's essay, the indeterminacy of violence and subjecthood is the site of politics. Similarly, the ambiguity at the heart of Weiner and Young's understanding of queer bonds is what makes them a site of political and theoretical purchase.

Like Johnson, the editors of "Queer Bonds" hold a privileged position as mediating thirds; also like her, they sit with contradiction rather than definitively conclude. For Weiner and Young (2011: 236), what makes queer bonds queer is "a *simultaneous* adhesion and dehiscence, a centripetal pull toward the social and a radical centrifugal drive away from it." There is value in remaining attentive to the ways in which this impossible simultaneity operates. More interesting than the existence of queer bonds is their paradoxical mechanism: the very impossibility of the persistence of queer sociality is its driving force. Rather than side with the antisocial or the utopian, the normative or antinormative, "Queer Bonds" teaches us that queer theory's greatest potential lies in its inability to escape dramatically negotiating between the two.

Notes

1. Rereading "Queer Bonds," I thought of many examples of work that, though unmentioned in the volume and disparate in scope, might fall under its titular phrase. A few include the following: Tim Dean's (2009) ethnography of bug chasers and barebacking culture, Christina Sharpe's (2011) poetic and historical work on the monstrous intimacies of slavery and its wake, Karen Barad's (2011) theories of queer ethics, quantum

physics, and atomic bonds, Lauren Berlant and Lee Edelman's (2013) back-and-forth about the unbearable social nonrelation, and Kadji Amin's (2017) recent queer theorization of politically unsavory objects.

2. Consider, for example, the Centers for Disease Control and Prevention's early "four H's" campaign, which warned that AIDS manifested primarily in the "high risk" groups "Haitians, hemophiliacs, homosexuals and heroin addicts" (Washington 2010: n.p.).

3. Robyn Wiegman makes a similar observation in her recent article "Eve's Triangles, or Queer Studies beside Itself" (2015). Wiegman reminds her readers that "when the normalization of AIDS remained a cogent and much needed political goal, Sedgwick renewed the call for a 'queer analysis, not a strictly gay one,' to address a 'disease that respects no simple boundaries of identity'" (ibid.: 50). Wiegman reads this particular invocation of "queer analysis" not as a renewed commitment to antinormative political projects in the post-AIDS-crisis moment but as a "confrontation with convergences" (ibid.).

4. Weiner and Young (2011: 230) make this claim with a wink, given that they themselves are publishing in one of the primary gatekeepers of that queer academic space: "For all the sexism, racism, and occasionally overt homophobia we still face in the academy, there do exist spaces (*GLQ* included) where leading an explicitly queer intellectual life in print as a mode of professional advancement names an institutionally viable and socially intelligible path across the profession."

5. Miller (2011: 368) goes on to claim that Johnson's alleged desire to be "brought out" constitutes a "perverse" (queer?) wish to depose the triangle in which she plays the mediating third in a conversation between two prominent critics: "But this time around, more remarkably, she seems interested in provoking a series in which she would occupy not the third but the second position, after Miller's essay on Barthes, and before. . . . You will have grasped the open secret harbored in the essay, the wish for a *third* essay to be called—inevitably—'Bringing Out Barbara Johnson,' in which Barbara would be granted, as opposed to the critical advantage of coming last, the writerly privilege of being primary."

References

Amin, Kadji. 2017. *Disturbing Attachments: Genet, Modern Pederasty, and Queer History.* Durham, NC: Duke University Press.

Barad, Karen. 2011. "Nature's Queer Performativity." *Qui Parle: Critical Humanities and Social Sciences* 19, no. 2: 121–58.

Berlant, Lauren, and Lee Edelman. 2013. *Sex, or the Unbearable.* Durham, NC: Duke University Press.

Berlant, Lauren, and Michael Warner. 1995. "What Does Queer Theory Teach Us About X?" *PMLA* 110, no. 3: 343–49.

Dean, Tim. 2009. *Unlimited Intimacy: Reflections on the Subculture of Barebacking.* Chicago: University of Chicago Press.

Johnson, Barbara. 1986. "Apostrophe, Animation, and Abortion." *Diacritics* 16, no. 1: 29–47.

Miller, D. A. 2011. "Call for Papers: In Memoriam Barbara Johnson." *GLQ* 17, nos. 2–3: 223–41.

———. "Anal Rope." 1990. *Representations* 32, no. 1: 114–33.

Sedgwick, Eve Kosofsky. 1987. "A Poem Is Being Written." *Representations* 17, no. 1: 110–43.

———. 1993. *Tendencies.* Durham, NC: Duke University Press.

Sharpe, Christina. 2011. *Monstrous Intimacies: Making Post-Slavery Subjects.* Durham, NC: Duke University Press.

Washington, Eric. 2010. "The AIDS Crisis Has Always Been Defined by What We Don't Know." *Colorlines*, December 1. www.colorlines.com/content/aids-epidemic-has-always-been-defined-what-we-dont-know.

Weiner, Joshua J., and Damon Young. 2011. "Queer Bonds." *GLQ* 17, nos. 2–3: 223–41.

Wiegman, Robyn. 2015. "Eve's Triangles, or Queer Studies beside Itself." *differences: A Journal of Feminist Cultural Studies* 26, no. 1: 48–73.

AFTER THE LOVE

Remembering *Black/Queer/Diaspora*

Jafari Sinclaire Allen and Omise'eke Natasha Tinsley

"Black/Queer/Diaspora," special issue edited by Jafari Sinclaire Allen. GLQ 18.2–3 (2012).

Dear Jafari,

So wonderful to hear your voice coming through the car yesterday. Since we never catch each other by phone more than twice a year, what a gift to write this together—because it means we *had* to find time to call! And because the only time I had was driving with Matt to pick up my diva-esque daughter, your goddaughter, Matt got to be in on the call too. (He wanted me to remind you of his *undying devotion*. Very insistent on that phrase.) You're endlessly missed in Austin, you know, and sometimes when I'm having a bad day I fantasize: what beautiful thing is Jafari wearing today, that makes the world a better place just by existing?

When Marcia and Jennifer generously asked us to think about the impact of "Black/Queer/Diaspora," I plucked my copy off the shelf for things most crucial to writing *Ezili's Mirrors*. But I never got past the table of contents. I ran my eyes down authors' names stacked in bold—Jafari, Omise'eke, Lyndon, Xavier, Vanessa, Ana, Matt—knowing I should be thinking about us as a scholarly field but thinking about us as friends. About searching for roti and gay clubs with you, Xavier, and Matt in London, at the conference where Matt presented work that made it into *GLQ* and Xavier shocked folks with descriptions of gay sex. About CSA in Curaçao, where Lyndon introduced me to Vanessa and I first got to hear the paper that became her article and we sat by the pool proclaiming black femme Pisces solidarity.

In other words, all I could think about is the ways "Black/Queer/Diaspora" came out of and built so many personal/professional relationships that have made this generation of black queer scholarship possible.

GLQ 25:1
DOI 10.1215/10642684-7275586
© 2019 by Duke University Press

Because I never made it past the contents before our call, you had to remind me how the introduction evokes this scholarly practice of black queer friendship, kinship, and love. "For black queers, survival has always been about finding ways to connect some of what is disconnected, to embody and re-member," you wrote. "The conventions of our guild—steeped in cool reason—avoid love as a *movida*. It is nevertheless evident in the works featured here and in the passion-filled (not easy, uncomplicated, or necessarily romantic) relationships between many individuals who do this work" (Allen 2012). This passage is marked by Matt's handwritten note "*Love* as a methodology," framed by flowery, vèvè-esque arrows.

Maybe you remember it differently. But I remember April 2009, when you convened the Black/Queer/Diaspora Work(ing) Group at Yale, as a time when the world felt full of promise. I was four months pregnant with Baia. Obama was just inaugurated. Young black queer scholars were being hired at prestigious institutions—Yale, UT—and many of us would soon be tenured. But as I write in early 2018 it feels like this promise has crumbled. I've had four miscarriages. Trump blustered into another year of transphobic, xenophobic, antiblack madness. Academic institutions haven't been able to force black queer faculty out, but undervalue and undermined us in ways we never foresaw. Why was Yale hemorrhaging black queer faculty by the time Baia started kindergarten? Why did UT just promote a professor whose work attacks queer families while those of us who live in them remain underpaid? Why does a next generation of black queer scholarship feel less possible now than ten years ago, and why have some in our field attacked friends when we have common enemies to fight?

It's impossible to look back on "Black/Queer/Diaspora" without sinking into how much I love the people in it. But it's equally impossible to read our names, think our stories together without mourning the ways black queer love has failed to make change in the academy. I look back and ask myself, what did we do wrong? Did our thirst for queer sociality lead us to underestimate institutions' racism, misogynoir, queerphobia? Don't forget, I'm a Pisces: I have to learn over and over again how the search for love makes us vulnerable.

Maybe you're thinking: *Omise'eke, you're a black lesbian writing a love letter to a black gay man to publish in GLQ. You're not afraid of vulnerability and you haven't given up on black queer love!* Of course, of course I haven't. Black queer love has failed this generation in academe, but it's also the only thing that's worked for us. I'm not still in this profession for my health. I'm here because you, Lyndon, Xavier, Vanessa, Ana, Matt, and so many others are here too, and I love seeing our black queer impossibility reflected in your disco balls and black sands. Remember Barbara: "What I write and how I write is done in order to save my own life. And I mean that literally. For me, literature is a way of knowing that I am not hallucinating, that whatever I feel/know *is*. It is an affirmation that sensuality is intelligence, that sensual language is language that makes sense" (Christian 1988). You, Jafari, and our writerly black queer sistren and brethren are that affirmation—that push toward remaking the world—that feels, tastes, moves like survival to me.

You mentioned *Sister Love: The Letters of Audre Lorde and Pat Parker*, so I rushed to buy it. I thought of us when Pat wrote: "Too often in the past, I have put letter writing off, because I thought whatever free time I had had to go to those survival things and if any energy left over would go to writing. However, it does occur to me that letter writing is both a survival thing and writing, plus it is so important to me to continue our conversation" (Enszer 2018). It's painful to read this knowing neither sender nor receiver *did* survive cancer. But because Pat took time to write Audre, this book now sits beside me as a map for what black queer sociality can—and can't—do. Right now, I want to take you really seriously and imagine: what if we take these letters as a model for what black/queer/diaspora scholarship does now? How can we care about black queerness in ways that are concrete, embodied, personal, sustainable? How might the tools we've relegated to the last century—tools we thought we could put away in the post–civil rights, post-Stonewall era—serve us in this moment?

Sister love,

Omi

Oh, Sister Love!

I am grateful to Marcia and Jennifer for inviting this conversation. Perhaps these love letters will inaugurate another way to mine our pasts and current feelings, for what is usable and sustaining. Let our letters be the beginning of starting the dance, again—a recursive "(re-)situat(ing) of our work through *conjunctural moments*" (Allen 2012: 214). Your words are always inspiring to me. On time, especially when I feel out of time. *Thiefing Sugar* (Tinsley 2010) came out one year before ¡Venceremos? (Allen 2011). "Black Atlantic / Queer Atlantic" provided a framework for us to begin our conversations in 2009. Last year I read galleys of *Ezili's Mirrors* (Tinsley 2018), breathless and awed, while my own second monograph awaited my courage to turn it in.

Yes! The letters between Pat and Audre are striking in their daily struggles—making a living and doing the work: illnesses, romances, children, shady editors, and Audre's too-familiar drama in academe—but also the sometimes very long intervals between. They remind me that I have to do better. Moving to Miami was supposed to be about "reclaiming my time." Still, I find there is much work to do, everywhere. And, as I keep rediscovering, not all of this work is "my work." You asked "what happened . . . ?": certainly, some of what we set out to do is somewhere buried under somebody else's agenda. While many of us get worn down by marginal employment in academe's precariat, for those of us situated in the Master's house of the tenured professoriat, it is *administrivia* that threatens to take us out.

In any case, what is on my heart most urgently, is to say I am so sorry that I was not there to lift your spirits or hold your hand through much of the pain you have endured—even with a note or a phone call. Matt's letter is coming, presently.

We have learned that while our love is not enough, it is what allows (some of) us to survive. Essex Hemphill wrote, "Counting t-cells on the shores of cyberspace, my blessing is this: I do not stand alone, bewildered and scared" (Frilot et al. 1995). He doesn't aver that there is nothing to cause fear or bewilderment. The facts and vulnerabilities are clear. Rather, not standing alone—even perhaps virtually, is the grace. "Black/Queer/Diaspora" emerged from relationships and could not be sustained without them—from pitching the idea to Ann, to the grace of all of you showing up—sanctifying that Anthropology conference room one semester after I had arrived at Yale from UT. Faculty meetings in that room provided an often violent but also invaluable education. But when I convened my classes there—smudged with incense—it is our engagement that I tried to model. *Friends*, we had come to work. It's a queer, Black thing that we find each other and convene in institutional spaces that (re)shape and sometimes mangle us, but as Christina reminds us, "We are not only known to ourselves and to each other through and by that force" (Sharpe 2016).

Rereading the introduction—written at one "current conjuncture" that has given way to another—I am struck at how unsettled we are. Deterritorialized. Some in generative ways, and in others, merely perhaps *without portfolio*. *Ezili's Mirrors* provides a beautiful model toward understanding and inhabiting unsettled and generatively deterritorialized space-time. I too have responded with the unsettled—traipsing very Black and queerly across continents and themes, renarrativizing the idea of Black/queer in clips, cases, vignettes, and memories. I am trying to offer an accounting of Black/queer habits of mind in *There's a Disco Ball between Us* (Allen forthcoming). Isn't this how we build a future for Baia, Georgia Mae, and our students? A palimpsestic "litany toward survival." Now, thriving is another question. What must we do? Who must we be, inside, for ourselves and to one another, to really win?

You invoke mourning. Is my private-public feeling mourning? Is it *tabanca*, or lovelorn? I'm hearing "Earth Wind & Fire" and Paul Gilroy in stereo: "After the Love Is Gone." My references are old (classic!). I know the insistence on (R&B) love seems hokey to many. Still, I believe that with everything that is wrong, "Every night / somethin' right / Would invite us to / begin the dance" (Earth, Wind & Fire 2014). Don't we have to continue to dance? Beginning again (and again . . . certainly). Sometimes less or more elegant or funky, but dance. I do not want to be misunderstood here, especially because I think some may mistake our love ethic and the insistence on Black/queer sociality in our issue as a description of a club of folks who cosign and adhere to the same politics. We know that's far from the truth. Agreement is not sine qua non of love. Nor is proximity, really. It is our willingness to begin again, even when "something happen(s) . . . '—violence, loss, forgetting, for example—' . . . along the way" (ibid.).

The introduction to the issue ends: "Here, the threads of our mourning clothes are laid down/bare" (Allen 2012: 237). I don't remember writing this, but it is there. Perhaps it is a love note from then, to us now. If we take off our mourning clothes, what do we put on? The bareness of our vulnerability? The beauty of our multihued Black flesh (that dances . . . *here in this place*) (Morrison 2016)? I look forward to meeting y'all in the clearing to find out, Sister-

-Love,

Jafari

Jafari,

I *should* let this end with your beautiful words, but this addendum comes because you've finally asked a question I have an answer to—via Beyoncé, of course. I stumbled on this from *Lemonade* stylist Marni Senofonte while reading about costumes for "Freedom": "When we started we were thinking about antebellum South, and Bey was talking about going back to these plantations," she explains. "There was a question of, 'Do we do authentic vintage or is it about wearing couture on these plantations?' And I was like, 'It's about wearing couture on these plantations!' You have fifty amazing women in there and Bey was in couture Givenchy up in the tree. It's a juxtaposition of what historically black women on a plantation were" (quoted in Carlos 2016). We still on plantations, brother, but I know we can both *rock the hell* out of a Givenchy dress.

References

Allen, Jafari. 2011. *¡Venceremos?: The Erotics of Black Self-Making in Cuba*. Durham, NC: Duke University Press.

———. 2012. "Black/Queer/Diaspora at the Current Conjuncture." *GLQ* 18, nos. 2–3: 217–18.

———. Forthcoming. *There's a Disco Ball between Us*. Durham, NC: Duke University Press.

Carlos, Marjon. 2016. "Beyoncé's Stylist Spills the Juice on the Fashion behind *Lemonade*." *Vogue*, April 25. www.vogue.com/article/beyonce-lemonade-stylist -interview-fashion-marni-senofonte.

Christian, Barbara. 1988. "The Race for Theory." *Feminist Studies* 14, no. 1: 77–78.

Earth, Wind & Fire. 2014. *The Essential Earth, Wind & Fire*. Columbia/Legacy, compact disc.

Enszer, Julie, ed. 2018. *Sister Love: The Letters of Audre Lorde and Pat Parker, 1974–1989*. New York: Midsummer's Night.

Frilot, Shari, Lewis Erskine, Essex Hemphill, Kobena Mercer, Barbara Smith, Urvashi Vaid, Jacqui Alexander, and Wayman Lamont Widgins. 1995. *Black Nations/Queer Nations? Lesbian and Gay Sexualities in the African Diaspora*. New York: Third World Newsreel. DVD.

Morrison, Toni. 2016. *Beloved*. London: Vintage.

Sharpe, Christina Elizabeth. 2016. *In the Wake: On Blackness and Being*. Durham, NC: Duke University Press.

Tinsley, Omise'eke Natasha. 2010. *Thiefing Sugar: Eroticism between Women in Carib- bean Literature*. Durham, NC: Duke University Press.

———. 2018. *Ezili's Mirrors: Black Atlantic Genders and the Work of the Imagination*. Durham, NC: Duke University Press.

QUEER INHUMANISMS

Dana Luciano and Mel Y. Chen

"Queer Inhumanisms," special issue edited by Mel Y. Chen and Dana Luciano. GLQ 21.2–3 (2015).

There are no new ideas, just new ways of giving those ideas we cherish breath and power in our own living.
—Audre Lorde, "Learning from the Sixties" (1982)

*W*hen we began work on our special issue, we were convinced that the phrase "queer inhumanisms" named not a new development but a longer history—perhaps several long histories—of thought, as yet unconsolidated under that particular sign. For this reason, we sought to move away from the progressive-temporal and oppositional frames encoded in such terms as *posthuman* or *antihumanist*. These frames, we believed, relied on the fantasy of a singular chronology of "human," asserting the solidity of a concept that has never, in truth, been stable. Even the more familiar *nonhuman*, we thought, focused too closely on the distinction between "human" and its others, risking its reconsolidation as an opposition. Instead, we wanted to emphasize the processual aspects of queer inhumanness, the way it invoked becoming, rather than dividing the world into two static and antagonistic camps; we meant to highlight the dynamic and diffuse encounters through which those two categories were continually re/constituted.

In avoiding both the anti- and the post-, we also wanted to move away from the pattern of consolidating a past in order to break with it and declare a new future for queer/nonhuman thought. This pattern has been much in evidence in recent years, both within queer theory more generally—witness the debates over antinormativity, anti-antinormativity, anti-anti-antinormativity, and so on—and within the nonhuman turn, especially among those thinkers who dismiss all poststructuralist thought as "correlationist" and therefore impossibly anthropocentric.

GLQ 25:1
DOI 10.1215/10642684-7275600
© 2019 by Duke University Press

We wanted, instead, to remain alive to the way histories are consistently remade to meet the needs of the present, to approach "queer theory" not as a singular, progressive history that the time has come to redirect, but as a flexible, ever-shifting collection of thought. This vitalizing approach to queer critical traditions is embraced explicitly in José Esteban Muñoz's *Disidentifications* (1997) and Roderick Ferguson's *Aberrations in Black* (2004), two books that were enormously influential for us. So we looked for antecedents for queer inhumanism in earlier writing, even in places that one wouldn't necessarily expect to find it. Audre Lorde, for instance, might not have located herself under the sign of inhumanism (or, for that matter, of "queer"). Yet alongside her emphasis on the active reconstruction of intrahuman relations, we find compelling accounts, in "Uses of the Erotic," of meaningful, not coincidental, intimacy with objects: the quasi-orgasmic pleasure of building a bookshelf, the subtler satisfactions of kneading a pellet of color into a block of margarine: "taking it carefully between our fingers . . . knead[ing] it gently back and forth, over and over" (Lorde [1984] 2007: 57). More than an analogy, the erotic, from a queer-inhumanist perspective, is also an effect of such contact, a component of transmaterial intimacy. If, as Kyla Wazana Tompkins (forthcoming) proposes, "Uses of the Erotic" constructs a theory of nonalienated labor, that theory encompasses economies of matter as well.

Our intent, in looking back at such influential texts, was not simply to locate moments that might speak to an inhumanist approach *avant la lettre*—to play a game of "spot the nonhuman" with texts of the past. Looking back was intended to help us come to a better understanding of what "queer" had meant, how it continued to unfold across time, backward as well as forward. We were concerned about a tendency within the nonhuman turn to use "queer" as a stand-in for the desire to defamiliarize—which meant that the turn to the nonhuman was always already queer, insofar as it unsettled long-standing (and shortsighted) intellectual habits. It wasn't the unsettling that concerned us; it was the potential narrowing of the meanings that "queer" might index, and of the archive that constituted "queer theory" to a handful of texts said to manifest its guiding tenets. In contrast, we wanted queer inhumanism to sprawl—to exemplify the range of methods, locations, sources, and commitments that live within and through queer thought. No single principle or critical gesture constrains the eighteen vibrant thinkers—Neel Ahuja, Karen Barad, Jayna Brown, Jack Halberstam, Jinthana Haritaworn, Myra Hird, Zakiyyah Iman Jackson, Eileen Joy, Eunjung Kim, Uri McMillan, José Esteban Muñoz, Tavia Nyong'o, Jasbir K. Puar, Susan Stryker, Kim TallBear, Jeanne Vaccaro, Harlan Weaver, Jami Weinstein—we had the privilege of including in the issue. Queerness, for them, necessarily emerged from multiple locations, moved in multiple directions. The collision between the "nonhuman turn" and queer thought was already—always already—spinning outward, difficult to pin down, impossible to contain. This was a good thing.

A lot has happened in the three years since the issue appeared. (As we wrote that sentence, we laughed until we cried.) The "nonhuman turn" has ceased to feel like a novelty—perhaps because so much fine scholarship on the topic has appeared; perhaps because increasing attention to the ongoing mass extinction event has underscored the need for interspecies thinking, emphasizing the ecological danger of anthropocentrism; or perhaps because the rhetoric of dehumanization has come to dominate the US political scene, manifesting as government policy. But whatever the reason, critical declarations of the need to "decenter the human" have come to feel almost axiomatic.

This too is a good thing. As we noted in the issue's introduction, queer inhumanism, as we understood it, would evolve of necessity. Queer inhumanism could never only be utopic, since it also indexed habits and histories of dehumanization. At the same time, we resist the dystopic mood that seems to have taken hold since the events of late 2016. We don't mean to dismiss the high stakes of the present—things *are* bad, and getting worse. But we are unpersuaded by calls to departicularize, to pursue universals, to simplify stakes, to abandon critique. Such arguments, we think, tend to assume the universality of the radically changed conditions to which they demand a response—an assumption we don't think is warranted.

"Queer Inhumanisms" embraces less familiar conjunctions—interconstitutions of race and environment, politics and microcosm—as an extension of intersectional analysis. In this sense, it too falls athwart of those self-nominated "public intellectuals" who maintain that November 2016 must sound the death-knell of "identity politics" (by which they inevitably mean political thinking that focuses elsewhere than cis-het whiteness) and its associated methods. The simplified version of crisis analysis that these naysayers exhort deplores any mode of thought which delineates paths to justice that seem, from their perspective, implausible. How, they object, can something like "thinking like a forest"—or worse, *feeling* like one—be integrated into extant environmental initiatives? The demand for "applicable" forms manifests beyond the realm of policymaking, insinuating intellectual and political crisis-reductionism even within fields of inquiry (science studies, ecocriticism, etc.) that might be deemed friendly to the "nonhuman turn." In the shadow of the current presidential administration, we are admonished to narrow our fields of inquiry and action in order to produce the unambiguous "yeses" said to be needed for political advocacy—yeses that often cluster unreflectively around the desire to return to an unmarked, unruffled whiteness. What does it mean, for instance, for scholars to proclaim that climate-change denial and other antiscience postures on the right must prompt antiracist or decolonial scholars to defer or abandon the critique of science?

"Politics," in many of these invocations, seems primarily to index legislative and/or electoral procedures. In this sense, the "crisis" response in critical thought perpetuates civic forms that rely, for their continued existence, on the denial of pervasive structural injustice and settler colonial logics. Yet even thinkers who do not demand immediate political legibility along these lines often produce articulations of the "nonhuman turn" that, in their reliance on the "new," reproduce colonial patterns by alternately appropriating and ignoring non-Western thinking. Pointing to long-standing theorizations of nonhuman sentience in indigenous thought, Métis scholar Zoe Todd suggests not only that there is little "new" about the new materialisms but also that there is nothing "new" about the conditions that the ontological turn is helping to sustain:

> The colonial moment has not passed. The conditions that fostered it have not suddenly disappeared. We talk of neo-colonialism, neo-Imperialism, but it is as if these are far away things. . . . The reality is that we are just an invasion or economic policy away from re-colonizing at any moment. So it is so important to think, deeply, about how the Ontological Turn—with its breathless "realisations" that animals, the climate, water, "atmospheres" and non-human presences like ancestors and spirits are *sentient* and *possess agency*, that "nature" and "culture," "human" and "animal" may not be so separate after all—is itself perpetuating the exploitation of Indigenous peoples. (Todd 2016: 16)

Todd's reflection on the partiality of the ontological turn's "*aha* moment"—its sudden realization, from a place of privileged unknowing, of "what many an Indigenous thinker around the world could have told you for millennia"—also, we think, applies to the pattern of responses to November 2016. For some of us, indeed, things took a sudden, desperate turn; for others, things went from bad to worse; while for many, many others, things remained pretty much as *worse* as they already were. Demanding a radical alteration of the terms on which intellectual inquiry can be conducted in response to the current political crisis would, in effect, mean weaponizing such histories of privileged unknowing against precisely the kinds of knowledge they have long, and comfortably, ignored.

A lot has happened, indeed; but things are not as different as they sometimes feel. Queer inhumanism, with its manifold, weaving intellectual histories, was always meant to exist with many companion thinkers. Our task, looking backward and forward, is to seek an intensified alignment with the burgeoning adjacencies of the present, in resonance and appreciation with the work done outside its name.

References

Ferguson, Roderick A. 2004. *Aberrations in Black: Toward a Queer of Color Critique*. Minneapolis: University of Minnesota Press.

Lorde, Audre. [1984] 2007. "Uses of the Erotic: The Erotic as Power." In *Sister Outsider: Essays and Speeches*, 53–59. New York: Crossing Press.

Muñoz, José Esteban. 1999. *Disidentifications: Queers of Color and the Performance of Politics*. Minneapolis: University of Minnesota Press.

Todd, Zoe. 2016. "An Indigenous Feminist's Take on the Ontological Turn: 'Ontology' Is Just Another Word for Colonialism." *Journal of Historical Sociology* 29, no. 1: 4–22.

Tompkins, Kyla Wazana. Forthcoming. *So Moved: Ferment, Jelly, Intoxication, Rot.*

THE INFLUENCE OF BARAD'S "TRANSMATERIALITIES" ON QUEER THEORIES AND METHODOLOGIES

Stephanie Anne Shelton

"Transmaterialities: Trans*/Matter/Realities and Queer Political Imaginings," by Karen Barad. GLQ 21.2–3 (2015).

There was a storm within the pages of *GLQ* in 2015. Karen Barad's "Transmaterialities: Trans*/Matter/Realities and Queer Political Imaginings" (2015) begins with metaphorical lightning zigzagging across the sky, illuminating—for just seconds of flash—the "charged yearnings and the sparking of new imaginaries" that she argues are inherent in the politicizations and explorations of origins, imaginings, and matter (387). Seizing on the role of galvanization in Mary Shelley's *Frankenstein*, Barad pulls from queer theory's past of monsters and the grotesque (e.g., Cohen 1995; Crowder 2007) to move into an intra-active past/present/future with seemingly impossible origins/promise stemming from "queer self-birthing" and "monstrous re/generations" (Barad 2015: 388).

Distilled from actual and fictional scientific efforts that attempted to unfold and re-create the origins of life itself, Barad recounts numerous desperate endeavors to harness lightning, and in "shocking brute matter to life," control the spark of life that is presumably all living matter's origin (ibid.: 389). The issue with such attempts for Barad is that there is no reason to "think that matter is lifeless to begin with," and that by employing lightning as the key to understanding, these explorers have "always danced on the razor's edge between science and imagina-

GLQ 25:1
DOI 10.1215/10642684-7275614
© 2019 by Duke University Press

tion" (ibid.). Barad pushes the exploration of origins just past that edge to examine the implications of this Frankenstein-esque lifegiving in relation to queer, particularly trans*, empowerment.

Given queer theory's importance in responding to moments such as the 1980s AIDS epidemic, decades of antiqueer political legislation, and related efforts, queer theory has often situated itself as "a theory of extinctions" (Ahuja 2015: 365), with emphases on topics such as (self-)annihilation producing a "tradition of queer negativity" (ibid.: 366). Barad honors this heritage of fear and rage, while building on and moving beyond it. In her consideration of others' efforts to galvanize flesh to life, she notes that these historical efforts at reanimation parallel the queer "monster," whose "presence of impurities" and "destruction of boundaries" make this queer creature truly grotesque to the general populace (Jack Halberstam, quoted in Barad 2015: 391). Specifically, Barad notes that the electricity, serving as a metaphor for efforts to arrest queerness, "can serve to demonize, dehumanize, and demoralize" (ibid.: 392). However, she notes, that a jolt of electricity "is also capable of bringing a heart back from a state of lifelessness. . . . It can also be a source of political agency. It can power and radicalize" (ibid.: 302). She argues that the would-be monster has agency and might harness its rage and despair to work toward empowerment.

To galvanize this agency, she considers society's positioning of some "bodies as natural against the monstrosity of trans embodiment" (ibid.: 392) and shifts to the notion of origin stories to explore the "normal" and the "monstrous." She notes the tradition of understanding creation as derived from a divine origin; a Creator breathed life into those forms. In contrast, she argues, monstrous/grotesque bodies are assemblages resulting from or/and requiring scientific interventions, for example, Frankenstein's stitched-together creature. To illuminate such monstrous origins, Barad turns to birth. She explores "natural" birthing in comparison/contrast with/to self-birthing through Susan Stryker's account of her partner giving birth. As Stryker stands in the delivery room, torn between the joy and the pain of the moment, she is "painfully aware that the physicality of birthing a being from her own womb is denied to her by the specificity of her constructed enfleshment" (Barad 2015: 393). Here Barad emphasizes that what might be only loss/sorrow is galvanized into a moment of self-actualization. Stryker's sense of pain is entangled with the joy of both the emerging baby and a powerful sense that through a "radically queer configuring of spacetimemattering," Stryker simultaneously witnesses their child's birth and her own. She emerges from "a self-birthed womb" that re/generates from what initially seemed a void, a nothingness. These two lives/bodies/selves coming into being through opposite/same originations shifts notions of what counts as creation/Creator, electrifying an "atmosphere silently cracking with thunderous possibilities" (Barad 2015: 393).

Barad's 2015 essay has had a profound influence on scholarship in the fields of education, health sciences, technology, and research methods. Indeed, "Transmaterialities" has reshaped queer theory and queered disciplines, through "Lightning Strikes."

Lightning Strike One: The Body

Given the ways that Barad's discussion borrows from both her scientific background and the fictionalized/actual attempts to bring the dead to life, it is unsurprising that her concepts have informed health sciences research and other forms of embodied inquiry. Annette-Carina van der Zaag's 2017 paper published in *Science & Technology Studies*, "Imaginings of Empowerment and the Biomedical Production of Bodies: The Story of Nonoxynol-9," considers the political implications of an HIV treatment drug on vaginal microbes. The paper acknowledges that queer theory in its more traditional sense is useful, in that this research also "foregrounds the performativity of sex(uality) and gender" (Barad 2015: 46), but that Barad's 2015 discussion propels the discussion in productive new directions, as her galvanized Franken-birthing "not only celebrates human-nonhuman hybridization, but also pays heed to the process through which the human comes into being." Van der Zaag uses this element of humanity and agency to theorize the role of empowerment in women's understandings of and interactions with the microbicide Nonoxynol-9.

Stephanie Springgay and Sarah Truman's (2017: 27) paper in *Body & Society* adopts a similar usage of queer theory that emphasizes Barad's amalgamations of (self-)creation, (re)generation, and animation in their "bodily methodologies." As with van der Zaag, the application here acknowledges a heritage of queer theoretical work that works to disrupt norms and shape research participants' discomfort into findings. In one part of the study, "participants listen to audio compositions that connect laundry detergent to fish, to capitalism and menstrual blood" (Springgay and Truman 2017: 46). The power of Barad's work in advancing these queer applications of sound, space, and body is in researchers and participants working to understand themselves, others, and matter as operating agentially through simultaneous "radical undoing of 'self'" (Barad 2015: 411) and regenerations (Springgay and Truman 2017). In both this and van der Zaag's work, Barad's acknowledgment of the origins of and shifts from queer theory matter a great deal, in that those origins are the basis of new understandings and (self-)creations.

Lightning Strike Two: Research Methodologies

Coming soon after the publication of Barad's article, Vickie Hargraves's (2016) discussion of researcher entanglements in the international journal *La Investigación Como El Enmarañamiento* relies heavily on Deleuzean and queer theorizing of assemblages and identity construction to explore the interactions between researchers and data. Barad's trans*materialities article is key to extending Hargraves's efforts in creative and playful new directions. Hargraves reflects that while long-standing methodological discussions examine the interplays between researcher, researched, and data, Barad's notion of self-birth and self-determinacy effect "different potentialities for [spacetimematterings] actualization" that electrify the "dynamic dance" that is research—pushing data analysis into new realms and possibilities (Hargraves 2016: 547). The notion of birth from a self/void "always holds potential" and emphasizes the alterity and possibilities found in research methods (ibid.).

Agency is similarly key to Janet Miller's 2017 postqualitative reflection on participatory action research (PAR), in the *International Journal of Qualitative Studies in Education*. In Barad's "reconfiguring [of] the apparatuses of bodily reproduction" (Miller 2017: 496), the notion of self-production becomes a powerful concept in participant-led research. Such a shifting of material and discursive norms, Miller argues, necessarily shifts notions of subjectivity. Informed by Barad's discussion, Miller theorizes on "the limits to [a subject's] knowing—its opacities—and thus . . . the limits of its capacities to given an account" of self to others (ibid.: 496). Ultimately, Barad's notion of identity as entangled, intra-active, and potentially self-originating queers PAR in ways that necessitate reconsiderations of participants' agency—including their abilities to challenge research's norms and push "the limits of our knowing" (ibid.). Much like in the other instances, there is an electrification of a field that builds on more established concepts of queer scholarship to emphasize possibility and hope for empowerment and action.

Drawing on new materialist and Deleuzean notions of virtuality and reality, Springgay and Truman's 2018 *Qualitative Inquiry* article "On the Need for Methods beyond Proceduralism" draws from Barad's work to counter growing arguments for postdata qualitative research. Springgay and Truman (2018: 208) argue researchers' need to "let go of agendas" and instead embrace "the speculative middle" in an effort to queer research approaches in ways that are flexible, speculative, and playful. Barad's (2015: 396) notion of a "void [that] is flush with yearning" and potential helps the authors to push both Deleuze's discussion of virtuality and a queering of qualitative research into spaces that originate from "nothingness," yet advance "ongoing thought" on the "dynamism between the virtual actual" (Springgay and Truman 2018: 208). These efforts to challenge both traditional and postqualitative methodologies offer new insights and possibilities across disciplines, as Barad's concepts influence research methods.

The Zigzagging Pathways of Lightning: A Conclusion

In her discussion of births and origins, Barad (2015: 408) imagines "the potential face of lightning yet to be born" and the "different possible pathways" that it might take as it zigzags downward to shatter the darkness. In doing so, Barad notes that the "path that lightning takes not only is not predictable but does not make its way according to some continuous unidirectional path" (ibid.: 398). Her own galvanizations of queer thought similarly storm, hiss, and pop across innumerable scholarly landscapes. An article only a few years old has shaped understandings in a range of fields, and in doing so has extended theoretical concepts and methodological applications. The many possibilities that Barad's article have sparked are "electrifying the atmosphere silently crackling with thunderous possibilities" (ibid.: 393). Given that every year since its publication "Transmaterialities" has informed queer theory and a range of scholarship, the booming of that thunderous potential will be deafening, and the continued illuminations of those lightning strikes will be undoubtedly blinding.

References

Ahuja, Neel. 2015. "Intimate Atmospheres: Queer Theory in a Time of Extinctions." *GLQ* 21, nos. 2–3: 365–85.

Barad, Karen. 2015. "Transmaterialities: Trans*/Matter/Realities and Queer Political Imaginings." *GLQ* 21, nos. 2–3: 387–422.

Cohen, Lawrence. 1995. "Holi in Banaras and the Mahaland of Modernity." *GLQ* 2, no. 4: 399–424.

Crowder, Dianne Griffin. 2007. "From the Straight Mind to Queer Theory: Implications for Political Movement." *GLQ* 13, no. 4: 489–503.

Hargraves, Vickie. 2016. "Research Becomes Entangled." *La Investigación Como El Enmarañamiento* 18, no. 3: 541–52.

Miller, Janet L. 2017. "Neo-Positivist Intrusions, Post-Qualitative Challenges, and PAR's Generative Indeterminancies." *International Journal of Qualitative Studies in Education* 30, no. 5: 488–503.

Springgay, Stephanie, and Truman, Sarah E. 2017. "A Transmaterial Approach to Walking Methodologies." *Body & Society* 23, no. 4: 27–58.

———. 2018. "On the Need for Methods beyond Proceduralism: Speculative Middles, (In)tensions, and Response-Ability in Research." *Qualitative Inquiry* 24, no. 3: 203–14.

Van der Zaag, Annette-Carina. 2017. "Imaginings of Empowerment and the Biomedical Production of Bodies: The Story of Nonoxynol-9." *Science & Technology Studies* 30, no. 4: 45–65.

POSSIBLE IMPOSSIBLES BETWEEN AREA AND QUEER

Ragini Tharoor Srinivasan

"Area Impossible: The Geopolitics of Queer Studies," special issue edited by Anjali Arondekar and Geeta Patel. GLQ 22.2 (2016).

*A*rea studies has always seemed to me rather queer. Queer in the sense that language is queer: promiscuous and ranging, given to misfires and infelicities, promising to reveal more than it can access or represent. Queer in the sense that its objects are queer: messy and incommensurable, irreducible to identitarian categories yet occasioned by identity, boundaried yet open, unbounded yet self-referential. Queer in the sense that interdisciplinarity is queer: a knowledge project premised on destabilizing its own objects, which points to the social, historical, and political construction of the disciplines between and against which its labors are situated. Queer in that it is antinormative. Queer in that it is impossible.

By that same token, area studies, that "hoary" Cold War–era "intelligence-gathering force for consolidating US power" (Arondekar and Patel 2016: 153), has always been and remains in need of queering. Queering, because those who study contemporary geopolitics and neoliberalism must attend to "the global expansion of normative society's modes of operation" (Tadiar 2016: 175). Queering, because the field's practitioners are called to "[work] with the difference of geopolitics through a notion of 'difference'" and in so doing to resist "any form of totalizing knowledge" (Arondekar and Patel 2016: 155). Queering, because it does not consistently, in José Esteban Muñoz's description of the queer, reject "the here and now" and insist "on potentiality or concrete possibility for another world" (quoted in Taylor 2016: 210).

"Area Impossible: The Geopolitics of Queer Studies" makes the case that area studies is queer and that it remains to be queered, while also posit-

GLQ 25:1
DOI 10.1215/10642684-7275628
© 2019 by Duke University Press

ing area studies as a critical field formation with the potential to provincialize queer studies. The issue aims, in Anjali Arondekar and Geeta Patel's (2016: 154) words, "to read the politics of queer and area studies as coincident—if not quite isomorphic—activities, to read both as heuristic practices that see form . . . as a placeholder that might partly express a promiscuous or incoherent desire or a desire whose content continues to be under erasure." The articles, performance pieces, and aesthetic meditations assembled are consequently as interested in the signs by which they are occasioned as they are in such desires. Contributors engage with and disavow their key terms (e.g., if Diana Taylor's "We Have Always Been Queer" owns its titular sign, then Keguro Macharia's "On Being Area-Studied: A Litany of Complaint," refuses to accede), while questioning how translated, untranslatable, and varied knowledges travel across fields. In the process, both area studies and queer studies are defamiliarized. The queer body, readers are reminded, is not just the sexed body but the body dismembered by the US imperial war machine and recomposed with prosthetic appendages (Mikadashi and Puar 2016: 221). "Language, organism, and race can be areas, too" (Tadiar 2016: 180).

Who, what, where and when—the issue attends equally to each interrogative—are the referents of area studies and queer studies? How might bringing these fields together enable scholars to tackle "the epistemological problem, the problem of reading, making sense of gender, race, and sexuality 'in a global context'" (ibid.: 174)? The "area" of area studies is in some sense an empty signifier, or a misdirecting one. Area studies renders places into areas, an operation that jettisons the particularity and history of some "where" for what it occasions in some other('s) name. The issue gives critical and locational specificity to "area studies" through articles that focus on Dalit studies, Caribbean studies, and African studies, while marshalling ethnographic, literary, and historical methods in service of their respective projects. Queer studies, in turn, is distinguished from queer theory, characterized by some contributors as a "finite collection of ideas about destabilizing gender and sexual norms" (Currier and Migraine-George 2016: 282).

If we are accustomed to thinking of the "area" as pointing, however provisionally, to a "where" and to "queer" as pointing, however tentatively, to a "who," then these essays ask equally to whom the area points and where queer directs us. How might we develop studies of areas that do not absorb queer bodies, voices, and experiences "as 'data' or 'evidence'" and read them instead "as modes of theory or as challenges to the conceptual assumptions that drive queer studies" (Macharia 2016: 185)? How might we develop queer studies that are not always already American in orientation, that do not reduce "areas" and their subjects to case studies, and that do not assume that the United States is "the prehensive force for everyone else's future" (Mikadashi and Puar 2016: 217)? What methods are adequate to a queer area studies and an area-aware queer studies that are alive to how scholarly objects, like our bodies, "betray us as much as they allow us to survive, live, love, and find each other" (Tadiar 2016: 178)?

These are some of the questions the issue provokes. Since first reading *GLQ* 22.2, I have returned to them often, as well as to two of the issue's many interventions. The first has to do with how thinking between area studies and queer studies might give us new purchase on the international division of labor, both economic and intellectual. On the economic question, Neferti Tadiar (2016: 177) observes that "when some national economies are presumed and disciplined to service the needs and wants of others, sexuality is not a 'mere' metaphor but the set of regulatory precepts of regional and global trade, of transnational production and governmentality." Sharma 2014 on power-chronography and Vora 2015 on gestational surrogacy and outsourcing are just two recent projects from outside area studies and queer studies that nevertheless take a consonant approach to the study of global biocapital and may be profitably read at this intersection. On the question of scholarly divisions of labor, Ashley Currier and Thérèse Migraine-George's essay plumbs the pernicious divide between those orientalists and Euro-American scholars who "know" authentic areas like "India" and "Africa" and the impure natives who study their diasporic, transnational, or otherwise hybrid derivations. This, too, is the impossible space between area and queer: the space between the desire to know, and not being able to not know it.

The second has to do with temporality as "an epistemic demeanor for the impossible nexus of area with sexuality" (Arondekar and Patel 2016: 165). Almost every essay in "Area Impossible" addresses the temporal, but Lucinda Ramberg's (2016: 243) essay on Dalit religiosity in South India is particularly attuned to how the "narrat[ion of] queer futurity" depends on fixing certain others "in the past." In ethnographic readings of Dalit women married to gods, or *devadasis*, and Dalit converts to Buddhism, Ramberg theorizes "recombinant time," a knotted, entangled temporality that "is a way of acting in time on time to recombine its elements, producing pasts forward and backward futures" (ibid.: 235). She is particularly interested in how "backwardness" is both attributed to the Dalit community and marshalled by that community as an aspirational condition; it is also, she argues, "a sexual condition and . . . feature of queer existence" (ibid.: 228). The term *belated* doesn't figure in Ramberg's essay, but parallels can be drawn to key postcolonial texts that also focus on the relationship between the denial of coevalness, broadly defined (Fabian 1983), and "belatedness as possibility" (Chakrabarty 2011).

I noted above that *GLQ* 22.2 defamiliarizes area studies and queer studies. It also refamiliarizes those of us who do not necessarily write under the signs
of "area" and "queer" with the critical potential of both. I am a scholar of South
Asian Anglophonism who is not considered a South Asianist by the disciplinary
conventions of area studies. I am a cisgendered female feminist theorist who presents as heterosexual. I am married and participating in the normative project of
reproductive futurism. I'm also, as I write this, the inhabitant of a queer, brown
pregnant body that carries within it a body that will be assigned male at birth. I'm
a woman of color who is, like many of those addressed or speaking in this issue,
too frequently asked to give an account of myself.

This "burden of always having to explain" (Taylor 2016: 208) is broached
in multiple essays as a condition shared by a range of nonnormative, nondominant,
or otherwise marginal subjects of both area studies and queer studies. At issue are
problems of language and translation, of inscrutable faces and bodies. "Women
have always been explaining themselves," Taylor writes; "feminists have always
been explaining themselves; people of color have always been explaining themselves; queer, transgender, and transsexual groups have always been explaining
themselves; indigenous peoples have always been explaining themselves" (ibid.:
213). The injunction to explain, the imperative to yield, the expectation of making available undergirds every journey from nobody to somebody, from nothing to
something, and from nowhere to somewhere.

Ronaldo Wilson's contribution dramatizes this journey through a scene of
being seen. Wilson is in a mask, wig, and heels at a conference bar. He is questioned by a she who "sorta-know[s]" him: "Why are you hiding?" (Wilson 2016:
192). The question pretends playfulness, if not quite innocence. It is asked of Wilson "simply for being present in the modes of performance in which [he] choose[s]
to operate" (ibid.: 201). Why are you hiding? The question, which demands an
explanation, presumes to know "you" and therefore to know that you are masked,
unyielding, unavailable. It is a question that, slightly modified, speaks to decades
of area studies scholarship: "what are you hiding?"—the gold, tea, sugar, your
women in purdah—and "where are you hiding it?"

Circling what he calls "the are(n)a of the story," Wilson reflects that his
"attempt was not to provide a spectacle to be seen but to disrupt the very sight of
being seen in order to expand the site of my own inquiry . . . to mark the impossibility of the marked subject" (ibid.: 193). In this scene of being seen and not
seen, of knowing what he is asked and refusing to deliver it, Wilson becomes what
Macharia (2016: 188) calls "the indifferent native," heir to "the sly native, the

trickster native, the desiring native, the sage native, the undeveloped native, the homosexual native, the queer native, the deracinated native," "witness to [his] own demolition" which he apprehends with an "indifferent gaze" (Chow 1993: 51–52).

The figure of the indifferent native with an indifferent gaze is one that perhaps best captures the project of "Area Impossible." Arondekar and Patel's introduction reads the poet Agha Shahid Ali on Kashmir, the embattled territory where Ali was born, caught between violently partitioned India and Pakistan, what he names "the country without a post office." "One cannot, as it were, know, or even learn about Kashmir," Arondekar and Patel (2016: 159) write. Yet, "even as one cannot not know it, Kashmir provisions the possibilities for epistemology without rendering itself as knowable, as the place constantly constituted as an object for geopolitical fracases, as the denouement in the games of geopolitics" (ibid.: 162). Kashmir is area, but as area it is queer: it is and it is not; it is known and unknowable. Like the fields of area studies and queer studies, Kashmir is always already home to many, even if, finally, it belongs to no one.

References

Arondekar, Anjali, and Geeta Patel. 2016. "Area Impossible: Notes toward an Introduction." *GLQ* 22, no. 2: 151–71.

Chakrabarty, Dipesh. 2011. "Belatedness as Possibility: Subaltern Histories, Once Again." *The Indian Postcolonial: A Critical Reader*, edited by Elleke Boehmer and Rosinka Chaudhuri. London: Routledge.

Chow, Rey. 1993. "Where Have All the Natives Gone?" *Writing Diaspora: Tactics of Intervention in Contemporary Cultural Studies.* Bloomington: Indiana University Press.

Currier, Ashley, and Thérèse Migraine-George. 2016. "Queer Studies/African Studies: An (Im)possible Transaction?" *GLQ* 22, no. 2: 281–305.

Fabian, Johannes. 1983. *Time and the Other: How Anthropology Makes Its Object.* New York: Columbia University Press.

Macharia, Keguro. 2016. "On Being Area-Studied: A Litany of Complaint." *GLQ* 22, no. 2: 183–90.

Mikadashi, Maya, and Jasbir Puar. 2016. "Queer Theory and Permanent War." *GLQ* 22, no. 2: 215–22.

Ramberg, Lucinda. 2016. "Backward Futures and Pasts Forward: Queer Time, Sexual Politics, and Dalit Religiosity in South India." *GLQ* 22, no. 2: 223–48.

Sharma, Sarah. 2014. *In the Meantime: Temporality and Cultural Politics.* Durham, NC: Duke University Press.

Tadiar, Neferti X. M. 2016. "Ground Zero." *GLQ* 22, no. 2: 173–81.

Taylor, Diana. 2016. "We Have Always Been Queer." *GLQ* 22, no. 2: 205–14.

Vora, Kalindi. 2015. *Life Support: Biocapital and the New History of Outsourced Labor.* Minneapolis: University of Minnesota Press.

Wilson, Ronaldo V. 2016. "The Are(n)a of the Story." *GLQ* 22, no. 2: 191–204.

COLLATERAL DAMAGE

Warfare, Death, and Queer Theory in the Global South

Oliver Coates

*"Queer Theory and Permanent War," by Maya Mikdashi and
Jasbir K. Puar. GLQ 22.2 (2016).*

"Can queer theory be recognizable as such when it emerges from elsewhere?"
(Mikdashi and Puar 2016: 215). Queer theory's encounter with the lives of marginalized peoples in the Middle East and Africa provides urgent answers to this
question. New technologies of warfare have led to the possibility that entire vil-
lages might be suddenly eliminated at the press of a button in a Western military
facility; at the risk of laboring the obvious, these individuals have no access to
the kinds of "future" often conceived in Western neoliberal culture. "Collateral
damage" is becoming an increasingly important term for scholars and activists
who want to draw on perspectives from queer theory to analyze these new forms
of remotely controlled death. But how did queer theory enter into a scenario that
might more typically be thought of as belonging to security or area studies?

As Maya Mikdashi and Jasbir Puar reveal, queer theory is intimately impli-
cated in this landscape of "permanent" and asymmetrical warfare. Queer subjects
in this context are not simply individuals who experience same-sex desire but all
those who, regardless of sexual identity, are placed in a queer relation to neoliberal
conceptions of death, life, and futurity. It is therefore no accident that Mikdashi
and Puar's subject matter deliberately parts company with queer theorists' favored
focus on visible queer communities, texts, and activism. They deliberately emphasize the ways in which queer theory forces us to confront stigmatized and marginal
forms of life without focusing on sexual identities that might be either unavailable
or unattractive to those in non-Western cultures. We might also think of what this
emerging queer theory tells Western readers about the prisons, homeless shelters,

GLQ 25:1
DOI 10.1215/10642684-7275642
© 2019 by Duke University Press

and working-class communities of their own supposedly "developed" neoliberal societies. Eschewing an easy focus on what they term "queer theory's general obsession [with] . . . the sexualized human form" (ibid.: 221), they instead draw our attention to precarious forms of life that exist at the margins of policymaking, media coverage, and activism in Washington, Paris, and London. They specifically avoid any easy attempt to universalize Western categories such as sexuality and LGBTQ rights, and instead show how queer theory can explore the lives of Afghani or Iraqi war veterans; they remain critical of the "homonationalism" or "queer imperialism" of millennial gay rights discourses, with their attendant devaluation of queer subjects who persist in forms of religious, linguistic, or cultural identification that fail to respect neoliberal projects of sexual self-determination.

If we accept a long-standing tendency within queer theory to position the "queer" as being disruptive, antinormative, and subversive to prevalent discourses of sexuality and biopolitics, then we find much provocative material in Mikdashi and Puar's article, as well as in Puar's (2007) earlier work on terrorism and the body. What has held queer theory back from this encounter? Too often, as the authors observe, queer theorists have simply been unwilling to accept that queer theory could address the experiences of a disabled war veteran in Kabul or a transgender prostitute in Bagdad. Put bluntly, "white, cisgendered, masculinist and middle-class queer histories" have tended to constitute the archive of queer theory. Other lives, Puar and Mikdashi contend, have been judged as somehow unworthy of queer theorists' attention. The Academy, as much as the military or NGOs, appears to consider such lives as being illegible and "collateral"; at best, they have been consigned to a different disciplinary framework, most often sexuality or area studies.

Mikdashi and Puar's 2016 article reminds us that this situation is untenable. Both scholars have made these arguments before, and similar critiques of queer theory have existed for years, but the 2016 article, itself a report on a roundtable on queer theory and area studies, coincides with a gathering momentum within queer and transgender studies (Mikdashi 2013: 351). It makes a concise, simple, and compelling case for queer theory to deprovincialize itself and move outside the West (Whab 2016: 707; Smith 2013: 180). This argument has been taken up in other work that has drawn explicitly on Achille Mbembe's notion of "necropolitics" to theorize the troubling forms of expendable life apparent throughout the South. Mbembe's term describes the hegemonic deployment of death as a form of sovereignty or "the subjugation of life to the power of death;" in a nightmare mirror image of Michel Foucault's argument about the use of life as a form of governance, necropolitics has reshaped our understanding of queer relationships with death, previously a subject of psychoanalytic theory (Bersani 2009; Mbembe 2003: 11–12, 39). Queer and transgender theories have played a vital role in this project and transformed our understanding of these collateral populations who face death and preciousness on a daily basis (Lamble 2013; Snorton and Haritaworn 2013).

Partly in the light of Puar's work, Jin Haritaworn (Haritaworn et al. 2015) has argued for a distinctive "queer necropolitics" that reveals how forms of life that are deemed worthwhile are sharply divided from those that are consigned to the garbage heap, as disposable and worthless. In an argument that recalls Judith Butler's theorization of "precarious life" in post-9/11 America, we might consider the contrast between the wealthy, white gay and lesbian couples imagined in neoliberal advertising campaigns aimed at the "pink pound," and an incarcerated transgender subject seeking urgent surgical interventions (Butler 2006). In a 2015 volume, Haritaworn and others (2015) have shown how working-class and marginal queers have repeatedly been marked by death as a form of social control. Like Puar's studies of maimed and collateral populations, necropolitics reveals those who are not yet dead, their lives neglected and subject to the chance drone strike, the possible drive-by shooting, or a malfunctioning batch of fake black-market pharmaceuticals; in other words, the living dead. Mikdashi and Puar contend that following the lengthy US war in Afghanistan, the country was left with the world's highest population of individuals relying on prosthetic body parts, often without adequate aftercare and support. The authors deliberately use the term *crippled* to distinguish between those who have received medical care and identification as *disabled*, and those simply left to live without any limb; Puar (2017) has recently advanced her theorization of physical impairment in this context.

These are the lives of queer and collateral subjects; their deaths are as yet unrealized, but they are always already sanctioned. Deprived of legal protection, one thinks of villagers subjected to drone strikes, collateral subjects can die at any time. These queer life stories run at odds with core assumptions within Western LGBTQ rights discourses; they are deprived of the self-realization deemed integral to the emergence of a sexual subject. Queer forms of living death marked by permanent war clearly preclude the possibility of middle-class self-discovery. The mobilization of living death, as evinced separately in the work of Mbembe and Haritaworn, is in itself of considerable interest to queer theorists, who have long been concerned with the politics of life, reproduction, and futurity (Edelman 2004). To live without the privilege of a future, or to have children who are not privileged as the bearers of futurity, are conditions that must develop queer theory's otherwise sophisticated accounts of biopolitics and reproduction.

Queer theory from elsewhere challenges a certain stagnation within metropolitan queer theory, or what Mikdashi and Puar (2016: 215) term "queer theory as American studies"; forms of life and death in the South speak far more closely to the interests of earlier queer theorists than contemporary middle-class queer life in the West. Yet this point must remain secondary; queer theory from elsewhere should not be judged on what it offers "to" its Western counterpart. Work at the intersection of queer theory and area studies needs primarily to engage closely with the specificity of non-Western cultures, histories, and languages; there is a continual danger of becoming subsumed into a generalized notion of "world sexualities." But given these caveats, interventions such as Mikdashi and Puar's force queer theory out into the world; they anticipate a traveling queer theory able to engage with non-Western places and peoples, whether in Kabul, Beirut, Kinshasa, or Lagos. This deprovincialized queer theory has the potential to generate a type of reverse ethnography through which Western readers can appreciate their own domestic practices of exclusion, particularly in the prison and health care systems, through newly critical eyes.

References

Bersani, Leo. 2009. *Is the Rectum a Grave? and Other Essays*. Chicago: Chicago University Press.

Butler, Judith. 2006. *Precarious Life: The Power of Mourning and Violence*. London: Verso.

Edelman, Lee. 2004. *No Future: Queer Theory and the Death Drive*. Durham, NC: Duke University Press.

Haritaworn, Jin, Adi Kuntsman, and Silvia Posocco, eds. 2015. *Queer Necropolitics*. Abingdon, UK: Routledge.

Lamble, Sarah. 2013. "Queer Necropolitics and the Expanding Carceral State: Interrogating Sexual Investments in Punishment. *Law and Critique* 24, no. 3: 229–53.

Mbembe, Achille. 2003. "Necropolitics." *Public Culture* 15, no. 1: 11–40.

McGlotten, Shaka. 2014. "Zombie Porn: Necropolitics, Sex, and Queer Socialities." *Porn Studies* 1, no. 4: 360–77.

Mikdashi, Maya. 2013. "Queer Citizenship, Queering Middle East Studies." *International Journal of Middle Eastern Studies* 45, no. 2: 350–52.

Puar, Jasbir. 2007. *Terrorist Assemblages: Homonationalism in Queer Times*. Durham, NC: Duke University Press.

———. 2017. *The Right to Maim: Debility, Capacity, Disability*. Durham, NC: Duke University Press.

Smith, Christen. 2013. "Strange Fruit: Brazil, Necropolitics, and the Transnational Reso-
    nance of Torture and Death." *Souls: A Critical Journal of Black Politics, Culture,
    and Society* 15, no. 3: 177–98.

Snorton, C. Riley, and Jin Haritaworn. 2013. "Trans Necropolitics: A Transnational
    Reflection on Violence, Death, and the Trans of Color Afterlife." In *The Transgender
    Studies Reader 2*, edited by Susan Stryker and Aren Aizura, 66–76. Abingdon, UK:
    Routledge.

Whab, Amar. 2016. "Homosexuality/ Homophobia Is Un-African'? Un-Mapping Transna-
    tional Discourses in the Context of Uganda' Anti-Homosexuality Bill/Act." *Journal of
    Homosexuality* 63, no. 5: 685–718.

GLQ FORUM / TWENTY YEARS OF PUNKS

Introduction

Nic John Ramos

A little more than twenty years ago, *GLQ* published Cathy J. Cohen's "Punks, Bulldaggers, and Welfare Queens: The Radical Potential of Queer Politics?" (hereafter referred to in this forum as "Punks"). Her groundbreaking article provided a fresh analysis of race and sexuality by arguing both are intertwined processes of power rather than discrete systems of identity making. In conceiving of power as an element that is *routed through* race, gender, sex, and class, Cohen's (1997: 437) article served as an invitation for scholars to join her in "search[ing] for a new political direction and agenda, one that does not focus on integration into dominant structures but instead seeks to transform the basic fabric and hierarchies that allow systems of oppression to persist and operate efficiently."

This special *GLQ* forum demonstrates how powerful her provocation was and *still is* by gathering responses from ten scholars who participated in one or more of four different events in 2017 to celebrate the twentieth anniversary of "Punks." These events included a Minority Scholars Committee panel at the American Studies Association conference in Chicago, a presidential roundtable panel at the National Women's Studies Association conference in Baltimore, and two separate symposiums held at the University of Maryland, College Park, and at the University of Michigan. The associations, universities, and people who hosted these events demonstrate the incredible influence of Cohen's article and her broader work on community activism and the academy (see list of events and participants at the end of this introduction).

For me, "Punks" has achieved the same level of kinship implied as asking people where they were when a human first landed on the moon. Be they stranger

GLQ 25:1

or longtime acquaintance, the article often works as shorthand in my conversations with colleagues and students to establish a common language to understand my approaches to the study of race, sexuality, and medicine. As this forum shows, "Punks" calibrates scholars across several generations, fields, and disciplines into a single conversation that, like Cohen's analysis of power, brings together what, at first, looks disparate into the same orbit of feeling and relation.

The forum opens with Cohen's reflection on the article she wrote more than twenty years ago. Her piece loosely frames the order of the forum's subsequent articles. Cohen openly worries about the erasure of Black feminist, lesbian, and gay activists in a history overwhelmingly narrated as white and gay. Her call to remember Black activism is more than just a concern about the racial and sexual representation of Blackness, lesbianism, and feminism in gay history *or* gayness, lesbianism, and feminism in Black history; it is an urgent reminder to heed the kinds of radical dreams, imaginations, and worlds their activism called forth *across* racial and sexual difference. Rather than flatten Black feminist, lesbian, and gay organizing as simply a "gay movement in response to HIV/AIDS," she wishes us to remember their work as also a "radical attack on the politics of respectability in Black communities" and as "a radical attack on the state violence perpetrated through Reagan's neoliberalism."

The erasure of this "queer potential of politics" animates the insights contained in the essays of Christina Hanhardt, Chandan Reddy, and L. H. Stallings. They each argue for the crucial role "Punks" played in developing a field of queer political history that is, as Hanhardt argues, "informed by intellectual work that has too often been left outside the dominant canon of *queer.*" In particular, all three essays connect "Punks" to its often-overlooked and/or taken-for-granted genealogical roots in Black feminism, the Black radical tradition, and racial capitalism.

Cohen and many of the authors also take time in their essays to answer her haunting subtitular question—"The Radical Potential of Queer Politics?"—with new questions about what *queer* might exactly be in an era of intersectionality, queer identity, and queer of color critique. C. Riley Snorton's musing on the temporality of queer thus launches readers into a discussion about the structural conditions of life today facing Black gay men, Black cis women, and Black trans feminine peoples found in the essays of Marlon Bailey, Jih-Fei Cheng, and Sarah Haley. As their essays argue, the structural entanglements of race and sexuality continue to make the subjects in "Punks" as vulnerable to violence as they were in 1997. Their work also challenges us to think again about queer ethical engagements with the "politics of respectability." Haley's essay on Black women with "coiffed, pressed hair protruded from netted veiled hats," for instance, challenges our assumptions about who can inhabit the category of queer.

Finally, while all the authors in this forum trace, gesture toward, and provide language to imagine new political alliances for our times, the last two essays, by Nayan Shah and Elliott Powell, strongly consider Cohen's provocative call for new coalitional politics and methods. Based on his forthcoming work on detained hunger strikers, Shah's essay further destabilizes the boundaries of identity to extend the radical potential of queer politics to include refugees, the incarcerated, and others affected by new and old turns in racial capitalism. Taking a slightly different turn, Powell's essay argues that music serves as a prime arena to explore where idea exchange, community making, and the launching of new politics regularly takes place.

Scholars and activists who participated in one or more of the four events listed below include Aliyyah Abdur-Rahman, Katherine Acey, Jafari S. Allen, Darius Bost, Elsa Barkley Brown, Kenyon Farrow, Chandra Ford, Dayo Gore, Dean Hubbs, David Hutchinson, Jennifer D. Jones, Jonathan Lykes, Michelle Rowley, and Lester Spence.

> "Punks, Bulldaggers, and Welfare Queens" Twenty Years Later: A Celebration of the Scholarship of Cathy Cohen. 2017. Tenth Annual DC Queer Studies Symposium at the University of Maryland, College Park, April 21.

> "Punks" @ 20: Revisiting Cathy Cohen's Queer Coalitional Vision. 2017. Lesbian, Gay, Queer Research Initiative Symposium at the University of Michigan, Ann Arbor, September 18.

> "Punks, Bulldaggers, and Welfare Queens": An Anniversary Celebration across Generations, Scholarship, and Disciplines. 2017. Minority Scholars Committee Professional-Development Session at the American Studies Association Annual Conference, Chicago, November 11.

> Twenty Years since "Punks, Bulldaggers and Welfare Queens." 2017. Presidential Panel at the National Women's Studies Association Conference, Baltimore, November 17.

Note

I would like to thank the editors and staff of *GLQ* as well as the conference planning committee and the members of the Minority Scholars Committee of the American Studies Association, especially Randy Ontiveros, Kandice Chuh, Siobhan Somerville, Laura Kang, and Alexandra Vazquez.

Reference

Cohen, Cathy J. 1997. "Punks, Bulldaggers, and Welfare Queens: The Radical Potential of Queer Politics?" *GLQ* 3, no. 4: 437–65.

DOI 10.1215/10642684-7275320

THE RADICAL POTENTIAL OF QUEER?

Twenty Years Later

Cathy Cohen

*A*s those who write for a living or for pleasure or for both know, the things we write are never created in isolation, but often speak to and reflect the issues, conditions, and hopes that are most prevalent in our time and space. For me, "Punks, Bulldaggers, and Welfare Queens" was shaped by numerous factors. Let me mention three. First was the HIV/AIDS crisis that took root on the coasts and across the country, overwhelming many communities, including especially Black communities (Cohen 1999). Second was the devastation of poor communities and communities of color that resulted from Ronald Reagan's implementation and Bill Clinton's enforcement of neoliberal policies and ideologies (Duggan 2012). The third factor was one of hope and stood in contrast to the loss generated by HIV/AIDS and neoliberalism. Here I am referring to the emergence and solidification of both Black feminist and Black gay and lesbian communities during the 1970s, 1980s, and 1990s (Springer 2005).

It is this third factor that I want to spend some space and time reflecting on, because I am worried about a process of erasure. Specifically, I am concerned with the erasure that happens through the rewriting of histories, where the politics of Black feminist and Black lesbians and gay men of the 1970s, 1980s, and 1990s are framed not as a radical attack on the politics of respectability in Black communities or a radical attack on the state violence perpetrated through Reagan's neoliberalism, or a radical articulation of Black gay life in all its fullness and idealism, and ordinariness, but instead the 1970s, 1980s, and 1990s become only a gay movement in response to HIV/AIDS, leading to a path-dependent result of professional organizations and assimilation.

This process of erasure or rewriting can be deadly because it inhibits our ability to know what happened before us, to know that there were radical Black queers who fought similar fights for liberation to those being waged today, who insisted on reimagining what liberation might look like, when it includes and makes central those on the margins of Black communities. We must remember that it was in the 1970s, 1980s, and 1990s that critical texts and documentaries were created from individuals such as Audre Lorde (1984), Barbara Smith (1983), Cheryl Clarke (1983), Pat Parker (1978), Marlon Riggs (1989), Joseph Beam (1986, 1991), and Essex Hemphill (1992)—to mention but a few. It is also during this period that organizations like the Combahee River Collective, the National Coalition of Black Lesbians and Gays, Kitchen Table Women of Color Press, Other Countries, Blackheart Collective, Blackout Magazine, Salsa Soul Sisters, Gay Men of African Descent, and eventually The Audre Lorde Project would all emerge to provide organizational structure to communities of Black gay folk committed to pursuing a radical agenda of Black liberation.

It was in many ways the intersection of the rich ways of thinking, imagining, and connecting, provided by Black feminist knowledge production, in and largely out of the academy, and the urgency of Black death confronting us through both HIV/AIDS and neoliberalism that produced the environment in which "Punks" was written. "Punks" was an articulation of longing for a radical formation that would not only save our lives but also see us—punks, bulldaggers, and welfare queens—as full members of Black communities, connected in struggle and helping produce a new era in the Black radical tradition.

The Radical Potential of Queer Today

While "Punks" was a long-form articulation of longing for a radical collective formation, the choice of queer, as a framework or identity that could serve as a foundation for collaborative struggle or at least make visible our shared location on the outskirts of traditional power, was offered up because it felt like an unresolved question about positionality and identity in Black communities. What I mean is that queer was not overidentified in Black gay and lesbian communities. Thus, while significant segments of white LGBT communities in the 1990s seemed to embrace the sexual fluidity and flattening of their power associated with being queer, many in Black LGBT communities approached the idea and term of *queer* with greater skepticism and reluctance (Battle et al. 2002). And because the idea of queer was not overdetermined as a personal/sexual identity, at least in Black communities, it left some space to use the idea of queer as a *provocation* to imagine how we might organize across varied communities defined as "the other" by the state and/or racial capitalism.

What is interesting about the current moment in relation to the use of queer is the space for provocation seems to be quickly closing. What I mean is that queer as a unifying framework for mobilization and action or that space available for interrogation and imagining of who could be included in a or the queer political project and what might be the political basis of queer unity is less available as more people adopt queer as a personal politicized identity, embodying a radical identitarian personal politics, as opposed to a collective position relative to state and capitalist power.

As I wrote in 1997, I was using the transformed idea of queer to "envision a politics where one's relation to power and not some homogenized identity is privileged in determining one's political comrades. I'm talking about a politics where the nonnormative and marginal position of punks, bulldaggers, and welfare queens, for example, is the basis for progressive, transformative coalition work. Thus, if there is any truly radical potential to be found in the idea of queerness and the practice of queer politics, it would seem to be located in its ability to create a space in opposition to dominant norms, a space where transformational political work can begin." In the vision of queer politics that motivated me in "Punks," individuals like Michael Brown and Rekia Boyd are important queer subjects not because of their sexual practice, identity, or performance but because they, as well as other young and poor folks of color, operate in the world as queer subjects: the targets of racial normalizing projects intent on pathologizing them across the dimensions of race, class, gender, and sexuality, simultaneously making them into deviants while normalizing their degradation and marginalization until it becomes what we expect—the norm—until it becomes something that we no longer pay attention to.

And while increasingly I see some of the most radical social movements today taking on the nomenclature of queer, I am also confronted by its adoption as a personal, politicized identity. Thus, I worry that as more individuals take on the identity of queer as an embodiment of sexual positionality, queer becomes less effective—if it ever was effective—as a unifying framework for solidarity work across domains of struggle and across identities. What I see now is a queer politics defined by bodies and practices and less about collaborative politics: what I might crudely call the queer politics of identity over the queer politics of positionality.

This adoption of queer as a personal, politicized identity is radical in the sense that those who embrace the identity of queer also often articulate an anti-capitalist, feminist, and nonnormative politics, committed to fighting with and struggling for those who are most marginal in our communities and the larger society. The personal politics of queer, as currently articulated, is also collectivized through the mobilization and identification of queer people. For example, the Movement for Black Lives is different from anything we have seen before in the Black radical tradition because so many of the organizations are led by Black queer feminists. But at the same time, through this formation, the radical potential of queer is reduced to an identity that is largely attached to sexual desire, practice, and performance. Thus, it becomes easier for us to identify the "queers" leading the movement—a good thing—than to detail what we mean by the queer politics of the movement.

Let me be clear: despite my reservations about queer as the basis for collective struggle on the left, the framework still animates my hopes and dreams about what is possible in this current moment of organizing. Many of the organizers in the Movement for Black Lives embrace a *Black feminist and queer analysis* independent of who their intimate and sexual partners are. For them, being queer can be both an identity and a position relative to oppressive state power. These folks refuse to conform to a politics of respectability and instead practice a Black feminist intersectional approach to organizing, highlighting the many identities that Black communities and Black bodies encompass, but with an eye on centering their work on those most marginal, Black women, Black poor people, Black trans and gender-nonconforming folk, and Black gay, lesbian, and queer folks. These organizations, like the Black LGBT organizations of the 1970s, 1980s, and 1990s, are led by young Black people, often on the margins, but demanding both recognition and an expansion of blackness. This may not be the radical potential of queer that I envisioned twenty years ago, but this combination of Black feminism and a commitment to queer as a continuation of the Black radical tradition may be our best hope for the radical movements and queer futures we all deserve.

References

Battle, J., C. J. Cohen, D. Warren, G. Fergerson, and S. Audam. 2002. *Say It Loud, I'm Black and I'm Proud: Black Pride Survey 2000*. New York: Policy Institute of the National Gay and Lesbian Task Force.

Beam, Joseph. 1986. *In the Life: A Black Gay Anthology*. Boston: Alyson Publications.

———. 1991. *Brother to Brother: New Writings by Black Gay Men*. Edited by Essex Hemphill. Boston: Alyson Publications.

Clarke, Cheryl. 1983. "The Failure to Transform: Homophobia in the Black Community." In *Home Girls: A Black Feminist Anthology*, edited by Barbara Smith, 197–208. New York: Kitchen Table–Women of Color.

Cohen, Cathy J. 1999. *The Boundaries of Blackness: AIDS and the Breakdown of Black Politics*. Chicago: University of Chicago Press.

Duggan, Lisa. 2012. *The Twilight of Equality? Neoliberalism, Cultural Politics, and the Attack on Democracy*. Boston: Beacon.

Hemphill, Essex. 1992. *Ceremonies: Prose and Poetry*. New York: Plume.

Lorde, Audre. 1984. *Sister Outsider: Essays and Speeches*. Berkeley, CA: Crossing Press.

Parker, Pat. 1978. *Movement in Black: The Collected Poetry of Pat Parker, 1961–1978*. Berkeley, CA: Crossing Press.

Riggs, Marlon T., dir. 1989. *Tongues Untied: Black Men Loving Black Men*. San Francisco, CA: Frameline.

Smith, Barbara, ed. 1983. *Home Girls: A Black Feminist Anthology*. New Brunswick, NJ: Rutgers University Press.

Springer, Kimberly. 2005. *Living for the Revolution: Black Feminist Organizations, 1968–1980*. Durham, NC: Duke University Press.

DOI 10.1215/10642684-7275334

THE RADICAL POTENTIAL OF QUEER POLITICAL HISTORY?

Christina B. Hanhardt

*I*n the opening to "Punks, Bulldaggers, and Welfare Queens: The Radical Potential of Queer Politics?," Cathy Cohen describes reports of racism at what was then the nation's largest HIV/AIDS organization, the Gay Men's Health Crisis (GMHC). She uses this example to frame two key contexts for her 1997 essay: the entrenched racism of many lesbian and gay institutions as well as the failed promises of so many anti-assimilationist *queer* alternatives. She then maps a new queer politics, one that troubles the default focus on a queer-versus-heterosexual dichotomy and is instead attuned to the stratifications of race, gender, and class and organized around a range of nonnormative kinship and gender roles, stigmatized pleasures, and criminalized practices—those of "punks, bulldaggers, and welfare queens." The essay closes by pointing to the political possibilities of coalition, including the AIDS Coalition to Unleash Power (ACT UP)'s participation in HIV/AIDS activism for needle exchange programs and within prisons.

Cohen's Black feminist left method of queer critique upended the assumptions of much of queer theory and politics at the time, in addition to other left social movement analysis and practice, and the essay's influence cannot be overstated. Cohen's take on three of the topical mainstays of queer theory—identity, normativity, and liberalism—is to trace their operation and mine their contradictions, offering *queer* not as an idealized position or a prescription but as a *relation* produced by the uneven and shifting dynamics of power. Her analysis of how sexual stigma adheres to nonnormative expressions of kinship, gender, and pleasure demonstrates the central function of queerness within the operation of racism and capitalism and the limited terms of political campaigns that organize around *queer* only as a placeholder either for lesbian, gay, bisexual, or transgender (LGBT) identities in isolation or for antinormative expressions that subsume the recognition of power-over into ahistorical abstracted ideals.

One of my favorite moments of the essay is when, after Cohen (1997: 453) has already outlined in great detail the tensions in Black, left, feminist, and queer theorizing, she writes that she will turn to give "a little history" because "as a political scientist a little history is all that [she] can offer." The next section gives much more than a *little* history, as Cohen proceeds to detail how sex and gender regulation have always been racialized, and racial subjugation articulated in sexual and gendered terms, in a history of "heterosexuals on the (out)side of heteronormativity" (ibid.: 452) that runs from the prohibition of marriage under slavery to antimiscegenation laws to debates about the so-called underclass.[1] As Cohen explains, her framework is informed by intellectual work that has too often been left outside the dominant canon of *queer,* especially that of Black feminism. Insofar that a "truly . . . transformative" queer politics has a history (in hitherto ignored intellectual pasts) *and* its future remains to be known (in titling the essay as a question about political "potential") (ibid.: 438), Cohen's look at heterosexuality outside heteronormativity has been crucial to new approaches to *queer political history*—be that in the adoption of a queer lens on the history of LGBT- or queer-identified activism, or the history of a range of political campaigns for and by the "non-normative and marginal" (ibid.).

This is the focus of the remainder of my brief comments: to show what Cohen's essay has offered, and continues to offer, to our understanding of the history and future of queer politics. Despite the tremendous influence of Cohen's vision on scholarship and activism of the past twenty years, many historians of LGBT politics have resisted the use of *queer* as an interdisciplinary and intersectional framework for analyzing power. But, as Cohen's essay shows, an expansive approach to the historical study of so-called *punks, bulldaggers,* and *welfare queens* is essential to fully grasping both how the LGBT movement (in organizations like the GMHC) got to be the way she described it in 1997 and if promising coalitions of the time (such as those ACT UP participated in) ultimately realized their transformative potential. This method also further facilitates the broad genealogy of the queer politics Cohen envisioned in 1997, and that we see in 2019.

First, Cohen's insistence on looking at the regulation of kinship and the complexity of stigma and criminalization paved the way for scholars to understand how different historical and social movement forces shaped the normative form of LGBT politics as counter to issues associated with racialized and gendered poverty (Ellison 2015; Esparza 2017; Hanhardt 2013; Holmes 2011). That is, from the 1960s through the 1990s, the gay movement gained momentum as activists made claims to neighborhoods and demanded the decriminalization of homosexuality and its removal from the *Diagnostic and Statistical Manual of Mental Disorders-II.* But this was also the time that new policing, economic development, and social welfare policies increasingly targeted single-mother households and the street life of the poor, especially people of color and those labeled mentally ill, who were gay and straight, trans and not. One result was the consolidation of a *homonormative* political agenda (Duggan 2003) at the very same time that LGBT- and queer-identified movements sought to expand their ranks.

Second, Cohen reminds us that our analysis of power shapes our interpretation of social movements, including how we find and define the very subjects and strategies of activism. The essay provides a framework for understanding the importance of the political activities of those outside the normative narrative for LGBT political history, including those whose lives have been structured as queer, be they political prisoners, single mothers receiving welfare, or those who move in and out of criminalized informal economies. To do so, she reminds readers that there are precedents for this model of analysis and strategy, especially in the Black feminist and LGBT writing and political organizing of the 1960s through 1990s that have too often been left out of the canon of LGBT and queer social movement history. There are many reasons for this exclusion within the historical literature: LGBT archives have been linked to social movements, and radical and marginalized groups tend not to donate their papers to archives that don't reflect their vision. And for many activists of the 1960s through 1990s, their work and their papers are still unfinished. In addition, historicizing coalition and participation in multiple campaigns, features of Black feminist and LGBT activism of the period, requires dispensing with the terms of movements that otherwise sort activism according to single issues, goals, or aspects of individuals' identities (Arondekar et al. 2015).

Cohen's essay provided a charge to think about the history of LGBT and queer politics differently, and such scholars as Jonathan Bailey (2017), Darius Bost (forthcoming), Treva Ellison (2015), Dayo Gore (2018), Emily Hobson (2016), Kwame Holmes (2011), Jennifer Jones (2014), Kimberly Springer (2005), and Emily Thuma (forthcoming) have responded with new histories of autonomous Black feminist and LGBT organizing, the LGBT and queer forces in Black political history, and multi-issue, multiracial, and coalitional organizing that undoes the false oppositions of queer versus heterosexual, and identity versus class, and that may or may not take on the monikers *LGBT* or *queer*. All of these studies reach outside the discipline of history, just as Cohen looked outside her discipline of political science to develop her theoretical framework. This interdisciplinary method often draws on Black feminist literary theory, seeks new terms within the words and experiences of Black women, and pulls apart dominant perspectives on the places of knowledge production and political practice. This includes Sarah Haley's (2016) history of Black women's challenges to Jim Crow modernity, Aimee Meredith Cox's (2015) ethnography of the performative and everyday *choreography* of young Black women in Detroit, and C. Riley Snorton's (2017) rich archive for the linked trajectories of blackness and transness from the nineteenth into the twenty-first century.

Although today the uses of *queer* are often similar to its uses in 1997—as a shorthand for an expanding acronym; placeholder for identities outside these categories; marker of single-issue LGBT militancy; or intersectional analysis of power—the last approach has played a key role in the leadership, vision, and practices of a new generation of radical Black political organizing. In a recent interview, Cohen, in a nod to her earlier essay, describes activism within the Movement for Black Lives as "using a queer lens to challenge the static nature of categories and identities," and having the "possibility . . . to think about the ways in which different bodies are marginalized and made to be queer in the eyes of the state as well as in their own communities" (Cohen and Jackson 2016: 782). Nonetheless, even as some mainstream LGBT organizations recognize the LGBT- or queer-identified leadership of the founders of #BlackLivesMatter, that has not always translated into finding common ground in or building coalitions for goals such as ending order maintenance policing or heightened municipal ticketing, a dynamic that continues to parallel many disciplinary approaches to LGBT- and even queer-identified social movement history.

In 1997, queer theory and LGBT social movement history had a strained relationship (Duggan 1995), and in 2019 much has remained the same. But "Punks, Bulldaggers, and Welfare Queens" was a foundational text that opened a door for approaches to queer political history that value and learn from a Black feminist left theoretical genealogy and method. This has been realized in some LGBT- and queer-identified social movement history and in other studies of resistance led by the "non-normative and marginal" that often draw the past right up to the present and are found outside the guarded borders of the discipline of history and the canons and institutionalized locations of queer theory and politics. Cohen's essay inspired many—and certainly me—to read and engage differently and to commit to the details of politics and history, for a future, queer and otherwise.

Note

1.   Here I want to emphasize this essay's transformative influence on my own scholarship, as I have tried to give "a little history" to exactly the types of cases that frame Cohen's essay: my book, *Safe Space*, asks how the mainstream LGBT antiviolence movement came to be as she describes the GMHC; my current research asks where we might put needle exchanges and prisoner solidarity projects in *queer* political history.

References

Arondekar, Anjali, Ann Cvetkovich, Christina B. Hanhardt, Regina Kunzel, Tavia
 Nyong'o, Juana María Rodriguez, Susan Stryker, Daniel Marshall, Kevin P. Murphy,
 and Zeb Tortorici. 2015. "Queering Archives: A Roundtable Discussion." *Radical
 History Review* 122: 211–31.

Bailey, Jonathan. 2017. "'As Proud of Our Gayness as We Are of Our Blackness': The
 Political and Social Formation of the African American LGBTQ Community in Baltimore and Washington, D.C., 1975–1991." PhD diss., Morgan State University.

Bost, Darius. Forthcoming. *Evidence of Being: The Black Gay Cultural Renaissance and
 the Politics of Violence*. Chicago: University of Chicago Press.

Cohen, Cathy J. 1997. "Punks, Bulldaggers, and Welfare Queens: The Radical Potential
 of Queer Politics?" *GLQ* 3, no. 4: 437–65.

Cohen, Cathy J., and Sarah J. Jackson. 2016. "Ask a Feminist: A Conversation with Cathy
 Cohen on Black Lives Matter, Feminism, and Contemporary Activism." *Signs* 41, no.
 4: 775–92.

Cox, Aimee Meredith. 2015. *Shapeshifters: Black Girls and the Choreography of Citizenship*. Durham, NC: Duke University Press.

Duggan, Lisa. 1995. "The Discipline Problem: Queer Theory Meets Lesbian and Gay
 History." *GLQ* 2, no. 3: 179–91.

———. 2003. *Twilight of Equality: Neoliberalism, Cultural Politics, and the Attack on
 Democracy*. Boston: Beacon Books.

Ellison, Treva C. 2015. "Towards a Politics of Perfect Disorder: Carceral Geographies, Queer
 Criminality, and Other Ways to Be." PhD diss., University of Southern California.

Esparza, René. 2017. "From Vice to Nice: Race, Sex, and the Gentrification of AIDS."
 PhD diss., University of Minnesota.

Gore, Dayo F. 2018. "Making Space for Pauli Murray: Transformations in a Queer Politics
 and Life." Article manuscript in author's possession.

Haley, Sarah. 2016. *No Mercy Here: Gender, Punishment, and the Making of Jim Crow
 Modernity*. Chapel Hill: University of North Carolina Press.

Hanhardt, Christina B. 2013. *Safe Space: Gay Neighborhood History and the Politics of
 Violence*. Durham, NC: Duke University Press.

Hobson, Emily. 2016. *Lavender and Red: Liberation and Solidarity in the Lesbian and
 Gay Left*. Berkeley: University of California Press.

Holmes, Kwame. 2011. "Chocolate to Rainbow City: The Dialectics of Black and Gay
 Community Formation in Postwar Washington, D.C., 1946–1978." PhD diss., University of Illinois, Urbana-Champaign.

Jones, Jennifer. 2014. "'The Fruits of Mixing': Homosexuality and the Politics of Racial
 Empowerment, 1945–1975." PhD diss., Princeton University.

Snorton, C. Riley. 2017. *Black on Both Sides: A Racial History of Trans Identity*. Minneapolis: University of Minnesota Press.

Springer, Kimberly. 2005. *Living for the Revolution: Black Feminist Organizations,
  1968–1980*. Durham, NC: Duke University Press.
Thuma, Emily. Forthcoming. *All Our Trials: Prisons, Policing, and the Feminist Fight to
  End Violence*. Urbana: University of Illinois Press.

DOI 10.1215/10642684-7275348

NEOLIBERALISM THEN AND NOW

Race, Sexuality, and the Black Radical Tradition

Chandan Reddy

(For Marcellus Blount)

*I*t's impossible to enumerate in this short space all the different and crucial interventions Cathy Cohen's 1997 *GLQ* essay made not only to queer studies, black and ethnic studies, and feminist studies but also to left politics, social movement activism, and grassroots organizing. I will make two main points, then. First, in relation to the latter, we ought to read Cohen's "Punks, Bulldaggers, and Welfare Queens: The Radical Potential of Queer Politics?" as part of what Cedric Robinson (2000) termed the Black Radical Tradition, a tradition produced through "an accretion over generations of collective intelligence gathered from struggle" (xxx). For Robinson, this tradition could be transformed "into a radical force," the purpose of which, "in its most militant manifestation . . . [is] the overthrow of the whole race-based structure" (xxxi). Cohen's essay built on the collective intelligence gathered by women of color, black feminist, and queer of color struggles from the 1970s onward, a canniness that "grows from the lived experience of existing within and resisting multiple and connected practices of domination and normalization" (Cohen 1997: 441). In this way, Cohen's essay also marks a transformation and rearticulation of tenets of the Black Radical Tradition, by noting and making explicit that in late capitalist modernity, the "whole race-based structure" is a *heteronormative order* that masks the very "interlocking systems of domination" it articulates together and depends on (Ferguson 2004).

Reading Cohen's essay today, we note continuities and departures between our moment and its own. Written in the "twilight of equality," as Lisa Duggan (2003) characterized that moment, the context of Cohen's essay was an ascendant global political economy of transnational production, neoliberal financialization, austerity, privatization, and racial security, the US face of which was the Clinton-era Crime Bill of 1994; the Welfare Reform Act, the Illegal Immigration Reform and Immigrant Responsibility Act, and the Counterterrorism Act all passed in 1996, just months before the essay's publication (Reddy 2005). Yet, if Cohen's essay elicits a diagnostic power and analytic importance that feels as galvanizing now as it did in its moment of publication, that is because the material and ideological architecture of that era, which Cohen (1997: 438) sought to diagnose in the interest of constructing a "new politics," lives on in our own, not only as lasting effects but as the source today of a capitalized infrastructure of racial incapacitation and administrative gendering (Spade 2015) that has only grown since the publication of "Punks" twenty years ago. In our moment, Cohen's call for a "new politics" is being answered in diverse ways, through projects and groups such as #Say Her Name, Hands Up United, Black Lives Matter, BYP 100, the Silva Rivera Law Project, African American Policy Forum, Familia: TQLM, water protectors, detention center hunger strikers, and youth movements to end incarceration. That is, like Kimberlé Crenshaw's intersectionality (1991), Angela Davis's (2003) and Ruth Wilson Gilmore's (2007) work on the prison-industrial complex, and the return and transformation of Black life itself as the violated bearer and immobilized source of value through confinement and repressive-state tactics of terror and death-dealing, the insights of "Punks" so infuse today's critical and activist discourses precisely because they were written from a black radical standpoint within the forming neoliberal order, a standpoint that exploits—for liberation, collective autonomy, communal survival, and economic redistribution—the structural contradictions immanent to the modes of accumulation that were becoming dominant twenty years ago. "Punks" doesn't just diagnose domination or unmask the complexity and cunning of power. It points a way forward, a way through. It focuses on contradictions that liberal, queer, and left critiques alike fail to see that point to modes and "subjects" of resistance otherwise foreclosed by power.

For example, as neoliberalism dismantled the gains of the civil rights welfare state, it formulated discourses of social efficiency, and increased personal autonomy and equal rights of privacy. These public discourses were crucial to the incorporation of homosexuality within the neoliberal state that the marriage equality movement produced and exploited for its own ends. Yet austerity, privatization, joblessness, and the wealth stripping of poor, working-class, and lower-middle-class Black and racialized immigrant families and neighborhoods in urban areas throughout the 1990s contradict these discourses of efficiency, personal autonomy, and universal privacy on which gay and lesbian rights projects depended. To seize on these contradictions from the standpoint of black radicalism is, according to Cohen, to find alternative coherencies and still-undisclosed relationalities that can constitute a "new" and radical political formation and fulcrum of punks, bulldaggers, and welfare queens that neoliberal and heteronormative logics of sexuality otherwise divide, alienate, distance, or figure as inhuman or unpolitical in their togetherness.

Second, I would like to suggest that Cohen's essay builds on Robinson's insight in *Black Marxism* that Western capitalism strives toward a racial totality, and as such, "racial antagonisms . . . [are] arrayed along a continuum from the casual insult to the most ruthless and lethal rules of law" (Robinson 2000: xxxi). For W. E. B. DuBois (2007), Western capital's reliance upon a racial totality accounted not only for the extra "psychological" wage demanded by the white working class in US society but also for the failure of contemporary historians and nearly all US citizens to see the "general strike" of four million enslaved workers that occurred right before their eyes. Likewise, following the works of Angela Davis (1983), the Combahee River Collective (1986), and Crenshaw (1989), who critiqued the various ways Black women's resistant agencies—as workers, women, racialized subjects—went unaccounted for, their standpoint made invisible, Black feminist and "queer" radical intellectuals such as Cohen (1997), Gilmore (1999), Joy James (1996), and Saidiya Hartman (1997) revealed the importance of gender and sexuality for the racial totality of neoliberal capitalism. Roderick Ferguson argued in *Aberrations in Black* (2004) that these queer/feminist rearticulations of the Black radical tradition disclosed the centrality of gender and sexual norms to the shaping and sustaining of violent racial capitalist orders both "within" the nation-state and across its practices of colonial and neocolonial empire. Furthermore, Jodi Melamed (2011) termed the US experience of neoliberalism detailed by the above scholars, neoliberal multiculturalism, the transformation of Western capitalism from a white supremacist and white liberal totality to a multicultural racial totality. Multiculturalism as a material edifice of US neoliberal capitalism is marked by the substantive inclusion of racialized elites into the promised multicultural capitalist totality through gender, sexual, and other bodily norms that paradoxically deepen and advance the violent racialization of nonelite and poor people of color. As Cohen brilliantly demonstrated in *The Boundaries of Blackness* (1999), in highly advanced US capitalism, or US neoliberalism, where Black elites are "solidly integrated at multiple levels into the state apparatus" (27), multicultural capitalism is a material phenomenon that works through gendered, sexual, and bodily norms (from the feminization of work to the criminalization of the "welfare queen"), such that the limited mobility offered to some marginal group member is often convergent with "the direct management of other, less privileged marginal group members to individuals who share the same group identity" (27). For Cohen, heteronormativity is crucial to the racial multicultural totality of neoliberal capitalism, sorting, dividing, and more finely partitioning marginalized sectors and communities for capitalist enrichment in unprecedented ways: "Heteronormativity interacts with institutional racism, patriarchy and class exploitation to define us in numerous ways as marginal and oppressed subjects . . . allowing our sisters and brothers to be used either as surplus labor in an advanced capitalist structure and/or seen as expendable, denied resources, and thus locked in correctional institutions across the country" (446). Yet, like DuBois's sense that his contemporaries were blinded to a slave general strike, Cohen brilliantly argues that under neoliberal multiculturalism, it is the ensemble of agents partitioned from each other—those "punks, bulldaggers, and welfare queens," cast as distinct objects of nonprofit management—whose self-activity is always in jeopardy of being missed, divided from one another by labor, feminism, antiracism, and queer politics.

What seemed elusive for Cohen at the time she wrote "Punks" was a queer politics whose charge came from engaging, living, and negotiating with the self-activity of those whose most powerful strength might be their ability to achieve concrete political alliance that defies the ordering principles of the hegemonic political order. These are formations created not through an identity, a coalition of interests, or even a shared position as "outsiders" to the heterosexual order. Rather, Cohen argued for the *active* creation of a different politics and political space in which the multicultural heteronormative order is made vulnerable precisely by its dependence on uneven, and historically distinct, interlocking systems of oppression.

Like other traditions of the oppressed, the Black Radical Tradition is a living tradition, keenly attuned to the calcifications, morphings, and resolidifications of sexualized racial orders, what Paul Gilroy (1995) called, using Amiri Baraka's words, the "changing same." In this way, as we return to Cohen's essay, we also note important discontinuities with the text in this moment, ones that, as Walter Benjamin reminds us, can fan the flames of resistance and the convictions of the oppressed that other worlds and worldings are possible. If Cohen's essay concludes by calling for a queer politics still too dim on the horizon for her to see at that moment, in her 2014 Kessler lecture Cohen turned her attention to the young Black activists of Ferguson, Missouri, discovering the "queer politics" she worried existed most fully only as unrealizable potentiality. During the height of the uprising and activism for social justice against predatory policing and municipal killing triggered by the callous murder of Mike Brown, the Ferguson activist Tory Russell of Hands Up United was interviewed by Gwen Ifill of the *PBS Newshour*: "So, let me ask you this . . . does this feel different to you? These protests we're seeing, these coast-to-coast rolling die-ins, the roadblocks, does this feel like a different stage?"

Russell responded, "Yeah, I mean it's younger, it's fresher. I think we're more connected than most people think. I don't, this is not the Civil Rights movement, you can tell by how I got a hat on, I got my t-shirt, and how I rock my shoes. This is not the Civil Rights movement. This is an oppressed peoples' movement. So when you see us, you gonna see some gay folk, you gonna see some queer folk, you gonna see some poor Black folk, you gonna see some brown folk, you gonna see some white people and we all out here for the same reasons, we wanna be free. We believe that we have the right over laws." For Cohen, Russell's *relational politics*— of some gay folk, some queer folk, some poor Black folk, some brown folk, even some white *people*—marked precisely the kind of "queer politics" she sought. Russell's remarks point to the ways that the institutionalization of the civil rights movement within the capitalist state paradoxically contributed to a multicultural heteronormative order in which the dispossessive and life-extinguishing tactics of neoliberal accumulation operate through the interlocking systems of race, gender, sexuality, class, migration, and citizenship. Yet they also point to the definitive and powerful insight of Cohen's "Punks, Bulldaggers, and Welfare Queens": as neoliberal capitalism exploits multicultural heteronormativity, it creates the conditions for the very alliances and connections it makes invisible and nearly unthinkable within liberal and radical politics alike. Just as DuBois reminds us how invisible the ubiquity of four million enslaved workers enacting a general strike against racial capitalism was in its own time, Russell interrogates the national public sphere's surprise and confusion over the geographically dispersed "general" insurgency that became for many visible only for the first time, remarking simply, of these incongruously diverse, momentarily unified "oppressed people's" history yet to be written: "We're more connected than most people think."

References

Benjamin, Walter. 2003. *Selected Writings, Volume 4, 1938–1940.* Edited by Michael W. Jennings. Cambridge, MA: Belknap Press of Harvard University Press.
Cohen, Cathy J. 1997. "Punks, Bulldaggers, and Welfare Queens: The Radical Potential of Queer Politics?" *GLQ* 3, no. 4: 437–65.

———. 1999. *The Boundaries of Blackness: AIDS and the Breakdown of Black Politics.* Chicago: University of Chicago Press.

———. 2014. Kessler Lecture. www.racismreview.com/blog/wp-content/uploads/2014/12 /Cohen_CLAGS_Transcript_121214.pdf.

Combahee River Collective. 1986. *The Combahee River Collective Statement.* Albany, NY: Kitchen Table.

Crenshaw, Kimberlé. 1989. "Demarginalizing the Intersection of Race and Sex: A Black Feminist Critique of Antidiscrimination Doctrine, Feminist Theory and Antiracist Politics." *University of Chicago Legal Forum* 43, no. 1: 139–67.

———. 1991. "Mapping the Margins: Intersectionality, Identity Politics, and Violence against Women of Color." *Stanford Law Review* 43, no. 6: 1241–99.

Davis, Angela. 1983. *Woman, Race, Class.* New York: Vintage.

———. 2003. *Are Prisons Obsolete.* New York: Seven Stories.

DuBois, W. E. B. 2007. *Black Reconstruction in America: An Essay toward a History of the Part Which Black Folk Played in the Attempt to Reconstruct Democracy in America, 1860–1880.* New York: Oxford University Press.

Duggan, Lisa. 2003. *The Twilight of Equality: Neoliberalism, Cultural Politics, and the Attack on Democracy.* Boston: Beacon.

Ferguson, Roderick A. 2004. *Aberrations in Black: Towards a Queer of Color Critique.* Minneapolis: University of Minnesota Press.

Gilmore, Ruth Wilson. 1999. "Globalisation and US Prison Growth: From Military Keynesianism to Post-Keynesian Militarism." *Race and Class* 40, no. 2–3: 171–88.

———. 2007. *Golden Gulag: Prisons, Surplus, Crisis, and Opposition in Globalizing California.* Berkeley: University of California Press.

Gilroy, Paul. 1995. *The Black Atlantic: Modernity and Double Consciousness.* Cambridge, MA: Harvard University Press.

Hartman, Saidiya. 1997. *Scenes of Subjection: Terror, Slavery, and Self-Making in Nineteenth Century America.* New York: Oxford University Press.

James, Joy. 1996. *Resisting State Violence: Radicalism, Gender, and Race in U.S. Culture.* Minneapolis: University of Minnesota Press.

Melamed, Jodi. 2011. *Represent and Destroy: Rationalizing Violence in the New Racial Capitalism.* Minneapolis: University of Minnesota Press.

Reddy, Chandan. 2005. "Asian Diasporas, Neoliberalism, and Family: Reviewing the Case for Homosexual Asylum in the Context of Family Rights." *Social Text*, nos. 84–85: 101–19.

Robinson, Cedric. 2000. *Black Marxism.* Chapel Hill: University of North Carolina Press.

Spade, Dean. 2015. *Normal Life: Administrative Violence, Critical Trans Politics, and the Limits of Law.* Durham, NC: Duke University Press.

DOI 10.1215/10642684-7275362

CATHY COHEN

The Quiet Storm Scholar That Queer Theory Needed

L. H. Stallings

For almost two decades Cathy Cohen's scholarship has epitomized a specific style and aesthetic unremarked on in queer theory wars, or beefs in hip-hop nomenclature. Cohen's approach to queer studies was both an innovation of sexual politics and a remix of deracinated culture wars. This is why, for me, playing and reflecting on Mobb Deep's original "Quiet Storm" (1999) and the "Quiet Storm (Remix) featuring Lil' Kim" is an apropos way to celebrate the twentieth anniversary of Cohen's now necessary and canonical essay "Punks, Bulldaggers, and Welfare Queens: The Radical Potential of Queer Politics?" (1997).

On the first verse of "Quiet Storm," Prodigy raps, "I put my lifetime in between the paper's lines. I'm the quiet storm nigga who fight rhyme," to capture the lyrical finesse of his style in rap battles. On the later "Quiet Storm Remix," Lil' Kim would drop scalding verses, "Light as a rock bitch, hard as a cock bitch," to signify her unique style. I take my inspiration from 1990s hip-hop because it is both thematically and aesthetically appropriate to what Cohen does in her essay, as it critiques the failures of queer theory and white queer studies in the 1990s. Not that I would ever equate Mobb Deep's oeuvre with white queer theory, but Cohen's essay is a notable reimagining of what queer theory and queer studies could do: "provide a space where transformational political work can begin" (438). The essay also, without explicitly stating an aesthetic intent, established through language that such a space could look and sound different. Black cultural studies and Black sexuality studies needed this essay to hype up a new generation for the work that is currently being done.

The video for Mobb Deep's remix was a Hype Williams production, but its red-light hue-filtered video was perhaps the least hyped video of Williams's career (the visual spectacle understated), owing to Mobb Deep's sonic sampling of Smokey Robinson's languid instrumental introduction from "The Quiet Storm" and the heavy bass line of Melle Mel's "White Lines." Unlike Smokey Robinson's version, there was nothing soft and warm about this Quiet Storm. "Punks, Bulldaggers, and Welfare Queens" establishes a tone that is quiet for its discursive moves and themes that were hard (serious). The essay sets the stage for the fugitive public that she would call for in her groundbreaking book *The Boundaries of Blackness: AIDS and the Breakdown of Black Politics* (1999) and a later essay, "Deviance as Resistance: A New Research Agenda for the Study of Black Politics" (2004).

The Lil' Kim refrain on Mobb Deep's remix of "Quiet Storm" is how I can best articulate the cogent Blackness and lesbian feminist maneuvering of what Cohen's now necessary and canonical essay did to LGBTQ studies and politics and queer theory. Beginning with the essay's title, Cohen enters into the mix of queer theory and links her concerns with language and discourse. Her use of the vernacular is the blackest clarion questioning as to whether queer studies can fulfill its radical potential. Specifically, the question mark that punctuates the end of her title asks the field if it can move beyond a white homonormative assimilationist agenda too often unable to deal with difference, a key strategy for pursuing a radical transformational coalitional politics. Judith Butler, Eve Kosofsky Sedgwick, Michael Warner, and Alex Doty are just a few of the queer theorists that culled the ideas of Sigmund Freud, Jacques Lacan, Jacques Derrida, and Michel Foucault into useful deployment of psychoanalysis and post-structuralism to shift LGBT studies from a strict enterprise of linear historical studies of lesbian and gay life. While Cohen does not use literary theory and philosophy as these authors did, she does perform close readings of cultural moments and texts and uses the vernacular to signal a foundational critique in the essay, that of class. Simply put, she remixes queer theory. Beginning in the vernacular allows Cohen to decenter white and upper-class narratives that shape sexual politics and sexual identity. Typically written as derogatory terms, much like queer was at some point, Cohen recognizes the nonnormative and marginal positions of punks, bulldaggers, and welfare queens as shaped by differences of race and class. Her use of the vernacular "creates a space in opposition to dominant norms" (Cohen 1997: 438), and those dominant norms typically ascribed to heterosexuality become incorporated in assimilationist agendas of LGBT communities that pay no attention to intersectionality. Much of the work in Black studies on respectability owes a great debt to the essay.

When Cohen asserts that radical queer politics should move away from "a simple dichotomy between those deemed queer and those deemed heterosexual" (ibid.: 440), since "varying relations to power exist among those who label themselves as queer" (ibid.: 449), she dismisses compulsory heterosexuality and assimilation politics. She provides Black feminist studies with an entirely new counterargument to the Moynihan madness and white queer theory with evidence of how class differences need to be addressed in queer politics. Assessing poor and working-class women as similarly marginalized for their sexualities, Cohen observes that queerness might provide a space in which politics can refuse stigmatization and stereotype and lead to new ideologies.

Cohen's assessment of identity and normativity alongside intersectionality certainly cleared out a space for another important work, *Black Queer Studies: A Critical Anthology* (Henderson and Johnson 2007). In many ways, Cohen's essay, republished in that collection, quietly demonstrated why Black queer studies would need to be invented, announced, and expanded to counter the limitations of queer studies. Like "Hot damn ho, here we go again," Lil' Kim's use of MC Lyte's verse from "10% Dis," a song about bite beaters and dope style takers, Cohen (1997: 453) does all of this while reminding readers that Black lesbian feminists such as the Combahee River Collective, Barbara Smith, and Cheryl Clarke have already radically complicated and challenged "reductive notions of heteronormativity articulated by queer activists and scholars." She subtly underlines the debt queer theorists owe Black feminists without calling them bite beaters, dope style takers, or knowledge colonizers.

That is why, even after twenty years in print, we can still sample the refrain from Mobb Deep's "Quiet Storm" to describe the significance of Cathy Cohen's "Punk, Bulldaggers, and Welfare Queens":

> Yo, it's the real shit
> Shit to make you feel shit
> Thump 'em in the club shit
> Have you wilding out when you bump this

References

Cohen, Cathy J. 1997. "Punks, Bulldaggers, and Welfare Queens: The Radical Potential of Queer Politics?" *GLQ* 3, no. 4: 437–65.

———. 2004. "Deviance as Resistance: A New Research Agenda for the Study of Black Politics." *Du Bois Review: Social Science Research on Race* 1, no. 1: 27–45.

———. 2006. *The Boundaries of Blackness: AIDS and the Breakdown of Black Politics.* Chicago: University of Chicago Press.

Henderson, Mae, and E. Patrick Johnson, eds. 2007. *Black Queer Studies: A Critical Anthology.* Durham, NC: Duke University Press.

Mobb Deep. 1999. "Quiet Storm." *Murda Muzik.* CD. Loud Music, Columbia Records.

———. 1999. "Quiet Storm Remix featuring Lil' Kim." *Murda Muzik.* CD. Loud Music, Columbia Records.

DOI 10.1215/10642684-7275376

THE TEMPORALITY OF RADICAL POTENTIAL?

C. Riley Snorton

This essay is an inquiry into the question that is the subtitle of Cathy Cohen's noted 1997 essay, "Punks, Bulldaggers, and Welfare Queens: The Radical Potential of Queer Politics?" As both a question and a fragment, "The Radical Potential of Queer Politics?" provides key insights into the temporality of queer's potential for radical politics. It is, in one sense, an invitation to read the conditional modality of *might* into this question: when and under what conditions might queer politics be radical? Or what are the temporalities of emergence for radical queer politics? These questions, and the occasion to reflect on them on the twentieth anniversary of the essay's publication, precipitates additional considerations about the potential of queer politics at the time of the essay's emergence, in the elapsed time, and in the tense of the future conditional.

As readers may note, Cohen's essay begins by situating the author in time. The first sentence reads: "On the eve of finishing this essay my attention is focused not on how to rework the conclusion (as it should be) but instead on news stories of alleged racism at Gay Men's Health Crisis (GMHC)" (Cohen 1997: 437). One might argue that there are, in fact, at least two temporalities being offered here—one experienced in the register of deadlines and scholarly time, and another in the register of contemporaneous politics. That these times are brought to bear on each other is an incitement to take time to listen and prioritize the lessons of the Left, as a proclamation that it is time to re/think what queer is becoming/might mean in terms of power.

This double gesture of time in the first paragraph provides context for the essay's title and the use of racially pejorative terms, such as "punks," a seemingly evergreen epithet for gay men that took root in the nineteenth century, "bulldaggers"—most frequently deployed in the early twentieth century to refer to masculine black women—and welfare queens, as a term that became particularly politically resonant in the late 1970s and early 1980s as a conservative catchphrase to explain and rationalize the decrease of federal social aid and increase in regulation for poor and working-class families in racist and sexist terms. The potential for queer politics to become intersubjective with the Black Radical Tradition is at least one of the essay's concerns, as it frames and discusses how misogynist, homophobic, and sexually restrictive policies are materialized in and through racial capitalism.

Kara Keeling provides a provocative genealogy for thinking about temporalities of emergence—one that brings the works of Karl Marx and Frantz Fanon into relation with each other—and draws our attention to the epigraph of the conclusion of *Black Skin, White Masks*, in which Fanon (1967: 174) quotes *The Eighteenth Brumaire of Louis Bonaparte*: "The social revolution . . . cannot draw its poetry from the past, but only from the future. It cannot begin with itself before it has stripped itself of all its superstitions concerning the past. Earlier revolutions relied on memories out of world history in order to drug themselves against their own content. . . . Before, the expression exceeded the content; now, the content exceeds the expression."

Keeling (2009: 565) explains that Fanon's interest in Marx indicates his concern about time as a psychopathology of colonialism: "As an epigraph to that conclusion, Marx's well-known formulation of the organization of time within the proletarian movement of the nineteenth century calls attention to Fanon's own interest in exploding the temporality of the colonial mode of representation of otherness and in revealing a temporality that raises the possibility of the impossible within colonial reality, black liberation." If, for Fanon, the notion of black liberation might be found in relation to an "organization of time within the proletarian movement of the nineteenth century," so one might ask how black liberation bears on the radical potential of queer politics as a question of temporality.

In *Black on Both Sides: A Racial History of Trans Identity*, I describe Cohen's analysis in "Punks, Bulldaggers, and Welfare Queens" as "an echo from the future" that explains how there is no necessary distinction between black lives mattering and trans lives mattering in our current formation of racialized gender (Snorton 2017: ix), particularly in a moment of spectacularized black and trans death as well as other modes of antiblack and antitrans violence, the rhythms of which Keeling (2009: 579) refers to as the "intolerable yet quotidian . . . historical index of belonging to our time." Perhaps this is what Cohen's double gesture of time helps make clear for organizers, critics, and teachers: of how political time might set the clock for scholarship in a model that enacts—not with definitiveness but as a question—how black feminist, queer, leftist thought disrupts the myth of linear temporality, of singular selves, of the insufferable identity politics of the unmarked.

As such, one might read Cohen's subtitular question alongside Fanon's final prayer—"oh my body, make of me always a man who questions"—to imagine a collective future of engaging in the political without guarantees and with principled uncertainty, as well as with a tenacity to do what Fanon (1967: 181, 179) espouses as a reminder to himself: to take "the *real* leap" of "introducing invention into existence." That is, and to return to the notion of potential, the future conditional of radical queer politics may have already occurred, for example, in the form of the Combahee River Collective Statement (1977); is occurring, arguably in the radical critiques offered from the Movement for Black Lives, the Black Youth Project, and Bailout Movements, among other groups led by self-identified queer and feminist leadership; and will emerge in unforeseeable ways as queer continues to be an asymptotic index of temporalities of radical black, feminist, and left politics. This, too, is what Cohen (1997: 482) suggests in the final lines: "The best I can do is offer this discussion as a starting point for reassessing the shape of queer/lesbian/gay/bisexual/transgender politics as we approach the twenty-first century. . . . Such a project is important because it provides a framework from which the difficult work of coalition politics can begin." In this, its twentieth year of circulation, I look forward to the many beginnings to have with Cohen's analysis and for the radical potential of queer politics that (might) have and will (continue to?) emerge.

References

Cohen, Cathy J. 1997. "Punks, Bulldaggers, and Welfare Queens: The Radical Potential of Queer Politics?" *GLQ* 3, no. 4: 437–65.

Combahee River Collective. 1977. "Combahee River Collective Statement." circuitous.org /scraps/combahee.html.

Fanon, Frantz. 1967. *Black Skin, White Masks*. Translated by Charles Lam Markmann. New York: Grove.

Keeling, Kara. 2009. "Looking for M—: Queer Temporality, Black Political Possibility, and Poetry from the Future." *GLQ* 15, no. 4: 565–82.

Snorton, C. Riley. 2017. *Black on Both Sides: A Racial History of Trans Identity*. Minneapolis: University of Minnesota Press.

DOI 10.1215/10642684-7275390

BLACK GAY SEX, HOMOSEX-NORMATIVITY, AND CATHY COHEN'S QUEER OF COLOR THEORY OF CULTURAL POLITICS

Marlon M. Bailey

*I*t is difficult to capture in this short amount of space and time the extent to which Cathy Cohen's scholarship has influenced my work, and shaped the fields in which I am situated, such as gender and sexuality studies, Black studies, performance, and HIV/AIDS prevention. Therefore, I decided to discuss how Cohen's queer of color theory of cultural politics guides my current project, which examines the impact of the HIV/AIDS epidemic on Black gay sexual subjectivities in the United States. I want to highlight these contributions in two points, and I draw from "Punks" and her 2004 article "Deviance as Resistance: A New Research Agenda for the Study of Black Politics." These articles have influenced my work that contemplates the daily experiences of Black gay men, and how HIV-related stigma and the AIDS epidemic shape our subjectivities in the United States.

Today I ask, how does Cohen's queer of color theory help me describe and examine the conditions under which Black gay men live that make us structurally vulnerable to HIV/AIDS, among other health disparities and social inequities. One of the most important contributions that "Punks" makes to my work is that it helps explain how power works under systems of domination, as well as in the margins. Cohen (1997: 438) encourages us to highlight and analyze power relations as opposed to "static, stable sexual identities and behaviors," for example, to understand how systems of domination work and how to collectively mobilize against them.

Second, I engage Cohen's (2004) notion of "deviance as resistance." I use this concept to analyze my ethnographic data on Black gay men's raw sex practices in this moment of our disproportionate representation in the HIV/AIDS epidemic in the United States. Hence I am interested in how this dimension of Cohen's queer of color theory of power delineates both the oppressive conditions under which Black gay men live and how we challenge, resist, and (sometimes) negotiate the obstacles to and constraints on our bodies, sexual health, and well-being.

Structural Conditions of Black Gay Life

What are the structural conditions under which Black gay men live? How does HIV/AIDS shape these conditions? Black gay men's disproportionate representation in the HIV/AIDS epidemic in the United States is the most vivid example of the severity of health disparities that we continue to experience after nearly four decades of the epidemic. Social inequality and health disparities are caused by convergent racism and homophobia and contribute to Black gay men's structural vulnerability to HIV. When I say structural vulnerability, I mean how Black gay men disproportionately experience the consequences of institutional racism, such as poverty, homelessness (including housing instability), under/unemployment, incarceration, health disparities, and violence perpetrated by law enforcement and civilians. While Black gay men live and navigate the realities of structural racism that, in part, affect their health outcomes, they also simultaneously experience institutional and communal homophobia that includes gay and HIV-related stigma, linked to violence, abuse, discrimination, and exclusion. In their study of Black gay men in the SF Bay Area, Emily Arnold and her colleagues (2014) describe these men as "triply cursed," because of their multiple experiences with homophobia and HIV-related stigma within the larger societal context of racism. In addition, in her intersectional study of Black gay and bisexual men, Lisa Bowleg (2013: 755) captures the ways in which these Black men's experiences are shaped by race, gender, and sexual oppression that challenges their mental health and overall social well-being.[1]

In "Punks" Cohen (1997: 438) argues that one's relationship to power, not some homogenized identities, should be the basis by which we come to understand the nature of social oppression, as well as what we do to mobilize against it. Cohen focuses on the intersectional identities of Black men, Black lesbians, and Black heterosexual women, all of whom are similarly situated within relations of power. I apply this theory to highlight Black gay men's relationship to power and structural vulnerability to the HIV/AIDS epidemic in ways that are dissimilar from other gay men. For instance, last year, the Centers for Disease Control and Prevention (2016) concluded that one in two Black gay men will become HIV positive within their lifetime. And in 2005 the CDC conducted a five-city study and released another startling report concluding that 46 percent of Black gay men are infected with HIV and 67 percent of those infected were unaware of their HIV seroconversion. Thus Black gay men's relationship to power is informed by our race, gender, sexuality, and HIV status, as well as our seemingly inevitable seroconversion. Being Black and seroconverting is substantially life altering for most multiply marginalized people, let alone Black gay men. Drawing from Cohen's work, I suggest that HIV is not merely a retrovirus; rather, it functions as a vector of power, a social category, which acutely shapes the quality and possibilities of life and the conditions of death, sometimes prematurely, for Black gay men. In my book, *Butch Queens Up in Pumps: Gender, Performance, and Ballroom Culture in Detroit*, I describe how one of my interlocutors, Noir Prestige, died in 2005 from complications of AIDS, and his hospice nurse told his partner, "We don't die like this anymore." I suggest that, even now, in 2018, some of us actually do (Bailey 2013: 217).

Homosex-normativity

In addition to convergent forms of anti-Black racism and homophobia that structure Black gay men's experiences within public health and other social institutions, dominant discourse and related approaches to HIV/AIDS prevention draw from and advance what I refer to as a homosex-normative discourse, not to be confused with Lisa Duggan's notion of "homonormativity," even though I draw from and extend her concept. By using homosex-normativity, I am precisely concerned about the management of gay sex practices rather than the neoliberalization of gay kinship and marriage (although there is, indeed, a correlation here). Public health paradigms for HIV prevention and overall sexual health promote/require repressing sexual urges and focusing on the fear of contracting not only HIV but other STDs as well. Instead of a primary emphasis on sexual desire, urges, and pleasure as healthy sexuality, emphasis is placed on reducing or eliminating risk at the expense of pleasure and sexual satisfaction. As Brandon Andrew Robinson (2013: 102) observes, for public health in the United States, sexual health discourse is centered on subordinating sexual urges to rational thinking and behavior. Furthermore, too often, white heterosexual health officials function as the paternalistic authorities on and managers of the sexual behaviors of Black gay men (ibid.). These encounters with public health authorities cause many Black gay men to internalize repressive and disciplinary discourses about their sexuality. By using the term *homosex-normativity*, I bring into focus the management of gay sex practices as part of the neoliberalization of gay life, marriage, and kinship, underpinned by an anti-Black racism. Homosex-normativity is a particular technology that public health uses to manage Black men's sex practices in the age of AIDS.

A basic assumption that underpins a homosex-normative logic of HIV prevention often promoted by public health and larger society is one that assumes that for all rational, self-loving gay men, avoiding seroconversion, or discontinuing sex if one seroconverts, is more important than satisfying and pleasurable sex. But for

the Black gay men in my study, the aforementioned is not always the most important issue. For instance, when asked about the role that HIV awareness plays in
his sexual decision-making, Tyrone, who is HIV positive from Indianapolis, said,
"I just don't see it as, I guess, that big of a deal because I got so much knowledge about HIV; I feel like it's not the end of the world. It's a lot more worse stuff
out there. I'd rather have HIV than diabetes or some other stuff you know." In
addition, for many of the interlocutors in my study, including those who were HIV
negative at the time, the fear of or concern for contracting HIV was not always a
primary factor in their sexual decision-making. Johnthon from Indianapolis, who is
HIV negative, made this point:

> There's a risk with sex either way it go. You know what I'm saying? So it's a
> choice I had to make. If I'm gonna have no sex or if I'm gonna have sex that
> I want to have an enjoy it. And if I'm gonna do it, if I'm gonna take the risk,
> I wanna enjoy it. I don't wanna take a risk and be like, damn, I took this
> risk for nothing and now I'm like, what the fuck did I do it for. So I'm gonna
> take the risk, I'm gonna make it mean somethin'.

I do not suggest that Black gay men do not think about or fear seroconversion and
that HIV never plays a role in their sexual decision-making. Instead, I argue that
other needs and priorities such as sexual pleasure, intimacy, connection, and satisfaction are also key factors, and in some cases, more important ones. Ultimately,
the assumption that, as a Black gay man, one's goal is to remain HIV negative at
any cost and adhere to an anti-Black homosex-normative regulatory regime that
requires less satisfying sex to make others feel comfortable and safe at his own
expense should not be the logic that underpins all HIV prevention and sexual
health models.

In "Deviance as Resistance," Cohen (2004: 27) calls for a "paradigmatic
shift" in African American studies to examine, detail, and highlight the agency of
those on the outside, on the bottom, of society who through their acts of noncon-
formity choose outside status, at least temporarily. Here I use Cohen to examine
how some Black gay men, through their raw and "high risk" sex discourse and
practices, contest and resist the homosex-normative logics that underpin HIV prevention strategies and discourse for Black gay men.

In my larger project, I analyze how Black gay men advance a form of sexual
noncompliance, sometimes unwittingly, by describing how they represent their raw
sex practices on gay networking and sex profiles, as well as ethnographic accounts
of the sex that Black gay men have where pleasure and risk are coconstitutive.

"Anything Goes" (raw sex) profiles on gay sex websites are an example of noncompliance or deviance as resistance. A raw sex profile on a dating and sex website not only tells a would-be suitor basic information about a person, such as race/ethnicity, age, height, weight, endowment, and so forth, but also HIV status and whether the individual uses substances and engages in group-sex situations, among other information that someone may find pertinent (Bailey 2016: 352).

> i jus wanna fuck raw . . .
> 33, 6'0", 190 lb, 34w, Athletic, Black Hair, Some Body Hair, Black,
> Looking for 1-on-1 Sex, 3some/ Group Sex, Misc. Fetishes, Cam2Cam.
> I like to fuck raw only . . . get at me . . .
> Conservative, Out No, Smoke Yes, Drink Occasionally, Drugs No, Zodiac
> Taurus.
> Top, 9" Cut, *Anything Goes*, HIV Positive, Prefer meeting at: My Place.

I'll make three points about this profile, which I've discussed elsewhere (Bailey 2016: 352):

> First, for this website, titling one's profile with the proclamation "i just wanna fuck raw. . ." is a radical claim because, while many men desire and engage in raw sex, most will not admit it.[2] He reveals his positive HIV status, which is also nonnormative for these websites, as many men who are HIV positive either falsely represent themselves as HIV negative or occlude the status from their profile altogether because of the extreme stigma associated with HIV. This Black man who has sex with men (MSM) (who is not out) is a sexual top, implying that he fucks bottoms raw and that he is into threesomes and group sex and not interested in a relationship (marked as romantic and monogamous). His claim to engage in this panoply of non-homosex-normative practices in the gay domain of this website can be viewed as a radical position and practice of sexual autonomy.

Second, when examining a profile like this, it is important to situate practices within the larger context of Black gay subjectivity and grapple with its contradictions and complexities. For Black gay men who engage in raw sex, for example, sexual pleasure and desire are often in conflict with social norms and gay identity. In addition, while many men may align with what is stated in the Black gay man's profile in practice, they are not willing to proclaim these practices publicly. It is very common for Black gay brothers to throw shade on other Black gay men who engage in raw sex and group sex, who are HIV positive in public, while engaging in the same practices themselves on the low. It is worth reiterating that non-homosex-normative Black gay men, viewed as bad sexual subjects, are stigmatized not only by larger society, particularly public health institutions, but also by other Black gay men.

Finally, the social context in which this Black gay man, who is HIV positive, has raw sex is very informative. Because of his status, he lives with a multiple social disqualification: Black, gay, and HIV positive, and has raw sex. This multiple disqualification constitutes the constraints under which he lives, and for him, the emphasis is placed on what he should not do sexually under the hegemony of safe sex. However, another dimension of his experiences is about his desire and pleasure—what he wants in terms of sex. Thus the politics of desire that may inform this Black gay man's sexual pursuits can be seen as a sociopolitical resistance to the hegemony of safe sex that produces shame and self-hatred for those who do not comply, combined with the sensual and tactical pleasure of skin-to-skin sexual contact. Ultimately, this profile articulates and reflects a radical epistemology of Black gay sex that unabashedly highlights sexual pleasure and risk as coconstitutive.

Cohen's queer of color theory of power, which informs her notion of "deviance as resistance," helps bring into focus how, through our existence and everyday survival, we embody sustained and multisited resistance to systems based on dominant constructions of race and gender that seek to normalize our sexuality and limit our life possibilities. Cohen brings clarity to our need to mobilize against homosex-normativity. To interrupt the myopic focus on modifying Black gay men's sexual behavior, we need to examine the forms of structural inequality that undermine our social and sexual health and well-being and our overall quality of life. While resistance to homosex-normativity is important for Black gay men, any form of sex normativity designed to limit and deny the desirable and pleasurable possibilities of consensual sex concerns all of Black society.

Notes

This essay is an excerpt from a larger essay, "Black Gay Men's Sexual Health, and the Means of Pleasure in the Age of AIDS," in the forthcoming collection *AIDS and the Distribution of Crisis*, edited by Jih-Fei Cheng, Alexandra Juhasz, and Nishant Shahani, published by Duke University Press. The research for this essay was funded by the Center for AIDS Prevention Studies (CAPS) in the Department of Medicine at the University of California, San Francisco, as part of the Visiting Professors Program. I also thank my Raw Sex Project research team for assisting me with this project.

1. Celeste Watkins Hayes and Michelle Tracy Berger, in their respective scholarship, have done extensive research on Black women's structural vulnerability to the HIV/AIDS epidemic.

2. This is also very radical and risky because in some states, particularly the one in which this person lives, "Duty to Warn" or compulsory disclosure laws require that those who are HIV positive must reveal their status before having sex with anyone, protected or not.

References

Arnold, Emily A., Gregory M. Rebchook, and Susan M. Kegeles. 2014. "'Triply Cursed': Racism, Homophobia, and HIV-Related Stigma Are Barriers to Testing, Treatment Adherence, and Disclosure among Young Black Gay Men." *Culture, Health and Sexuality* 16, no. 6: 710–22. doi:10.1080/13691058.2014.905706.

Bailey, Marlon M. 2013. *Butch Queens Up in Pumps: Gender, Performance, and Ballroom Culture in Detroit*. Ann Arbor: University of Michigan Press.

———. 2016. "Black Gay (Raw) Sex." In *No Tea, No Shade: New Writings in Black Queer Studies*, edited by E. Patrick Johnson, 239–61. Durham, NC: Duke University Press.

Bowleg, Lisa. 2013. "'Once You've Blended the Cake, You Can't Take the Parts Back to the Main Ingredients': Black Gay and Bisexual Men Descriptions and Experiences of Intersectionality" *Sex Roles* 68: 754–67. doi:10.1007/s11199-012-0152-4.

Centers for Disease Control and Prevention. 2005. "HIV Prevalence, Unrecognized Infection, and HIV Testing among Men Who Have Sex with Men—Five U.S. Cities, June 2004–April 2005." *Morbidity and Mortality Weekly Report*, June 25. www.cdc.gov/media/mmwrnews/2005/n050624.htm#mmwr1.

———. 2016. "HIV among Gay and Bisexual Men," September 2017. www.cdc.gov/hiv/pdf/group/msm/cdc-hiv-msm.pdf.

Cohen, Cathy J. 1997. "Punks, Bulldaggers, and Welfare Queens: The Radical Potential of Queer Politics?" *GLQ* 3, no. 4: 437–65.

———. 2004. "Deviance as Resistance: A New Research Agenda for the Study of Black Politics." *DuBois Review* 1, no. 1: 27–45.

Robinson, Brandon Andrew. 2013. "The Queer Potentiality of Barebacking: Charging, Whoring, and Breeding as Utopian Practices." In *A Critical Inquiry into Queer Utopias*, edited by Angela Jones, 101–28. New York: Palgrave Macmillan.

DOI 10.1215/10642684-7275404

AIDS, BLACK FEMINISMS,
AND THE INSTITUTIONALIZATION OF QUEER POLITICS

Jih-Fei Cheng

I teach Cathy Cohen's 1997 essay, "Punks, Bulldaggers, and Welfare Queens: The Radical Potential of Queer Politics?" ("Punks"), for introductory courses in the Department of Feminist, Gender, and Sexuality Studies at Scripps College, which was founded in Claremont, California, in 1926 during the Jim Crow era, as a white-serving women's liberal arts college. Scripps College was built on Tongva Indigenous lands using the settler colonialist Mission Revival style of design that the school conceives as "uncommon beauty, attributed to the founder's vision that the College's architecture and landscape should reflect and influence taste and judgment" (Scripps College n.d.). While feminist and queer studies have become somewhat requisite among US women's liberal arts colleges, many of these schools were founded by white suffragists who, as the Black feminist, journalist, and anti-lynching activist Ida B. Wells (1991: 151–52) documented, campaigned for voting rights on an anti-Black platform. Therein lies the liberal paradox embedded in the institutionalization of feminist and queer politics for which "Punks" persists as an interventional pedagogical tool.

In the fall of 2015—my first semester teaching at Scripps College—students of color across the Claremont Colleges Consortium staged walkouts, rallies, and marches as part of the international "Blackout" to protest anti-Black racism in school systems and other institutions. During the 2016–17 academic year, our queer and trans of color communities at the Claremont Colleges lost two student activist leaders. One of these students—a young Black woman and daughter of immigrant parents—was in my Introduction to Queer Studies course. She was, and is, a powerful leader who held many in her coalition-building work that ranged from addressing institutional racism to anti-Zionist activism. She was a science major who wished to bring women of color feminisms and queer and trans of color critique to her lab research on HIV antibodies. We had met during my office hours to discuss her work. We also sat on campus-wide committees tasked to address social and economic inequities and initiate structural changes. She was a residential adviser who passed away in her dorm room (Bramlett 2017; Zunguze Family 2017).

Tatissa Zunguzē.

Tatissa's leadership and coalitional organizing—staged against her multiple encounters with structural and everyday violence—are guided by genealogies of Black feminist and queer thought. Black feminist and queer intellectual projects continue to serve as antiracist and decolonizing pedagogical tools precisely because of their historical interjections into systems of oppression, including white feminist scholarship and other white-centered and/or heteropatriarchal canons of higher education. Black cis-women, gender-nonconforming (GNC), trans, and/or queer faculty, students, staff, and coalitional community members continue to demand engagements with Black feminist, trans, and queer studies to confront the mundane racism and institutional oppositions that form our stubbornly and persistently white-dominated US educational settings.

In "Punks," Cohen (1997: 438) questions the radical potential for queer politics because its settling into institutions elides the operations of power by "reinforc[ing] simple dichotomies between heterosexual and everything 'queer.'" "Punks" foregrounds Black feminist interventions into queer politics by calling attention to the then-recent resignation of three Black board members from the first and largest AIDS service organization of its time, Gay Men's Health Crisis (GMHC), over its alleged racism. In turn, Cohen calls for a "new politics" where the "*nonnormative* and *marginal* position of punks, bulldaggers, and welfare queens, for example, is the basis for progressive transformative coalition work" (ibid.). It is through the "intersection of oppression and resistance" of these nonnormative and marginal positions, Cohen (ibid.: 440) submits, that multi-issued, coalitional organizing could manifest the radical potential of queer politics. Cohen states,

> Both the needle exchange and prison projects pursued through the auspices of ACT UP New York point to the possibilities and difficulties involved in principled transformative coalition work. In each project individuals from numerous identities—heterosexual, gay, poor, wealthy, white, black, Latino—came together to challenge dominant constructions of who should be allowed and who deserved care. No particular identity exclusively determined the shared political commitments of these activists; instead their similar positions, as marginalized subjects relative to the state—made clear through the government's lack of response to AIDS—formed the basis of this political unity. (ibid.: 460)

Since, until the mid-1990s, there lacked effective antiretroviral medications that could maintain the health of those living with HIV, the mounting toll of deaths during the early years of the AIDS pandemic pointed to the "interlocking systems of oppression" and structural violence borne from the dismantling of the US welfare state, including health care and housing, and the diversion of funds toward the arms buildup and military imperialism. Yet Cohen also emphasizes the crucial role of Black and intersectional feminisms as key to the radical and transformative potential of queer politics and cites Kimberlé Crenshaw, Barbara Ransby, Angela Y. Davis, Cheryl Clarke, Audre Lorde, and the Combahee River Collective, among others (Cohen 1997: 441–42). She illuminates the operations of power that have persisted before (and, now, after) AIDS was widely seen as a "death sentence" by pointing to the historical regulation of women of color who continue to be rendered perverse and criminal as "single mothers, teen mothers, and, primarily women of color dependent on state assistance" (ibid.: 455). As Roderick A. Ferguson has shown in his theorization of the field of "queer of color critique," the stigmatization and demonization of these nonnormative and marginal Black and other people of color subjects through sociological documents, such as the 1965 Moynihan Report, led to the dismantling of the welfare state (Ferguson 2004). Furthermore, Ferguson (2012) contends, the liberal implementation of "diversity" initiatives in higher education reflects the management of Black and other radical social movements through the simultaneous inclusion of ethnic, gender, and sexuality studies and the continued marginalization of people of color in higher education. Put simply, the proliferation of the AIDS pandemic is historically and persistently tied to the institutionalization of Black feminist and queer studies alongside the ongoing structural violence that Black and other people of color, and especially Black cis-women, GNC, trans, and queer peoples, experience as liminal subjects across the institutions of scholarship, art, media, and politics.

For instance, elsewhere (Cheng 2016), I have assessed how there is a trend among recent critically acclaimed popular films addressing AIDS activist historiography whereby people of color have been nearly disappeared from the historical record. I contend that this is because the white men who direct and appear in these films are invested in telling a story about political progress since the earlier years of the AIDS crisis. Rather than examine the root causes for AIDS as embedded in histories of colonialism, racism, patriarchy, and socioeconomic inequality that block access for US people of color and the global South, the director David France of the feature-length documentary film *How to Survive a Plague* (2012) tells a false story meant to convince audiences that biomedical interventions generated and distributed by corporate pharmaceuticals, like pre-exposure prophylaxis (PrEP), will solve the pandemic (Shahani 2016). However, this narrative of social and biomedical progress comes at the cost of jettisoning the fact that the AIDS pandemic manifested precisely because of structural inequalities experienced by nonwhite peoples.

Moreover, the historical video footage adapted into films like *How to Survive a Plague* is extracted from earlier AIDS activist films and the personal archives amassed through a large network of video artists (Cheng 2016). These archives were donated to institutions, like the New York Public Library. Film directors accessed these public archives and used the footage. As I intend to show in future writing, France left out the extensive activist leadership and on-camera discussions by Black women, people of color, and their white allies that relay their experiences and interventions into the AIDS crisis despite their marginalization by white-dominated institutions and mainstream media (Juhasz 1995).[1]

As of this writing, the Tacoma Arts Collective (n.d.) continues to protest the book and touring exhibition, *Art AIDS America*, for nearly banishing artists of color, especially Black artists. Reina (Tourmaline) Gossett, a Black trans activist and artist, codirected with Sash Wortzel the film short *Happy Birthday, Marsha!* (2017), which focuses on the influence and activism of Marsha P. Johnson, who was "HIV positive, a sex worker, and an incredible performer and member of the group Hot Peaches." Johnson also cofounded the Street Transvestites Action Revolutionaries (STAR) with Sylvia Rivera (Gossett 2017). Yet Gossett has had to contend with the aforementioned France, who stands accused of appropriating much of Gossett's labor and research on Johnson's life while amassing funding and a media platform that far exceed Gossett (Weiss 2017). Eventually, France's feature-length film version, *The Death and Life of Marsha P. Johnson* (2017), was distributed via Netflix's video-on-demand.

Prompted by such systemic erasures, VisualAIDS (2017) commissioned Erin Christovale and Vivian Crockett to cocurate "Alternate Endings, Radical Beginnings"—a "video program [that] prioritized Black narratives within the ongoing AIDS epidemic" for the 2017 annual "Day with(out) Art." "Alternate Endings, Radical Beginnings" includes video shorts by Gossett, Mykki Blanco, Cheryl Dunye, Ellen Spiro, Thomas Allen Harris, Kia LaBeija, Tiona Nekkia McClodden, and Brontez Purnell. Each of these works transforms time and memory by reimagining and recalling the presence of Black cis-women, GNC, and trans peoples precisely at the moments and sites where they were excluded or forgotten to exist. Dunye's earlier film, *The Watermelon Woman* (1997), was a watershed for the New Queer Cinema movement. The experimental film yields critical insight into how the memories of Black feminist and queer women fall out of official archives. Official archives, then, must be recast to assert Black queer women's pasts, presences, and futures. In each of the works and conditions cited above, Black cis-women,

GNC, trans, and queer people speak out on their own behalf, but also on behalf of a queer radical imagination that seeks liberation for all. This form of Black feminist thinking and action is rooted in the Black Radical Tradition (Combahee River Collective 1979; Robinson 1983; Kelley 2003; Moten 2003; McLane-Davison 2016; Taylor 2017).

Writing more recently, Cohen (Cohen and Jackson 2016) recognizes the powerful and collectivized vision and work of "young black women who identify as queer" that have built a "leaderful movement with cis and trans women taking positions of power," including Black Lives Matter. She contends,

> Young people who have taken classes on black queer studies and black feminist theory through ethnic studies, African American studies and gender and sexuality departments are using the lessons taught in those classes to inform the organizing practices they are deploying on behalf of and in partnership with black people who may never see the inside of our classrooms. These young activists, who blend the politics of the academy and the politics of liberation, daily make black queer studies relevant to a changing world. (Cohen 2016: xiii)

In response to Tatissa's passing, Black queer and trans students across the Claremont Colleges Consortium gathered their pain and anger and transformed it into direct action. During the spring of 2017, Claremont McKenna College brought pro-police speaker Heather MacDonald to campus. MacDonald has advocated for the use of police against the Black Lives Matter movements. Overnight, in the tradition of nonviolent protest, Black queer and trans students organized and led other students to block access to the venue. They stood front and center while white students and other students of color strategically positioned themselves as a buffer between Black students and campus security, who did not intervene when hecklers not only shouted and taunted but took to shoving the nonviolent protestors. Students chanted "black lives matter" and "black lives—they matter here." They cited solidarity with immigrants faced with the militarization of the US-Mexico border as well as Palestinians living under Israeli apartheid. As a result, the event was effectively shut down. These students of color transformed their grief into a deep well of care and coalition building. They continue to build movements led by Black queer and trans intellectuals, writers, and artists. They teach me the radical potential of queer politics.

Ironically (or not), there are those who presumably identify as antiracists who describe such nonviolent protest tactics and aforementioned chants, which echo AIDS activists who adopted these strategies from earlier social movements including Black-led social movements, as seemingly incoherent and "meaningless slogans" (Casil 2017). There are even those who would, in stark self-contradiction, laud the Black-led civil rights movement as decidedly nonviolent while, in the same breath, describing these student protestors as "violent." The presumption is that white supremacists could be called to their senses because they are, at the bottom of their hearts, benevolent even if misguided people. Yet there is no history that shows that white people have been willing to dismantle white supremacy without the combined approach of civil rights protest and Black militancy (Singh 2004). On many occasions, I have heard decriers of Black protest urge, instead, that Black protestors conduct research and write articles—as if they have not and are not already doing so.

Given the increase in racial profiling and Black imprisonment and murder, intensified border patrolling and immigrant detention, hyperprivatization of all social safety nets, and ballooning college tuition and educational debt, alongside Donald Trump's aim to dismantle the National Endowment for the Arts and the National Endowment for the Humanities, one has to wonder how invested sectors of "civil society" are in the institutionalization of Black feminisms and the concurrent silencing of Black cis-women, GNC, trans, and queer peoples, even though people from all sectors benefit from the historical advancements made by Black feminists. Meanwhile, the "alt right" is ramping up attacks against students of color and ethnic, feminist, trans, and queer studies scholars by claiming that expressions of white supremacy amount to "freedom of speech" and "academic freedom" when, in fact, proclaiming the right to terrorize Black subjects and other people of color enacts the opposite. Allowing white supremacy to parade as "freedom" disassembles the public sphere and tears down academic freedom.

What if, then, we as non-Black people take up Black feminist work to ask such questions as: How would we understand the AIDS pandemic differently if we consider it the outcome of histories of settler colonialism, Native displacement, massive resource extraction, and anti-Blackness? How might we understand this, specifically, from the experience of Black cis-women, GNC, trans, and queer peoples in the midst of the enduring AIDS pandemic? How might Black feminisms form a foundation for challenging the liberal inclusion of "alt-right" discourse and action in academe?

Citing the radical tradition of Black feminisms as central to his approach to the study of anti-Blackness and AIDS, Adam Geary (2014: 23) explains that a "materialist epidemiology and its Marxist inheritance allows [him] to connect the health research that [he] read with materialist traditions in Black, feminist, queer, and cultural studies, especially those connected, if in complex ways, to the Marxist tradition. These critical, radical traditions are essential for elaborating the histories of struggle, violence, and domination that have made an AIDS epidemic possible and structured its development." Before Tatissa's passing, we had read Geary's work in class. She shared with me her excitement at the potential in engaging in a materialist epidemiology of AIDS that keeps at its core Black feminist, queer, and trans analyses.

Black students, staff, faculty, and community leaders cannot be expected to tirelessly research, write, produce culture, and organize against enduring racism, heteropatriarchy, and AIDS while others appropriate or even disparage such work. As non-Black faculty, staff, students, artists, and participants in social movements, we must teach and learn from Cohen's article as a genealogy of Black feminisms that make the radical potential of queer, trans, and AIDS studies and activism possible. "How" to engage Black feminisms and its continued critical importance to social movements while addressing the insistently low yet highly significant representation of Black people in scholarship, the classroom, and the pandemic is something we must continually ask and push ourselves to do.

Notes

My heartfelt gratitude goes to Tatissa Zunguzē and all the students who have foregrounded Black feminisms in the struggles for social and economic justice; to Cathy J. Cohen for creating a living document through which to manifest the intellectual, cultural, and political interventions of Black, feminist, and queer studies; to the editors of *GLQ*, Alexandra Juhasz, Nishant Shahani, C. Riley Snorton, and Abigail Nubla-Kung for their extensive feedback and support in this writing; and, finally, to my dear friend and comrade, Nic John Ramos, who organized the "Punks" commemorative panel at the 2017 Annual Meeting of the American Studies Association.

1. My forthcoming monograph examines the contemporary adaptation of video activist footage from the earlier years of the AIDS crisis, including footage from the documentary film *Voices from the Front* (1992) by the Testing the Limits Collective, which reveals the intentional foregrounding of Black feminisms and the crucial leadership of Black and other women of color AIDS activists.

References

Bramlett, Matthew. 2017. "Loss of Student Leaves College Community in Mourning." March 9. www.claremont-courier.com/articles/news/t22468-student.

Casil, Amy Sterling. 2017. "Don't Expect Nothing in Return from Scripps College: They Just Want Your Money." *Medium*, April 23. medium.com/real-in-other-words/dont -expect-nothing-in-return-from-scripps-college-they-just-want-your-money -79699d345897.

Cheng, Jih-Fei. 2016. "How Survive: AIDS and Its Afterlives in Popular Media." *WSQ: Women's Studies Quarterly* 44, nos. 1–2: 73–92.

Cohen, Cathy J. 1997. "Punks, Bulldaggers, and Welfare Queens: The Radical Potential of Queer Politics?" *GLQ* 3, no. 4: 437–65.

———. 2016. Foreword to *No Tea, No Shade: New Writings in Black Queer Studies*, edited by E. Patrick Johnson, xi–xiv. Durham, NC: Duke University Press.

Cohen, Cathy J., and Sarah J. Jackson. 2016. "Ask a Feminist: A Conversation with Cathy J. Cohen on Black Lives Matter, Feminism, and Contemporary Activism." *Signs: Journal of Women in Culture and Society* 41, no. 4: 775–92.

Combahee River Collective. 1979. "Combahee River Collective Statement." circuitous.org /scraps/combahee.html.

Dunye, Cheryl, dir. 1997. *The Watermelon Woman*. VHS. New York: First Run Features.

Ferguson, Roderick A. 2004. *Aberrations in Black: Toward a Queer of Color Critique*. Minneapolis: University of Minnesota Press.

———. 2012. *The Reorder of Things: The University and Its Pedagogies of Minority Difference*. Minneapolis: University of Minnesota Press.

France, David, dir. 2011. *How to Survive a Plague*. DVD. New York: Sundance Selects.

Geary, Adam M. 2014. *Antiblack Racism and the AIDS Epidemic: State Intimacies*. New York: Palgrave Macmillan.

Gossett, Reina. 2017. "Reina Gossett on Transgender Storytelling, David France, and the Netflix Marsha P. Johnson Documentary." *Teen Vogue*, October 11. www.teenvogue .com/story/reina-gossett-marsha-p-johnson-op-ed.

Juhasz, Alexandra. 1995. *AIDS TV: Identity, Community, and Alternative Video*. Durham, NC: Duke University Press.

Kelley, Robin D. G. 2003. *Freedom Dreams: The Black Radical Imagination*. Boston: Beacon.

McLane-Davison, Denise. 2016. "Lifting: Black Feminist Leadership in the Fight against HIV/AIDS." *Journal of Women and Social Work* 31, no. 1: 55–69.

Moten, Fred. 2003. *In the Break: The Aesthetics of the Black Radical Tradition*. Minneapolis: University of Minnesota Press.

Robinson, Cedric J. 1983. *Black Marxism: The Making of a Black Radical Tradition*. London: Zedd.

Scripps College. n.d. "About Scripps College." catalog.scrippscollege.edu/content.php
    ?catoid=9&navoid=628 and www.scrippscollege.edu/about/glance (accessed March
    17, 2018).

Shahani, Nishant. 2016. "How to Survive the Whitewashing of AIDS: Global Pasts, Trans-
    national Futures." *QED: A Journal in GLTBQ Worldmaking* 3, no. 1: 1–33.

Singh, Nikhil Pal. 2004. *Black Is a Country: Race and the Unfinished Struggle for
    Democracy.* Cambridge, MA: Harvard University Press.

Tacoma Arts Collective. n.d. "STOP ERASING BLACK PEOPLE." stoperasingblack
    peoplenow.tumblr.com/ (accessed March 1, 2017).

Taylor, Keeanga-Yamahtta. 2017. *How We Get Free: Black Feminism and the Combahee
    River Collective.* Chicago: Haymarket Books.

VisualAIDS. 2017. "Alternate Endings, Radical Beginnings." VisualAIDS. www
    .visualaids.org/projects/detail/alternate-endings-radical-beginnings.

Weiss, Suzannah. 2017. "'The Death and Life of Marsha P. Johnson' Creator Accused of
    Stealing Work from Filmmaker Reina Gossett." *Teen Vogue*, October 8. www
    .teenvogue.com/story/marsha-p-johnson-documentary-david-france-reina-gossett
    -stealing-accusations.

Wells, Ida B. 1991. *Crusade for Justice: The Autobiography of Ida B. Wells.* Chicago:
    University of Chicago Press.

Zunguze Family. 2017. "In Memoriam: Tatissa Zunguze SC '18 Remembered for Scripps
    Leadership, Passion for Social Justice." *The Student Life*, April 14. http://tsl.news
    /news/6706/.

DOI 10.1215/10642684-7275418

THE RADICAL POTENTIAL OF BLACK FEMINIST EVALUATION

Sarah Haley

On June 19, 1979, two hundred Black women boarded buses from their homes to the Los Angeles Police Department headquarters. Coiffed, pressed hair protruded from netted, veiled hats. They wore their best black dresses, buttoned to the top. They carried white carnations. Only rarely did their stoic expressions break, except to remind each other that they had to maintain their silence, the elders silently shushing the youngers. Was this a gesture of queer political intimacy? Was this a queer political event? Perhaps. It was for love, literally and figuratively.

It was a protest funeral for Mrs. Eulia Love,[1] and as such, it was indeed a choreography of radical queer potential of the sort that Cathy Cohen (1997) urges us toward in her transformative essay "Punks, Bulldaggers, and Welfare Queens." On January 3, 1979, Love was gardening in her front yard on Orchard Avenue in South LA. Gardening was therapeutic, as she suffered from what family members described as acute depression. She was impatient with city bureaucracy, having only just received the social security she was due after her husband's death several months before, and by that time the bills had accumulated. As she did her gardening that January morning, she was approached by an employee of the Southern California Gas Company, who informed her that he was there to shut her gas off for nonpayment (Board of Police Commissioners 1979: 4). She attempted to explain that she could now pay the $22.09, the minimum amount due to maintain her gas service. Yet according to some reports, when he insisted that he had to stop service, she hit his arm with the shovel she had been using. She returned inside and told her daughter Sheila that she "was trying to pay them, talk to them, and they just rolled up the window" (Mitchell and Shuit 1979). The gas employee left, and Mrs. Love went to the Boys Market down the street to pay her bill; the market attendant informed her that they only accepted payment for bills that were current, and since her account was past due she could not pay her bill there directly. So she purchased a money order for $22.09 intending to pay the bill that day (ibid.).

In the meantime, the gas employee had filed a police report describing Mrs. Love as "foaming at the mouth." Later that afternoon, armed with this description, two different SOCAL gas company employees, William Jones and Robert Aubry, went back to Love's house to await a police escort to execute the gas shutoff. Mrs. Love, unaware that the police were on their way, resumed her gardening, trimming the branches of a tree on her lawn with a knife. Shocked when two police officers showed up at her house, she began pacing and yelling that she could make her minimum payment, showing them the money order for $22.09. The police drew their guns and demanded that she drop the knife that was still in her hand (Board of Police Commissioners 1979: 1–8).

Eulia Love turned to go into her house, and the police advanced toward her. Love turned around, still holding the knife, as she faced Officer Hopson crouched, with a gun outstretched in both hands, and Officer O'Callaghan with a gun in his right hand and a baton in his left. She was surrounded. As she started to lower the knife, O'Callaghan knocked it from her hand with the baton. She picked it up again as if she was going to throw it, perhaps to protect herself, or perhaps to toss it far away from her in demonstration of her retreat. O'Callaghan and Hopson then each fired six rounds of bullets, inflicting eight bullet wounds. Hopson walked over to Love, rolled her dead body over, and placed handcuffs on her wrists. She was pronounced dead one minute later, at 4:26 p.m. (ibid.: 7–9). Police Chief Daryl Gates determined that O'Callaghan and Hopson's actions were "in policy" and that no disciplinary action would be taken (Farr 1979). In June, when the LA Police Commission published an extensive investigative report about the shooting, organizers planned the silent gathering. Young Black girls from Audubon Junior High School sent letters to Tom Bradley, Los Angeles's Black mayor. One student, Margo Willis (n.d.), ended her letter with a series of questions including: "What will it be like when I grow up? Will I get shot for not paying a bill on time? What will it be like after my generation?"

Might Margo Willis's questions inform queer politics? Eulia Love's placement on the hetero side of the queer-hetero divide that Cohen obliterates for its erasure of raced and classed subjectivities in "Punks, Bulldaggers, and Welfare Queens" surely accounts for the fact that police murders of black subjects, particularly Black women, have been cast out of the purview of mainstream queer protest.[2]

What do we make of the two hundred women who came to demand accountability decked out in their funeral best? In a sartorial drama and choreography of political mourning can we conceive of the silent protest as a register of the nonnormative? Is it possible that the production of carnations and netting and heels and hats and silence in the absurd space of the headquarters of Love's murderers was not an appeal for protection through respectability but instead a dramatization of the nonnormativity of black un/gender? Police Chief Gates was enjoying a rather normal dinner at home when he heard the news of Love's shooting, the sort of dinner that Love would never again have with her daughters, severed as her claims to normative motherhood, domesticity, and privacy were by her abrupt removal from the earth. Although he never saw her, to Gates (1992: 197), Love was "frightening to behold, 175 pounds, snarling, screaming invective. . . . This was hardly the poor widow portrayed in the *Herald*, but an out-of-control woman with a history of mental problems, who was threatening to kill anybody who came near her." Excised from the category of poor widow, with its connotations of normative sexuality and femininity, Love was a threat in life and in death to the LAPD's reputation: Gates bemoaned that upon hearing of the shooting, "the community had already convicted the officers. Next would come the lynching" (ibid.: 198–99). Love's murder rests alongside lynching in a different way: as an index of the continuing centrality of black sexual counternormativity in the production of gendered racial capitalism.

How might we evaluate the queer politics of such a funeral? Of a Black woman's life valued at approximately $22.09? Of the questions raised by young Margo Willis? Of the absurd bureaucracy of capitalism that made it impossible for Love to pay her bill even when she had the money? Of the time and frustration imposed on the economically precarious through errands and money orders and long lines and wait times and administrative refusals to accept payment that rendered young daughters orphans?

"Punks, Bulldaggers, and Welfare Queens" not only altered queer studies and Black studies by providing new theoretical grounds from which to think about such questions of gender, sexuality, race, and political economy but also offered new political terrain on which to take action. Specifically, Cohen (1997: 441) focuses on the disjuncture, "evident in queer politics, between an articulated commitment to promoting an understanding of sexuality that rejects the idea of static, monolithic, abounded categories on the one hand, and political practices structured around binary conceptions of sexuality and power on the other hand." She contends that the radical potential of queer politics is limited by activists who evoke a "single-oppression framework" (ibid.). Cohen teaches us that the production of white queer subjectivity has, in mainstream configurations, relied, at least in part, on the disavowal of Black female precarity and violation. We are forced to reckon with the proximity between the state's production of racial heteronormativity through violence and homonormative productions of subjectivity through erasure. The funeral protest exposes the intersection of impossibility and possibility— of the impossibility of redress and resurrection, and the possibility of Black life produced by collective insistence on alternative terms of political and economic order and alternative modes of sociality. It was a rejection of the state's ruse of criminalization; this is significant for queer politics if we are to understand the

stakes of radical recuperations of the term *queer*, a term that came into early political discourse precisely as a project of antiblack criminalization.

As early as the 1890s, in southern newspaper accounts, *queer* was used
widely to refer to excessive bodies. In these discourses, all the queers were Black
and all Blacks were criminal. In 1897, for example, there were at least forty-three
articles published in Atlanta newspapers, especially the *Atlanta Constitution*, revil-
ing Black life as queer, and this queerness was almost always demonstrated through
criminality.[3] These stories invariably took place in the city's municipal court with
sensational headlines describing Black bodies as excessive and delinquent. This
is all the more significant because queer was not an adjective used to describe a
range of nouns. Besides criminalized Black people, journalists only used queer to
describe strange objects and animals found in the city in a regular column called
"Queer Things in Georgia." Queer was defined by uncontrollable Black bodies that
could only be interpreted and governed through policing and incarceration. The
criminalizing discourse of queerness produced a white supremacist subjectivity that
excised blackness from the category of the human. "Punks, Bulldaggers, and Welfare Queens" exposes a problematic recuperation of "queer" as a political terminology that rejects sexual subordination with inadequate regard for the role of racial
and economic terrorization in the production of gender and sexual normativity. As
Cohen (1997: 451) argued, "queer politics and much of queer theory seem in fact to
be static in the understanding of race, class, and gender and their roles in how heteronormativity regulates sexual behavior and identities." Queer politics, then, was
problematic in its propensity to "collapse our understanding of power into a *single
continuum of evaluation*" (ibid.: 452; emphasis added).

A radically queer, complex evaluation of life and politics might organize
around the racial and gendered economies of $22.09. The march for Eulia Love
offers a glimpse into the possibility for social movement formation that centers
lives effaced under the weight of multiple axes of oppression; these effacements
are legitimized under the broad political rubric of another term of order that Cohen
has so powerfully illuminated in her radical oeuvre: deviance. It is Cohen's evaluation that propels us toward the formation of political analyses and organizing
platforms that recognize the stakes of queer assessment. Eulia Love, Michelle Cus-
seaux, Eleanor Bumpurs, and Korryn Gaines, to name only a few Black women
whose deaths at the hands of police were justified by discourses that depicted them
as criminally insane, that portrayed their bodies as excessive and uncontrollable,
reflect a long historical continuity; though they were not called queer by the police
who shot them, their murders reflect the work of policing and terrorization that the
term *queer* was meant to accomplish at least as far back as the late nineteenth cen-

tury; like Cohen's formative work, the gathering for Eulia Love offers a reminder of the queer potential of Black feminist evaluation to challenge political economies of death and dispossession.

Notes

1. In official documents Eulia Love's first name is variously spelled Eula and Eulia. I have used Eulia for consistency.
2. This is not to ignore the historical support for criminalized women of color by radical gay and lesbian activists and contemporary racial justice organizing that centers black feminist and queer politics. We see examples of this groundbreaking work by the Movement for Black Lives, Survived and Punished, the Free Bresha Meadows Campaign, the Free CeCe Campaign, BYP 100, and significant writing on the historical and contemporary relationship between racial justice, incarceration, and queer politics by Emily Thuma, Emily Hobson, and Charlene Carruthers, among others. Notably, both the scholarship and organizing on these radicalisms is indebted to Cathy Cohen's work. What I mean to suggest is that both historical and current mobilizations around sexual justice and queer politics (especially mainstream accounts and campaigns) often elide the regimes of racial/state violence that poor women and women of color face when such violence *seems* not to have a direct link to gender violence or sexual identity.
3. These are merely a few examples of headlines from the *Atlanta Constitution*: "Lively Police Items: Queer Prisoners Fight," May 9, 1897, 13; "At Judge Andy's Matinee: Queer Characters Were before the Recorder for Petty Offenses," December 29, 1897, 10; "Must Get a Shirt: Recorder Makes a Queer Demand of a Prisoner," September 20, 1897, 10; "Queer Police Court Terms: Used by Negroes Who Frequent Police Circles," September 20, 1897, 5; "He Declined to Dress," June 14, 1897, 3.

References

Board of Police Commissioners. 1979. "The Report of the Board of Police Commissioners Concerning the Shooting of Eulia Love and the Use of Deadly Force." Mayor Tom Bradley Administration Papers (Collection 293), box 1955, folder 8. UCLA Library Special Collections, Charles E. Young Research Library, UCLA.

Cohen, Cathy J. 1997. "Punks, Bulldaggers, and Welfare Queens: The Radical Potential of Queer Politics?" *GLQ* 3, no. 4: 437–65.

Farr, Bill. 1979. "DA Won't Prosecute Two Officers in Eulia Love Killing." *Los Angeles Times*, April 18.

Gates, Daryl F. 1992. *Chief: My Life in the LAPD*. New York: Bantam Books.

Mitchell, John, and Doug Shuit. 1979. "Facts Disputed: Eulia Love: Anatomy of a Fatal Shooting." *Los Angeles Times*, April 16.

Willis, Margo. n.d. Letter to Tom Bradley. Mayor Tom Bradley Administration Papers (Collection 293), box 1368, folder 2. UCLA Library Special Collections, Charles E. Young Research Library, UCLA.

DOI 10.1215/10642684-7275432

PUTTING ONE'S BODY ON THE LINE

Nayan Shah

*I*n "Punks" Cathy Cohen tracks my twenties in Chicago and my political attraction and dilemmas with Queer Nation's rhetorical and performative strategies that could galvanize defiance against normativity yet deny disparities of racialization that collapsed variant sexualities and gender into "reductive categories of straight and queer." Cohen (1997: 457–58) advocates putting intersectional analysis into the practice of coalition building to embrace and proliferate potential allies across difference and focusing on targeting the marginalized "relationship to dominant power which normalizes, legitimizes and privileges" and also pathologizes, denigrates, and demonizes people and lifeworlds.

I would like to carry her provocation of the "question of the radical potential of queer politics" to my current research on the political and bodily struggles of hunger strikers in detention. I am ruminating anew on Cohen's concluding remarks in the final section on destabilizing identity and radical coalitional work. My research on mass prison hunger strikes from 1909 to 2017 examines how bodily defiance struggles across the globe tested carceral institutions and precipitated crises of medical care. In the twentieth century, hunger striking moved from the isolation of prison onto the public stage, becoming central to political defiance. Political allies harnessed print and television media, amplifying through press accounts, public rallies, and sympathy fasts the perspective and bodily experience of prisoners. The struggle of the hunger strikers captivated the public, fueled controversy, and quickened the prisoners' political goals of mobility and removal from detention. The book's last chapters explore the intersectional strategies and challenges of creating alliances of solidarity for migrants and refugees with publics in the United States and Australia.

One of these strategies that leveraged mobility as a way to produce a spectacle of public protest is the Sikh freedom ride organized in April 2014 in response to hunger-striking Punjabi asylum seekers, who had spent eight months to over a year in an El Paso detention center, despite passing credible fear interviews. The Jakara youth movement in Fresno organized a caravan to draw attention to the struggles of the hunger-striking detainees. Deep Singh, cofounder of Jakara, explains that the inspiration to take action for El Paso detainees came in a discussion with Fresno-based Mexican American and Hmong groups that underlined the "common issues in the different communities" that are riven by state surveillance, immigration deportation, and incarceration (quoted in Romero 2014).

The organizing structure of "caravans" created durational and spatial protest performances that dramatized the urgency of mobility, and drew attention to rallies that publicized the struggles of and solidarity for isolated detainees. The Sikh youth traveled to a Gurdwara in Bakersfield and a Sikh service organization in Pacoima to rally support in their ethnic and religious communities for Punjabi detained immigrants. At a rally organized in the Los Angeles community of Artesia, the youth shared the stage with Latinx and South Asian activists. After driving through the night, the caravan arrived at the El Paso detention center, where some youth were able to interview detainees and share their stories with both local communities and the media afterward. Cayden Mak, who identifies as mixed race and transgender, leads the Asian American immigrant activist organization, 18 Million Rising, and created the hashtag #ELPASO37 to give the caravan a digital platform for grassroots activism to publicize the journey and connect incarcerated asylum seekers from South Asia, the Middle East, Africa, Mexico, and Central America and their allies.

These social justice alliances between Sikh American youth and Latinx and Hmong youth, and the advocacy for asylum seekers from across the globe, put in practice Cohen's call to build coalitions that recognized race, ethnic, spiritual, sexual identities, and bridged shared experiences of oppression and challenge to immigration policing and carceral systems. Rather than focus on identity as a limit to creating collective purpose, the networks emphasized intersectional practices of alliance building that could question the normalizing of immigrant and racialized criminality (Cohen 1997: 460).

The challenges of alliance building reverberate in the decision by three Latinx activists, Deyaneira García, Jorge Gutiérrez, and Jennicet Gutiérrez, in May

2016 to launch a hunger strike in a city park outside Santa Ana Jail after months of protests and negotiations on behalf of transgender immigrants facing deportation. Protesting alongside members of Orange County Immigrant Youth United, Familia-TQLM (Trans Queer Liberation Movement), and DeColores Queer Orange County, they demanded that US Immigration and Customs Enforcement (ICE) end the detention of transgender immigrants and challenged the Santa Ana city council to terminate its contract with ICE to hold trans immigrants in its sixty-four-bed segregated "pods" facilities specifically designed to detain trans and queer women (Reichard 2016). The transgender activist Jennicet Gutiérrez emphasized the vulnerability of transgender women to being "targeted" and "murdered" and how detention provides no protection from violence (Stanley 2015).

The protests emphasized the structural system of mass incarceration and immigrant detention as a trans, queer, Latinx justice, and freedom struggle. Contesting Santa Ana prison authorities' claims of the safety of their facilities for trans immigrants, Jorge Gutiérrez, a thirty-one-year-old transgender immigrant rights advocate who founded Familia: TQLM, questioned the $27 million debt servicing that propelled the need for revenue and the city's contracts to harvest $7 million a year from the federal government for holding trans and queer immigrants. He argued, "You know where the best place for our queer and trans brothers and sisters is? It's with their communities." "In detention, no matter where, we are harassed, we are made fun of, we are threatened, we are misgendered. We are denied medical access. If you complain about this, they put you in solitary confinement and say it's for your 'safety'—and that is punishment. I believe that is torture. Trans women who have been detained verify this. The Human Rights Watch report verifies this." The protest fast in front of Santa Ana Jail was part of a larger struggle that Jorge Gutiérrez expressed willingness to "put my body out on the line in Santa Ana to protect our communities and families, this is part of a national fight to stop the raids, deportations and close down detention centers" (quoted in Vasquez 2016).

Putting one's body on the line echoed the national mass hunger strikes six months before that connected the struggles in detention centers when hundreds of Punjabi, Bangladeshi, Ghanaian, Congolese, and Central American, Colombian, and Ecuadorian detainees participated in hunger strikes in seven ICE detainee centers from California to Texas, Louisiana, Florida, Georgia, and Alabama in October–December 2015. The intersectional coalition building and national solidarity campaign on behalf of hunger-striking immigrants was launched as the "Freedom Giving" campaign put in counterpunctual relief the extreme national feasting during Thanksgiving Weekend 2015. The #FreedomGiving campaign condemned the reach of the carceral system into the civil confinement of undocumented immigrants and asylum seekers, repudiating all detentions, deportations, and the ICE bed quotas that structurally sustains a profit-based incarceration industry.

On a local level, these campaigns against the detention and deportation of immigrants intersected with multiple and complex ways in which the US prison system produces people of color as queer, deviant, and dangerous to justify their intensified and extended cycles of incarceration (Vitulli 2012). In December 2015, at Yuba County jail, six women prisoners joined in a hunger strike to support Rajashree Roy, who faced deportation to Fiji, even though she was eight when she came to the United States to join her father after being abandoned by her mother and abused by relatives. At sixteen she was arrested for robbery and battery. Once released from prison, she struggled to survive and feed her children while in an abusive relationship, and she was arrested for misdemeanor petty theft. Because of her prior convictions, the district attorney set bail at $1 million and offered a twenty-five-to-life sentence; Roy accepted a plea bargain of seven years in 2011. She won early release in November 2014, but when Roy stepped foot out of jail, she was picked up by ICE and slated for deportation to Fiji, away from her children (Sohrabji 2015). In Yuba County jail, Roy organized with women imprisoned on a variety of convictions. Roy and her fellow hunger strikers at Yuba County Jail issued a statement: "We are locked up together and refuse to be divided into immigrants and citizens. None of us belong in this cage separated from our families. We join the brave immigrant hunger strikers across the country in fasting to force recognition of our humanity." Roy received free legal representation, and her struggle was publicized by Asian Americans Advancing Justice–Asian Law Caucus, which works with low-income Asian Pacific Islander immigrants in deportation proceedings. Members of ASPIRE, a pan-Asian, undocumented youth-led group affiliated with the legal nonprofit, conducted solidarity fasts outside the jail and insisted on an "end to the unjust policing and the criminalization of all communities of color" (Sohrabji 2015). In 2016 Roy was released from detention and became an advocate for those in detention, lobbying legislators for alternative justice reforms for those whose record of incarceration makes them vulnerable to deportation (Wu 2016).

These creative and conscientious examples of movement building initiated through prisms of ethnic, gender, and sexual identity have the capacity to share resources and concerns, and forge networks of alliance and support. The political activism and social media spotlighted the well-being of particular immigrant detainees and in the process poignantly revealed the pervasive carceral system's inhumanity. The system of civil detention, which borrowed from the prison industrial complex and criminalization, fostered trenchant critiques of the US prison systems' endemic racism, enumerating the ways it warehouses people of color and produces prisoners as racially other, deviant, and queer. In local jails, populations mixed and shared similar struggles against the structures of unjust policy, anemic legal recourse, widespread criminalization, vulnerability to violence, and relentless caging and confinement. Their critiques of the US prison system, communicated through allies and advocates, reverberated to challenge how the prison-industrial complex polices gender normativity, punishes gender and sexual deviance, and destroys and distorts kinship and social worlds of people of color. These grounds of struggle fed dreams of prison abolition across identities and locations (Vitulli 2012; Stanley 2015).

References

Cohen, Cathy J. 1997. "Punks, Bulldaggers, and Welfare Queens: The Radical Potential of Queer Politics?" *GLQ* 3, no. 4: 437–65.

Reichard, Raquel. 2016. "Immigrant & LGBT Rights Leaders Start Hunger Strike to #EndTransDetention." *Latina*, May 18. www.latina.com/lifestyle/our-issues/hunger -strike-end-transgender-immigrant-detention.

Romero, Ezra David. 2014. "Caravanning to El Paso, Fresno Sikhs Protest Year-Long Detention." Valley Public Radio, April 25. kvpr.org/post/caravanning-el-paso -fresno-sikhs-protest-year-long-detention.

Sohrabji, Sunita. 2015. "Indian American Mom in Jail Facing Deportation to Fiji." *India West*, December 16. www.indiawest.com/news/global_indian/indian-american-mom -in-jail-facing-deportation-to-fiji/article_89342814–a420–11e5–9cbb-4f7c2b15d391 .html.

Stanley, Eric, and Nat Smith, eds. 2015. *Captive Genders: Trans Embodiment and the Prison Industrial Complex*, 2nd ed. Oakland, CA: AK Press.

Vasquez, Tina. 2016. "Hunger Strikers to ICE: End Transgender Immigrant Detention." May 17. rewire.news/article/2016/05/17/hunger-strikers-ice-transgender-immigrant/.

Vitulli, Elias Walker. 2012. "Queering the Carceral: Intersecting Queer/Trans Studies and Critical Prison Studies." *GLQ* 19, no. 1: 111–23.

Wu, Gwendolyn. 2016. "How a Former Detainee Is Advocating for Prison and Immigration Reform." *Take Part*. www.takepart.com/article/2016/07/22/yuri-kochiyama -fellowship.

DOI 10.1215/10642684-7275446

COALITIONAL AURALITIES

Notes on a Soundtrack to Punks, Bulldaggers, and Welfare Queens

Elliott H. Powell

*A*s a scholar of Black popular music, it might seem odd that I am contributing to this discussion of Cathy Cohen's foundational article "Punks, Bulldaggers, and Welfare Queens." Music is, after all, virtually absent from Cohen's powerful reimagining of radical queer politics. And yet, I believe that there are significant ways that Black popular music and "Punks" can and do find meaning in each other. Indeed, the punk, bulldagger, and welfare queen, Cohen's exemplary nonnormative sexual categories whose relation to power inform an intersectional queer analysis and politics, have historical and contemporary legacies in Black popular music. For example, Tavia Nyong'o's work (2005) has reshaped the contours of punk rock by considering the history and circulation of the "punk" in African American culture; the butch bulldagger is found throughout much of Black music history from early twentieth-century blues songs like Lucille Bogan's "B.D. Women" to contemporary rappers like Young M.A; and, as feminist hip hop scholars like Tricia Rose (2008) have long pointed out, the welfare queen trope is one that frequently frames rappers' (irrespective of gender) responses to Black women's sexualities.

But while Cohen is interested in these *individual* marginalized subjects, she's more concerned with theorizing a broad-based *collective* political vision that centers the overlapping experiences of oppression among these marginalized subjects. Cohen (1997: 441) critiques the single-issue framework of mainstream queer politics that privileges nonheterosexual identity as the sole site of oppression (and that thus ignores social formations like race) to instead propose a different kind of liberatory project, one that is intersectional and leftist based, and that is organized around "those who stand on the outside of the dominant constructed norm of state-sanctioned white middle- and upper-class heterosexuality." Cohen refers to this new queer politics as "principled coalition work" and does so because it radically challenges the homogenizing logics of sameness that frame most articulations of coalitions. To pursue principled coalition work, then, as far as I'm imagining it, is to redefine coalitions as a relational politics of collective resonance. To resonate is to resemble, but not exactly to be the same. In particular—and this is where I find its connection to music most salient—to resonate is to amplify and animate; it is to simultaneously vibrate out and vibe with in unexpected, unintended, and uneven ways; and it is to then mark, draw, and produce a collective with those who share and experience such resonance, but are differently affected by it.

This kind of relational politics of collective resonance, this kind of refusal to elide varied histories and lived realities of marginalized people, is what makes Cohen's article so important in, of, and for Black popular music. To that end, what I want to do is briefly think through what principled coalitional work sounds like. How might we imagine the workings of these kinds of sono-social and sono-political performances of collectivity—what we might call "coalitional auralities?" Simply put, I want to make a case for the soundtracks of punks, bulldaggers, and welfare queens. And to do so, I want to choose a somewhat unlikely candidate, Miles Davis, and his often-overlooked and forgotten 1972 album *On the Corner*.[1]

It is with *On the Corner* that Davis, for the first and only time, sought to appeal to the youth of the Black Power generation. Sonically, the album is a jazz-funk album that draws inspiration from Black Power musical favorites like James Brown, Sly Stone, and the Last Poets. Visually, the album cover uses the mode of cartoons to represent the then-contemporary street corner life, hence the album's title, of Black working-class and working-poor urban ghettos. The cover depicts men dressed in Black Panther Party–inspired black leather jackets and berets as well as men wearing Pan-African colors of red, black, and green with phrases like "Free Me" emblazoned on their clothing, gesturing to the "Free Angela" and "Free Huey" slogans during Angela Davis and Huey Newton's incarcerations.

And yet, as *On the Corner*'s music and album cover speak to dominant Black Power ideologies, the album also reframes them. Indeed, *On the Corner* is Davis's only studio album to contain South Asian musicians and instrumentation, and the album cover also features female sex workers and what appears to be a gay Black man, a punk—he is sporting a midriff, often extends his pinky finger, and is giving devastating side-eye on the cover.

When I interviewed Bangladeshi *tabla* player Badal Roy about the recording process of *On the Corner*, he informed me that Davis instructed him to "play like a nigga" (pers. comm., July 26, 2016). I read this directive not through ethnoracial essentialist logic but through the Afro-Asian coalitional lens of what Vijay Prashad (2000) calls "model minority suicide." The model minority category was not as firmly rooted in US politics and culture in 1972 as it is today, but, as Susan Koshy (2001) notes, 1970 was the only time that the US Census counted South Asians as white. This Census change worked in tandem with the class- and normative-

kinship-biased legislative provisions of the Immigration Act of 1965 that disproportionately increased the number of middle- and upper-class Asian immigrant
nuclear families in the United States, and thus created a political and cultural
assimilative space and incentive through which South Asian immigrants like Roy
could identify with whiteness, middle-classness, and nuclear housing formations
through and against the criminalized, policed, and often deemed sexually nonnormative, Black working-class communities. Such context allows us to interpret
Davis's charge to Roy to "play like a nigga" as a call to reject the hailing of white
middle-class normativity—that is, "model minority suicide"—and to form alliances between marginalized communities against such race, gender, class, and
sexual normative systems of oppression. *On the Corner* makes audible such coalitional auralities through the linking of Roy's tabla playing and James Mtume's
Afro-diasporic drumming. In fact, Roy and Mtume's collaborative sounds are the
result of recording techniques that spliced and sutured together different recording sessions, further manipulated Mtume and Roy's playing so that their percus-
sive patterns refused the sonic norms governing their instruments' traditional (and
masculinist) histories, and then juxtaposed their playing against each other. And
it is due to this kind of queer approach to recording that Roy and Mtume appear
as sharing the same aural space and creating an interlocked, homosocial, and
Afro–South Asian sonic collective.

Such queering in the music of *On the Corner* is made even more evident
on the cover itself. Its inclusion of Black women sex workers and the Black punk
centers the subjectivities that Cohen insists we organize our queer politics around
because their sexual practices render them outside the privilege of heteronormativity and homonormativity. Cortez "Corky" McCoy was the album's illustrator.
McCoy and his wife and collaborator Sandra McCoy were known for their erotic
representations of Black women for the Black pornography outlet, *Players*, a magazine where, during McCoy's stint with them, the poet Wanda Coleman served as the
editor and sought cultural work whose nonnormativity was "wholly unaccounted
for in the black arts movement or the womanist movement" (Stallings 2015: 69).
McCoy brings such radical depictions of black women's sexuality in *Players* to *On
the Corner* in the form of sex workers, recasting the corner as not simply a race-
and class-based space of Black working-class and working-poor life but also a site
of sexual labor and desire.

McCoy extends such sexual valences of the corner by also drawing a Black
man posing on the outskirts of the street corner and whose gender expression is
vastly different from the other men on the cover. When I asked McCoy about this
character, he told me, "Do you know why he's off to the side? Because that's where

Figure 1. *On the Corner*, by Miles Davis, Columbia Records, album cover (front),
1972. Artwork by Cortez McCoy

we push gay people. . . . This country is a great marginalizer" (pers. comm., September 27, 2016). McCoy's words speak to his drawing of the punk character not as
a liberal assimilative representation of inclusion but a depiction that underscores
Black queer men's marginality. It is this marginality that positions him and the
female sex workers in relation to each other, gesturing toward nonnormative marginality as the basis through which to organize a leftist-inspired street corner political vision. And when paired with the Afro–South Asian sonics of the album, *On
the Corner* destabilizes a kind of coalitional project that is trapped within category-
based identity politics and enacts a more progressive politics of transnational and
comparative work; it creates Cohen's push toward principled coalition work.

      And yet, how do we interpret *On the Corner*'s coalitional auralities in the
face of Davis's documented history of sexism, misogyny, and domestic violence?[2]

Figure 2. *On the Corner*, by Miles Davis, Columbia Records, album cover (back),
1972. Artwork by Cortez McCoy

Rather than ignore this history or argue that it undoes the transformative work of
the album, I contend that we must go back to Cohen (1997: 480) and take heed
of her argument that principled coalition work "is not an easy path to pursue"
because it requires us to uncomfortably confront "the relative power and privilege"
of our positionalities that "challenge dichotomies such as . . . enemy/comrade." *On
the Corner*, as an album by a Black man who beat women and whose career and
life are shrouded in rumors of his nonnormative sexual desires and practices, is a
prime candidate for the complex struggles and challenges of coalition building. It
is a cultural work that visually and sonically represents the process, and not the
product, of principled coalition work. And as such, it is an emblematic soundtrack
for how we might see and sound the kinds of political possibilities of and for organizing around punks, bulldaggers, and welfare queens.

Further Listening

As a bonus, here are a few albums that I believe also soundtrack "Punks" (in chronological order): Rick James's *The Flag*; Lil' Kim's *Hard Core*; Missy Elliott's *Miss E . . . So Addictive*; and Janelle Monáe's *Electric Lady*.

Notes

1. This analysis is part of my current book project, *The Other Side of Things*.
2. I want to thank Bettina Judd for pressing me on this question.

References

Cohen, Cathy J. "Punks, Bulldaggers, and Welfare Queens: The Radical Potential of Queer Politics?" *GLQ* 3, no. 4 (1997): 437–65.

Koshy, Susan. 2001. "Morphing Race into Ethnicity: Asian Americans and Critical Transformations of Whiteness." *Boundary 2* 28, no. 1: 153–94.

Nyong'o, Tavia. 2005. "Punk'd Theory." *Social Text*, nos. 84–85: 19–34.

Prashad, Vijay. 2000. *The Karma of Brown Folk*. Minneapolis: University of Minnesota Press.

Rose, Tricia. 2008. *The Hip Hop Wars: What We Talk about When We Talk about Hip Hop—and Why It Matters*. New York: Civitas.

Stallings, L. H. 2015. *Funk the Erotic: Transaesthetics and Black Sexual Cultures*. Urbana: University of Illinois Press.

DOI 10.1215/10642684-7275460

BLACKINESIS

Erin Gray

Wandering: Philosophical Performances of Racial and Sexual Freedom
Sarah Jane Cervenak
Durham, NC: Duke University Press, 2014. 220 pp.

Intellectually ambitious and beautifully written, Sarah Jane Cervenak's *Wandering: Philosophical Performances of Racial and Sexual Freedom* is a timely contribution to interdisciplinary scholarship on the opaque powers of Black expressive culture. Working at the intersections of performance studies, Black critical theory, and political philosophy, Cervenak attends to philosophical performances of Black spiritual and epistemological diversion in abolitionist texts, novels, plays, performance art, and photography. Wandering as Black philosophical performance, she argues, is an antisurveillance strategy that disturbs Enlightenment demands for transparency and empirical truth while potentiating other philosophical and political horizons.

Cervenak advances her argument in four chapters and an analytic conclusion. Moving elegantly between philosophical exegesis, critical analysis, and close reading of artistic texts, *Wandering* unfolds a complex argument that belies the book's slim packaging. In the first two chapters, Cervenak examines the dialectic of comportment and waywardness, reason and affectability in Enlightenment and Black Enlightenment discourse. The book's second half looks to Black literary and artistic mobilizations of wayward thought that resist readability to "disaggregate freedom from the empirical measures" of respectability that underwrite liberal notions of freedom (18). Inspired by Audre Lorde's argument that Black women may turn to "erotic guides from within," Cervenak bases her analysis on a Black feminist tradition that takes the interior "as a philosophical site of radical desire, guidance, errant performativity, and healing" (13). The importance of this philosophical desire does not stem from its availability to interpretation.

GLQ 25:1

Undertaking a bold critique of performance studies scholars who read performances for verifiably political content, Cervenak grounds the philosophical power of Black performances of racial and sexual freedom in their failure to heed positivist demands for legibility. She builds on Jayna Brown's assertion in *Babylon Girls* that Black women's kinetic refusals of racist discourse are not contingent on analytic frameworks of bodily enunciativity or physical mobility. Against the racist codification of Black bodies as affectable matter and Black movement as criminally trespassive, interior kinesis in the form of prayers and daydreams and "in the motion of a rambling tongue" generates forms of thought and being that exceed the racially particular conceits of universal reason (6).

Black epistemological desire and spiritual wandering emerge, then, in sharp contrast to the violent wandering that facilitated the European Enlightenment. The first chapter opens with the Nigerian artist Yinka Shonibare's 2008 installation, *The Age of Enlightenment–Immanuel Kant* as Cervenak sets up the groundwork for her analysis of the "performative antagonism" at the heart of Enlightenment philosophy. Unearthing Enlightenment discourse's errant schema, Cervenak demonstrates that "reckless roaming" was a primary method of the Enlightenment; philosophers of reason, morality, and justice forged a discourse of transparent and universal reason by moving into and against other bodies and territories (7). In conversation with Black and postcolonial feminist critics, Cervenak explores how ideas of race and gender in the writings of Immanuel Kant and Jean-Jacques Rousseau "perversely enact the very mythical scene and unregulated performances which the Age of Enlightenment was said to straighten out" (30). This "intrusive itinerancy" formed the ecstatic underside of Enlightenment writings on reason and ethics, serving as the groundwork for reason to emerge as a discourse of racialized transcendence (7, 28).

Where Kant and Rousseau strayed violently from the straight-and-narrow course demanded by European cultures of secular reason, members of the Black Enlightenment, Cervenak posits, wandered in an "ethical, harm-free embodiment of self-interest—a recuperative, deregulated, interior kinesis" (20). In the second chapter, Cervenak focuses on a performative tension between self-determined uplift and divinely inspired waywardness in writings and speeches by David Walker, Martin Delany, Harriet Jacobs, and Sojourner Truth. She interprets Jacobs's omission, in *Incidents in the Life of a Slave Girl*, of the sensational details of her experiences as Flint's slave and Dr. Sands's mistress not as an assent to the principles of moral propriety that structured Victorian feminism; rather, Jacobs refused abolitionists' desire for her to narrate, through transparent and "impassioned speech," her sexual and maternal trauma. Jacobs's informational withholdings from her readers enact what Cervenak describes as a "phantasmatic straying into the ante-articulate—a place of hurt and spirit" that engenders "other coordinates of freedom" (62). The chapter concludes with a meditation on Sojourner Truth as the ur-figure for Black feminist practices of wandering. Because of her illiteracy and metaphysical propensities, Truth is frequently caricatured or dismissed altogether in narratives of Black radicalism; her relationship with God, Cervenak writes, "was determined to be unreadable and unassimilable into counterhegemonic project of racial and gender sense making" (89, 91–93). Yet Truth's prayerful sojourns countered the state's anti-Black surveillance apparatus through a spiritual counterkinesis that, like Jacobs's writings, extended "the terrain of reason to include the wayward, unpredictable, and errant" (17, 62).

Chapter 3, "Writing under a Spell: Adrienne Kennedy's Theater," recuperates the surrealist aesthetics of *Funnyhouse of a Negro* (1964) and *The Owl Answers* (1965) as an extension of slave narratives' cryptic fugitivity. Where critics have read Kennedy's Black female characters' daydreams, spirit connection, and self-talk as evidence of psychosis and internalized racism, Cervenak argues that the plays' textual polyvocality interrupts the "regulation of Black female desire at the heart of post-Enlightenment subject production" (19). In *Funnyhouse*, Sarah's desire "not to be" refuses surveillance and localizability. This "errant drive toward self-transgression" expresses Sarah's "grip" on other worlds that emerge from the underside of the surreal (105, 107). The fourth chapter engages the narrative difficulty of Gayl Jones's *Mosquito* by listening for "that which eludes capture" (19). Cervenak again counters the critical backlash to Black women's experimental writing, arguing that the verbose character of the novel is the result of an improvisatory strategy to produce a different kind of traveler's tale. Tracking the protagonist's movements across the Southwest United States as well as her encounters with American Indians and migrants seeking sanctuary, the novel's interlocking stories keep her "out of view" while enacting a coalitional ethos resistant to legislation. The book's conclusion, "Before I Was 'Straightened Out,'" engages Adrian Piper's *Everything* series (2003), William Pope. L's *Thunderbird Immolation* (1978), and Carrie Mae Weems's *Roaming* series (2006) as scenes of subaltern devastation, diminution, and stillness that conjure, via meditative restraint, Black forms of vitality.

Throughout *Wandering*, Cervenak refuses hermeneutic mastery in favor of a methodology akin to the critical and generous listening modeled by critics like Fred Moten and Tina Campt. Attuning her readers to those qualities of a text that exceed representation, as well as to quotidian practices of refusal frequently overlooked in masculinist political histories, Cervenak takes up a contradiction at the heart of affect studies: how do scholars write about nonlinguistic and preconscious processes without denuding them of their nonrepresentational intensity? Cervenak underscores the political urgency of this contradiction for Black subjects whose movements have functioned as the criminalized underside of Enlightenment and post-Enlightenment conceptions of reason and being. Though Cervenak refuses the diagnostic character of argumentation to avoid the anti-Black epistemic violence she critiques in *Wandering*, this reader was not convinced by Cervenak's claims that she was not reading her chosen texts, or even that reading as such should be avoided. Cervenak's contributions to Black feminist cultural studies—particularly long-standing epistemological debates around experience and evidence—will be more compelling if she engages the literature on reparative and surface reading.

This book will be of interest to students of Black women's innovative writings, philosophies of race, the abolition of slavery, performance studies, fugitivity, and Black optimism, as well as those pessimists who take seriously the forms of life and sociability that emerge in struggle and suffering. Cervenak's discussions of epistemological desire and Black women's interiority are relevant, too, to readers of queer and sexuality studies. Her conceptualization of wandering complicates the affective valence of dissemblance, Darlene Clark Hine's (1989) term for the "cult of secrecy" that some Black women fashioned to protect themselves from racist discourses of seduction. No longer simply a strategy for maintaining a respectable mask, dissemblance may encompass a fuller range of messy, discomfiting, antisocial, and irresolute practices undertaken by Black women to protect—and exercise—their erotic power.

Reference

Hine, Darlene Clark. 1989. "Rape and the Inner Lives of Black Women in the Middle West." *Signs* 14, no. 4: 912–20.

Erin Gray is a postdoctoral fellow and assistant professor of media, culture, and communication at New York University.

DOI 10.1215/10642684-7275674

HEMISPHERIC TRANSLATIONS

Cole Rizki

Translating the Queer: Body Politics and Transnational Conversations
Héctor Domínguez Ruvalcaba
London: Zed Books, 2016. x + 194 pp.

It is, by now, axiomatic that *queer*—a once pejorative and injurious signifier—was recuperated by activists and theorists alike in the early 1990s. The possibility of linguistic and affective resignification is, in part, what continues to load queer with the promise of radical destabilizing force. But as Latin American studies scholars, among others, have repeatedly attested, the same cannot be said when queer moves into other languages. Some Latin Americanists like Brad Epps (2007: 227) note that, as an English-language signifier, queer loses its potent affective charge in translation: rather than resignify harm, queer enacts it through academic imperialism, dressed as metropolitan theory. Indeed, queer sheds its thick verbal and corporeal history through travel; it becomes a concept without affective memory or place (ibid.: 234). Scholars such as Juan Pablo Sutherland and María Amelia Viteri are similarly critical of queer's conceptual limitations, yet they find promise in a contestatory queer politics. Such a politics would attend to the singularity of "the popular, the mestizo, critical activisms, and crises of representations of the masculine and feminine" while interrogating the fixity of categories such as Latino or queer, as these terms get "relocated, reappropriated, and translated" throughout the Américas (Sutherland 2009: 29; Viteri 2014: xxvii). Acknowledging the potential for imperialist injury and spectacular failure, Héctor Domínguez Ruvalcaba's *Translating the Queer: Body Politics and Transnational Conversations* joins this latter group of scholars, inciting Latin American studies to recuperate queer as a site of possibility.

Translation is central to Domínguez Ruvalcaba's project. Rather than semiotic practice, translation signals processes of mediation between bodily and cultural systems of meaning. *Translating the Queer* thus capitalizes on the natural affinity between translation and queering: as processes, both disrupt meaning and place "identity" into crisis. Domínguez Ruvalcaba's monograph is directly informed by the groundbreaking edited collection *Translocalities/Translocalidades:*

Feminist Politics of Translation in the Latin/a Américas, in which editors Sonia E. Alvarez et al. (2014: 2) develop "translocalities/*translocalidades*" as a conceptual framework. Translocation expands US Third World feminist "politics of location" to suggest a particular mediation of the subject that "link[s] geographies of power at various scales (local, regional, national, global) with the subject positions (gender/sexual, ethno-racial, class, etc.) that constitute the self" (Laó Montes 2007: 122). Simultaneously, translocation indexes circuits of multidirectional and continuous border crossings that mediate subject positions and ideas as both travel throughout the hemisphere. This dual sense of translocation informs Domínguez Ruvalcaba's work.

Divided into four chapters, *Translating the Queer* surveys an extensive corpus of contemporary scholarship on canonical Latin American literature, social movements, and cultural production, moving chronologically from the colonial period to the present. The conversations highlighted will be familiar to Latin Americanists, and, as such, this text will be most useful to nonspecialist readers or undergraduates as an introductory volume. Each chapter examines relationships between translation, queerness, and major areas of inquiry such as coloniality, modernity, and neoliberalism. Chapter 1 surveys Latin Americanist colonial studies scholarship centering the bond between queerness and coloniality. Drawing on Aníbal Quijano's formulation of "coloniality" as the arrangement of material and sociocultural relations that structure power in the Américas, Domínguez Ruvalcaba extends "coloniality" to "sex." This move allows him to consider how the "coloniality of sex" produces and regulates sexual perversity, translating indigenous sexual and gender practices as deviant by punishing "difference as a way of correcting gender expressions and sexual practices" (21).

In other chapters, Domínguez Ruvalcaba highlights incompatibilities between US-based and Latin American systems of sex and gender political organizing. Chapter 3, for example, focuses on Latin American LGBT social movement activism from the 1960s onward, stressing that these rights movements aimed, in part, to protect "Latin American identity from North American domination" (111). Domínguez Ruvalcaba underscores that Marxism and socialism have deeply influenced social movement organizing; class struggle—rather than identity politics— was a cornerstone of much early LGBT activism such as Argentina's Frente de Liberación Homosexual. The Left, however, largely did not recognize sexual diversity as a revolutionary identity, and gay and lesbian activisms of the 1960s and 1970s can be characterized by a "tension between the revolutionary left and the politics of homosexuality" (102).

Translating the Queer's final turn to trans politics is perhaps its least convincing move. Here Domínguez Ruvalcaba claims that "trans identity is one of the most dynamic stages from which to 'queer' the hegemonic culture" (133). By figuring trans identity as a "stage from which to 'queer,'" *Translating the Queer* risks reinstalling founding tensions between US-based queer and trans theory in which queer theory at times mobilized trans identity as evidence for gender's instability. Rather than transpose these frictions onto Latin Americanist scholarly and cultural production, a queer politics of translation might instead provincialize not only "queer" and "trans" but also any presumed relationships between them. Such a tactic would generate alternate readings of the ties that structure theories of bodies and desires in the Américas. Despite these lapses, *Translating the Queer* will serve readers who wish to familiarize themselves with existing scholarly conversations in Latin American queer studies.

References

Alvarez, Sonia E., Claudia de Lima Costa, Verónica Feliu, Rebecca J. Hester, Norma Klahn, and Millie Thayer, eds. 2014. *Translocalities/Translocalidades: Feminist Politics of Translation in the Latin/a Américas.* Durham, NC: Duke University Press.

Epps, Brad. 2007. "Retos y riesgos, pautas y promesas de la teoría queer." *Debate Feminista* 36: 219–72.

Laó-Montes, Agustin. 2007. "Afro-Latinidades: Bridging Blackness and Latinidad." In *Technofuturos: Critical Interventions in Latina/o Studies*, edited by Nancy Raquel Mirabel and Agustin Laó-Montes, 117–41. Lanham, MD: Lexington Books.

Sutherland, Juan Pablo. 2009. *Nación marica: Prácticas culturales y crítica activista.* Santiago, Chile: Ripio Ediciones.

Viteri, María Amelia. 2014. *Desbordes: Translating Racial, Ethnic, Sexual, and Gender Identities across the Americas.* Albany: State University of New York Press.

Cole Rizki is a PhD candidate in the Program in Literature at Duke University.

DOI 10.1215/10642684-7275688

REALIZING A DIFFERENT LACAN?

Meridith Kruse

The Ethics of Opting Out: Queer Theory's Defiant Subjects
Mari Ruti
New York: Columbia University Press, 2017. x + 252 pp.

Ruti offers numerous subclaims across this ambitious book, including a critique of Butlerian reiteration and a case for Tim Dean's impersonal ethics. All, however, are largely animated by her central argument that Lee Edelman's Lacan of negativity and destruction, widely accepted as dogma in queer theory, is incomplete and should be revised. While Edelman interprets Lacanian negativity as a matter of self-annihilation, Ruti counters that, for Jacques Lacan, an individual's plunge into self-shattering jouissance is better seen as an ethical act by a defiant subject unwilling to give ground on the "truth of their desire" (8). Although certainly posing a risk to one's social viability, such an act also has the potential to spark feisty agents of political rebellion whose "opting out" of the dominant order can include a fierce loyalty to cherished objects and loved ones (8). In Ruti's view, Antigone exemplifies this dynamic when she defies the hegemonic, symbolic order (Creon's Laws) and risks her own subjective incoherence out of a commitment to the truth of her desire, which is itself animated by intense loyalty to her brother (55). On the book's back cover, in praise of this unique intervention in our field, Heather Love remarks: "By joining Lacanian fidelity to desire with the impulse to repair, Ruti points the way toward a queer ethics that is antinormative without being antisocial." Within the field of queer theory, Ruti hopes that this different, more relational portrait will help clarify the value of Lacanian concepts for affect-oriented scholars who may have avoided such tools because of Edelman's influence as well as bridge the divide between "those who have chosen to follow Lacan (Bersani, Edelman, Dean)" versus "Foucault (Halperin, Huffer)" (4).

In her fourth chapter, "Beyond the Antisocial-Social Divide," Ruti begins work toward these goals by charting points of convergence among adversaries in the antisocial-social debate. For Ruti, the contours of this face-off are exemplified by antisocial theorists such as Edelman, who "tend to emphasize—along Lacanian lines—the constitutive role of negativity in human life," in contrast to scholars such as "Munoz, Eng, and Love," who focus on more social, "circumstantial and context-specific forms of negativity, wounding, decentering, and suffering" (131). Out of a desire to soften this disagreement, Ruti utilizes her alternative, relational Lacan to argue that "the recognition of the subject's constitutive lack-in-being should not, in principle, keep critics from acknowledging the importance of more circumstantial forms of wounding (and vice versa)" (131). For Ruti, then, the tension between scholars such as Edelman and Love could be reduced if each were able to admit how their common interest in specific kinds of negativity inform each other. Interestingly, Ruti asserts that Lynne Huffer's latest book, *Are the Lips a Grave?* (2013), offers a productive example of this kind of valuable bridgework that crosses the antisocial-social divide as Huffer accounts for the role of *both* constitutive and social forms of wounding to develop her ethics of sex (132–33).

Across *The Ethics of Opting Out*, then, the gesture of reconciliation (bridge building, finding common ground) begins to function as an unquestioned good that implicitly validates Ruti's numerous efforts to secure convergence. At first glance, this focus on alleviating disagreements would appear to be a laudable goal. Given Ruti's citation of Huffer's work, however, I would argue it is vital to recall that Huffer ties her specific sense of ethics in *Are the Lips a Grave?* to a messy, "rift-restoring" convergence that seeks to *preserve differences* when locating sites of "fractured common ground" so that a lively "politics of disagreement" can occur that honors, rather than erases, alterity (7–8). With Huffer's sense of ethics in mind, I now want to consider the stakes of Ruti's claim that Huffer's Foucauldian desubjectivation represents "the same celebration of incoherence" as Edelman's Lacanian self-shattering jouissance (142). Rather than merely a minor quibble, it is my sense that Ruti's equation of these two concepts erases key distinctions between Huffer and Edelman (as well as Michel Foucault and Lacan) which are vital to preserve if queer theory is to address a host of pressing ethico-political concerns.

Typically seen as occupying divergent theoretical positions, Ruti groups Huffer with Edelman because, in her view, both typify a harmful trend in queer theory to unreflectingly push for ever-more intense destructions of the Enlightenment subject in a way that disregards the struggles of everyday people to persist and survive. However, in equating Huffer's Foucault with Edelman's Lacan, Ruti ignores Huffer's important work in *Mad for Foucault* to remind queer theory of Foucault's argument, across *The History of Madness* (1961), that the Freudian-Lacanian psyche represents not a site of rebellion but the very culmination of positivistic science and bourgeois morality that continues to silence and repress unreason. In her fourth chapter, "Unraveling the Queer Psyche," for example, Huffer demonstrates how the Freudian Oedipus complex functions as a violent internal-izing "fold," depositing bourgeois moral norms of shame and guilt "inside" the modern sexual subject such that the psyche becomes a sly site of "caged freedom" (125–33). As a result, Foucault's efforts to undo the modern rationalist subject via his archival practice include an attempt to unravel the trappings of the Freudian-Lacanian unconscious (which Edelman and Ruti leave in place). Importantly, Huffer links Foucault's nonpsychoanalytic pursuit of desubjectivation to his archi-val practice, where he not only strives to hear the traces of lives snuffed out by reason but also to grasp ethical forms of freedom with immediate relevance for our world. Thus, when Ruti disparages the value of Foucauldian desubjectivation and assimilates it to Edelman's self-shattering jouissance, queer theory again misses out on Foucault's incisive critique of psychoanalysis and loses touch with a range of vital, nonpsychoanalytic tools for pursuing an erotic ethics of living.

To circle back to my opening question, then, does Ruti succeed in offer-ing queer theory a *different* Lacan? It would appear to be a matter of perspective. For American scholars primarily familiar with Edelman's work, Ruti's portrait of a more relational, socially oriented Lacan might seem unique. But for those who are cognizant of Foucault's genealogy of psychoanalysis in *The History of Mad-ness* (1961) as well as Gilles Deleuze and Félix Guattari's ongoing efforts to not only critique structuralist interpretations of Lacan but also adapt certain psycho-analytic ideas for their more radical schizo-analysis, Ruti's work will appear quite staid. Already in *Anti-Oedipus* ([1972] 1983), for example, Deleuze and Guattari pinpoint the specific Lacanian theory of desire that Ruti embraces as something to discard and move beyond because of its repression of desiring-production. "Lacan's admirable theory of desire appears to us to have two poles," they note, "one related to 'the object small *a*' as a desiring-machine, which defines desire in terms of a real production . . . and the other related to the 'great Other,' as a signi-fier, which reintroduces a certain notion of lack" (27). As is widely known, Deleuze and Guattari will deploy this first pole of desire to chart a radically different, transversalist notion of the unconscious. Meanwhile, Ruti and Edelman remain tethered to this second pole as they promote a Lacanian desire tied to the great Other and a constitutive lack-in-being that Deleuze and Guattari denounced long ago for its suppression of both desiring-machines and antifascist modes of thinking and living. As a result, one might say that the value of *The Ethics of Opting Out* lies less in its newness per se than in its ability to remind queer theory of how far it has yet to go to acknowledge the vital transformations to Lacan, ethics, and desire wrought by the innovative thinkers circulating around May '68.

References

Deleuze, Gilles, and Félix Guattari. [1972] 1983. *Anti-Oedipus: Capitalism and Schizo-phrenia*. Minneapolis: University of Minnesota Press.

Foucault, Michel. [1961] 2006. *The History of Madness*. New York: Routledge.

Huffer, Lynne. 2010. *Mad for Foucault: Rethinking the Foundations of Queer Theory*. New York: Columbia University Press.

———. 2013. *Are the Lips a Grave? A Queer Feminist on the Ethics of Sex*. New York: Columbia University Press.

Meridith Kruse is a lecturer in the writing program at the University of Southern California.

DOI 10.1215/10642684-7275702

A QUEER ETHIC OF CONFLICT AND THE CHALLENGE OF FRIENDSHIP

David S. Byers

Conflict Is Not Abuse: Overstating Harm, Community Responsibility, and the Duty of Repair
Sarah Schulman
Vancouver: Arsenal Pulp Press, 2016. 299 pp.

Conflicts, according to Sarah Schulman in her most recent book, are varied, sometimes mundane, and often consequential challenges to dominant understandings. Conflicts can range from simply showing up in interaction, for people whose social identities and sexualities are contested, to active resistance to state and intergroup violence, marginalization, and oppression. Schulman's deceptively simple contention is that such conflicts are so uncomfortable for most people that we pervasively misunderstand or misrepresent them as potentially leading to serious psychological, social, and physical harm. Intentionally or not, we overstate the danger of necessary and inevitable conflict and frame it as abuse.

The obfuscation of necessary conflict relates in part to a defense of consolidated power and control—when people with more power feel narcissistically injured when those with less power pose a challenge. Schulman offers various case studies of this threatening interaction across power differentials, including driving (or walking, or selling loose cigarettes) while Black in the United States, having sex while HIV+ in Canada, and resisting the occupation of the West Bank and siege on Gaza as a Palestinian.

In the last example, Schulman provides a careful analysis of social media posts about Israel's assault on Gaza in 2014, pointing to the Israeli government's anxious control of the narrative through shunning and dehumanizing Palestinian resistance. As I first sat down to read Schulman's book, sixteen-year-old Ahed Tamimi was arrested for allegedly slapping and kicking two Israeli soldiers patrolling her village in the occupied West Bank (see Goldman 2017). Arrests of children and adolescents in the West Bank are common, usually for throwing stones at the occupying army (see "Imprisonment of Children" n.d.). Tamimi's case has received unusual attention because her family filmed the incident and the Israeli education minister later suggested that she be imprisoned for life as punishment. She was released in July 2018 after eight months in prison. In a less well-known but as common example, Munther Amira, a Palestinian social worker, was arrested and held for six months for nonviolent protest of Tamimi's imprisonment (see "Social Work and Non-Violent Resistance" 2018). Schulman's point about overstating harm to justify state control could hardly be more evident. The Israeli social psychologist Niza Yanay (2013) offers a similar psychoanalytic reading of the Israeli military's violent response to challenges to its supremacy. Building on a Fanonian conceptualization of colonialist anxiety, Yanay critiques the dominant power's disavowed yet frustrated yearning for the subjugated group's validation.

In Schulman's analysis, these overestimations of harm can also play out at the interpersonal level, even when the person claiming abuse may have less or similar structural or institutional power as the person accused. She offers several provocative examples, including sexual interactions in professional settings characterized too quickly and simply as sexual harassment, student demands for "trigger warnings" in college coursework to avoid uncomfortable content, and conflations of violence and abuses of power in intimate relationships. In a particularly disturbing example, she recounts an incident between two female friends in a long-term, high-conflict relationship. One of them threw a heavy object at the other, causing a broken bone, and weeks later the woman who was injured called the police to have her former partner arrested. Schulman suggests that the conflict might have been better resolved by seeking remediation and parting ways. Instead, the injured friend sought recourse for her pain and anger with punitive and likely ineffective legal measures, effectively recentering the state.

The tradition of psychoanalytic, feminist, and queer theorization about conflict and power across micro and macro levels of interaction—between individuals, between individuals and the state, and between states—inevitably leads to additional distortions. Schulman's work, however, largely finds coherence because of her strategy of locating disparate problems within a personal frame of reference through an ethic of bystander accountability. In each example, from Gaza to an East Village apartment, Schulman insistently implicates herself—as a member of the community and a friend who plays a role.

Many of us are drawn into the group enactments Schulman describes, overstating the harm of interpersonal interactions to justify punishments of uncomfortable differences through shunning and scapegoating. This justification undermines our ability to engage productively in conflict and address dangerous abuse when it occurs. The slippage happens actively between us, yet we can interrupt the circuit by acting as what Schulman terms "good friends"—relations that, regardless of other formal and informal ties, facilitate questioning and accountability. We otherwise tend to egg each other on in escalating claims of abuse through notions of exceptionalism, whether in shared response to past trauma or relying on assumptions about the group's supremacy. Schulman's premise that traumatized groups often behave like groups organized around supremacy is an old yet still challenging one in psychoanalytic contexts. Byers (2016: 343) has theorized that targeted and traumatized people seek "accountable recognition" of social pain from peers—introjections of credible care to counter expectations of violence and indifference that can allow traumatized people to reconstitute and reengage across differences. Schulman centers her analysis not on social pain but instead on the difficult recognition of the conflict itself.

Here, too, is where a friend can help. Whether we are family members, teachers, students, colleagues, social workers, postal workers, lovers, and others who can also be friends, Schulman's new book offers an often persuasive new (and old) strategy for queer ethical engagement: a model of friendship that assumes conflict and difference, where we depend on each other to ask questions and hold each other accountable.

References

Byers, David S. 2016. "Recognition of Social Pain among Peers: Rethinking the Role of Bystanders in Bullying and Cyberbullying." *Smith College Studies in Social Work* 86, no. 4: 335–54.

Goldman, Lisa. 2017. "Nabi Saleh Is Where I Lost My Zionism." *+972 Magazine*, December 24. 972mag.com/nabi-saleh-is-where-i-lost-my-zionism/131818/.

"Imprisonment of Children." n.d. Addameer: Prisoner Support and Human Rights Association (accessed December 26, 2017). www.addameer.org/the_prisoners/children.

"Social Work and Non-Violent Resistance." 2018. International Federation of Social Workers, June 13. www.ifsw.org/social-work-and-non-violent-resistance.

Yanay, Niza. 2013. *The Ideology of Hatred: The Psychic Power of Discourse*. New York: Fordham University Press.

David S. Byers is assistant professor at the Graduate School of Social Work and Social Research at Bryn Mawr College.

DOI 10.1215/10642684-7275716

About the Contributors

Jafari S. Allen is the director of Africana Studies and the Miami Initiative on Intersectional Social Justice, as well as an associate professor of anthropology, at the University of Miami. Allen's scholarship and teaching has opened new lines of inquiry and offered reinvigorated methods of narrative theorizing in anthropology, Black diaspora studies, and feminist and queer studies. His new book—*There's a Disco Ball between Us: An Ethnography of an Idea*—will appear from Duke University Press in 2019. Allen is the author of *¡Venceremos? The Erotics of Black SelfMaking in Cuba* (Duke University Press, 2011) and editor of the special double issue of *GLQ* titled "Black/Queer/Diaspora." Allen is currently working on two research projects, is beginning research on a third monograph, "Structural Adjustments: Black Survival in the 1980s," and is serving as lead Co-PI on the interdisciplinary research team "Reproducing Race in Miami."

Marlon M. Bailey is an associate professor of women and gender studies in the School of Social Transformation at Arizona State University. His book, *Butch Queens Up in Pumps: Gender, Performance, and Ballroom Culture in Detroit* (University of Michigan Press, 2013), was awarded the Alan Bray Memorial Book Prize by the GL/Q Caucus of the MLA. Some of Marlon's essays appear in *Signs*, *Feminist Studies*, *Souls*, *Gender, Place, and Culture*, and several book collections. Marlon's essay "Black Gay (Raw) Sex" appears in *No Tea, No Shade: New Writings in Black Queer Studies* (Duke University Press, 2016), edited by E. Patrick Johnson.

Gabby Benavente is an English PhD student at the University of Pittsburgh. Her interests include trans, queer, environmental, activist, and queer studies and how these fields can help imagine worlds that wrestle with legacies of violence.

Andy Campbell is an assistant professor of critical studies at USC-Roski School of Art and Design. His book "Bound Together: Leather, Sex, Archives, and Contemporary Art" is under contract with Manchester University Press.

V Varun Chaudhry is a PhD Candidate in the Department of Anthropology at Northwestern University. His work focuses on the institutionalization of "transgender" in nonprofit and funding agencies through ethnographic research in Philadelphia, PA. V's research has been generously supported by the Social Science Research Council, the Wenner-Gren Foundation, the Sexualities Project at Northwestern, and the Center for the Study of Women in Society at the University of Oregon. His writing appears or is forthcoming in *Critical Inquiry* and *American Anthropologist*.

Mel Y. Chen is associate professor of gender and women's studies and director for the Center for the Study of Sexual Culture at the University of California, Berkeley. Since their 2012 book, *Animacies: Biopolitics, Racial Mattering, and Queer Affect* (Duke University Press), Chen's current project concerns intoxication's role in the interanimation of race and disability. Elsewhere, Chen has been thinking about and writing on slowness, gesture, inhumanisms, and cognitive disability and method. Chen coedits the "Anima" book series at Duke and is part of a small and sustaining queer-trans of color arts collective in the San Francisco Bay Area.

Jih-Fei Cheng is an assistant professor of feminist, gender, and sexuality studies at Scripps College. He has worked in HIV/AIDS social services, managed a cultural center, been involved in media production and curation, and participated in queer and trans of color grassroots organizations in Los Angeles and New York City. Cheng's research examines the intersections between science, media, surveillance, and social movements. His first book manuscript tracks how the experimental videos of feminist and queer of color AIDS activists produced during the US early crisis years (1980s to early 1990s) continue to intervene into contemporary popular media, scientific conceptions, and social movements. Cheng's published writings appear in *Amerasia Journal*; *Catalyst: Feminism, Theory, Technoscience*; and *Women's Studies Quarterly*, among others.

Oliver Coates is a college supervisor in history at Cambridge University and an associate researcher at Institut des mondes africains, CNRS, Paris. His research focuses on West African society and culture, and has been published in *Research in African Literatures*, *Journal of African Cultural Studies*, and *History in Africa*.

Cathy J. Cohen is the David and Mary Winton Green Professor of Political Science and former chair of the department. She has served as the deputy provost for graduate education and is the former director of the Center for the Study of Race, Politics, and Culture at the University of Chicago. Cohen is the author of two books, *Democracy Remixed: Black Youth and the Future of American Politics* (Oxford University Press, 2010) and *The Boundaries of Blackness: AIDS and the Breakdown of Black Politics* (University of Chicago Press, 1999), and coeditor with Kathleen Jones and Joan Tronto of *Women Transforming Politics: An Alternative Reader* (New York University Press, 1997). Her work has been published in numerous journals and edited volumes including the *American Political Science Review*, *GLQ*, *NOMOS*, and *Social Text*. Cohen is principal investigator of two major projects: The Black Youth Project and the Mobilization, Change and Political and Civic Engagement Project. Her general field of specialization is American politics, although her research interests include African American politics, women and politics, lesbian and gay politics, and social movements.

Rachel Corbman is a doctoral candidate in women's, gender, and sexuality studies at Stony Brook University. Her dissertation, "Conferencing on the Edge: A Queer History of Feminist Field Formation, 1969–1989," is a history of the acrimonious feminist conflicts over women's studies and gay and lesbian studies in the 1970s and 1980s.

Carolyn Dinshaw, Dean for the Humanities and Silver Professor of Social and Cultural Analysis and English at New York University, is founding coeditor (with David M. Halperin) of *GLQ*. For their work on the journal they received the Distinguished Editor Award from the *Council of Editors of Learned Journals* in 2006.

Allen Durgin, PhD, teaches writing at Columbia University in the City of New York and is a course director of University Writing: Readings in Gender and Sexuality.

Elizabeth Freeman is professor of English at the University of California, Davis, and former coeditor of GLQ (2011–17). She is the author of *The Wedding Complex: Forms of Belonging in Modern American Culture* (2002) and *Time Binds: Queer Temporalities, Queer Histories* (2010), both published by Duke University Press.

John S. Garrison is an associate professor in the Department of English at Grinnell College. He is author of *Friendship and Queer Theory in the Renaissance* (Routledge, 2014), *Glass* (Bloomsbury, 2015), and *Shakespeare and the Afterlife* (Oxford University Press, 2018), as well as coeditor of *Sexuality and Memory in Early Modern England: Literature and the Erotics of Recollection* (Routledge, 2015) and *Making Milton: Writing, Publication, Reception* (Oxford University Press, 2019).

Julian Gill-Peterson is assistant professor of English and gender, sexuality, and women's studies at the University of Pittsburgh. They are author of *Histories of the Transgender Child* (University of Minnesota Press, 2018) and coeditor of "The Child Now," a special issue of *GLQ* (2016).

Chase Gregory is a PhD candidate in the Program in Literature and the Program in Gender, Sexuality, and Feminist Studies at Duke University.

Sarah Haley is an associate professor of gender studies and African American studies at UCLA. She is the author of *No Mercy Here: Gender, Punishment, and the Making of Jim Crow Modernity* (University of North Carolina Press, 2016).

David M. Halperin is the W. H. Auden Distinguished University Professor of the History and Theory of Sexuality at the University of Michigan, where he is also a professor of English and women's studies. He is the author or editor of ten books, including *One Hundred Years of Homosexuality* (Routledge, 1990), *The Lesbian and Gay Studies Reader* (Routledge, 1993), *Saint Foucault* (Oxford University Press, 1995), *What Do Gay Men Want?* (University of Michigan Press, 2007, 2009), *Gay Shame* (University of Chicago Press, 2009), *How to Be Gay* (Belknap/ Harvard University Press, 2012), and *The War on Sex* (Duke University Press, 2017). He cofounded *GLQ: A Journal of Lesbian and Gay Studies*, which he coedited from 1991 to 2005.

Christina B. Hanhardt is associate professor in the Department of American Studies at the University of Maryland, College Park. She is the author of *Safe Space: Gay Neighborhood History and the Politics of Violence* (Duke University Press, 2013), which won the 2014 Lambda Literary Award for Best Book in LGBT Studies.

Scott Herring is James H. Rudy Professor of English at Indiana University. He is the author, most recently, of *The Hoarders: Material Deviance in Modern American Culture* (University of Chicago Press, 2014).

Heather Love teaches English and gender studies at the University of Pennsylvania. She is the author of *Feeling Backward: Loss and the Politics of Queer History* (Harvard University Press, 2009), the editor of a special issue of *GLQ* on Gayle Rubin ("Rethinking Sex"), and the coeditor of a special issue of *Representations* ("Description across Disciplines"). Love has written on topics including comparative social stigma, compulsory happiness, transgender fiction, spinster aesthetics, reading methods in literary studies, and the history of deviance studies.

Dana Luciano is associate professor of English at Rutgers University, where she teaches courses in queer studies, environmental humanities, and nineteenth-century American literature. Recent work includes "Queer Inhumanisms," a special issue of *GLQ: A Journal of Gay and Lesbian Studies*, coedited with Mel Y. Chen (June 2015) and *Unsettled States: Nineteenth-Century American Literary Studies* (New York University Press, 2014), coedited with Ivy G. Wilson.

Whitney Monaghan is an assistant lecturer in film and screen studies at Monash University. Her background is in screen, media, and cultural studies and her research examines queer screen media. She is the author of *Queer Girls, Temporality and Screen Media: Not "Just a Phase"* (Palgrave Macmillan, 2016).

John Petrus is an assistant professor of Spanish at Grinnell College. His research focuses on Latinx intimate narratives of the HIV/AIDS crisis.

Elliott H. Powell is assistant professor in the Department of American Studies at the University of Minnesota. His research sits at the intersections of race, sexuality, and popular music. Recent publications appear or are forthcoming in *philoSOPHIA: A Journal of Continental Feminism*, *The Black Scholar*, the *Oxford Handbook of Hip Hop Studies*, and other venues.

Nic John Ramos is the Mellon Postdoctoral Fellow of Race in Science and Medicine at Brown University. He received his PhD in the Department of American Studies and Ethnicity at the University of Southern California in 2017. His research examines the role reproductive politics played in sustaining the exclusion and management of poor and queer people of color in post-1965 health institutions originally designed to alleviate poverty.

Chandan Reddy is associate professor of gender, women, and sexuality studies and the Program for the Comparative History of Ideas at the University of Washington, Seattle, where he teaches courses on racial capitalism, settler and overseas colonialism, sexuality, and US modernity. He is coeditor (with Jodi Byrd, Alyosha Goldstein, and Jodi Melamed) of the *Social Text* special issue "Economies of Dispossession: Indigeneity, Race, Capitalism" (June 2018). His book *Freedom with Violence: Race, Sexuality, and the US State* (2011) from Duke University Press won the Alan Bray Memorial award for Queer studies from the MLA as well as the Best Book in Cultural Studies from the Asian American Studies Association, both in 2013. He is currently at work on a new book project titled "Administrating Racial Capitalism."

Richard T. Rodríguez is associate professor of media and cultural studies at the University of California, Riverside. The author of *Next of Kin: The Family in Chicano/a Cultural Politics* (Duke University Press, 2009), he is at work on two projects: "Undocumented Desires: Film Fantasies of Latino Male Sexuality" and "Latino/U.K.: Postpunk's Transatlantic Touches."

Nayan Shah is professor of American studies and ethnicity and history at the University of Southern California. He is the author of *Stranger Intimacy: Contesting Race, Sexuality, and the Law in the North American West* (University of California Press, 2011) and *Contagious Divides: Epidemics and Race in San Francisco's Chinatown* (University of California Press, 2001). Shah was coeditor of *GLQ: A Journal of Lesbian and Gay Studies* from 2011 to 2014.

Stephanie Anne Shelton is assistant professor of qualitative research in the College of Education at the University of Alabama. Her research interests include queer and feminist approaches to qualitative inquiry and examining intersections of genders and sexualities with other identity elements, especially in secondary education. Recent publications have appeared in *Sex Education*, *Journal of Black Sexuality and Relationships*, *Journal of Language and Literacy Education*, *Qualitative Inquiry*, and *Teaching and Teacher Education*.

C. Riley Snorton is professor of English and gender and sexuality studies at the University of Chicago. He is the author of *Black on Both Sides: A Racial History of Trans Identity* (University of Minnesota Press, 2017) and *Nobody Is Supposed to Know: Black Sexuality on the Down Low* (University of Minnesota Press, 2014).

Ragini Tharoor Srinivasan is assistant professor of English and social, cultural, and critical theory at the University of Arizona. Her essays on contemporary literature, postcolonial and feminist theory, and Indian globalization may be found in a range of venues, including *ARIEL*, *The Comparatist*, *Interventions*, *Qui Parle*, *Verge*, *Women and Performance*, and the *Oxford Research Encyclopedia*. Srinivasan is also an award-winning journalist and former magazine editor, with bylines in international publications including the *New Yorker* online, *Public Books*, *Los Angeles Review of Books*, the *Caravan*, *Guernica*, and *Himal Southasian*. More information is available from www.raginitharoorsrinivasan.com.

L. H. Stallings is professor of women's studies at Georgetown University. She is the author of *Mutha Is Half a Word! Intersections of Folklore, Vernacular, Myth, and Queerness in Black Female Culture* (Ohio State University Press, 2007). Her second book, *Funk the Erotic: Transaesthetics and Black Sexual Cultures* (University of Illinois Press, 2015), explores how black sexual cultures produce radical ideologies about labor, community, art, and sexuality. It has received the Alan Bray Memorial Award from the MLA GL/Q Caucus and the 2016 Emily Toth Award for Best Single Work by One or More Authors in Women's Studies from the Popular

Culture Association/American Culture Association (PCA/ACA). It was also a 2016 finalist for the Twenty-Eighth Annual Lambda Literary Awards for LGBT studies.

Susan Stryker is an associate professor of gender and women's studies at the University of Arizona and founding coeditor of *TSQ: Transgender Studies Quarterly*.

Omise'eke N. Tinsley is associate professor of African and African diaspora studies and associate director of the Center for Women's and Gender Studies at the University of Texas, Austin. Her research focuses on queer and feminist, Caribbean, and African American performance and literature. In November 2018, University of Texas Press will release her *Beyoncé in Formation: Remixing Black Feminism*, a black femme-inist reading of Beyoncé's *Lemonade*. Her recently published second monograph, *Ezili's Mirrors: Black Queer Genders and the Work of the Imagination* (Duke University Press, 2018), explores spirituality and sexuality in twenty-first-century black queer literature, dance, music, and film from the Caribbean and African North America. In addition to *Thiefing Sugar: Eroticism between Women in Caribbean Literature* (Duke University Press, 2010), she has published articles in journals including *GLQ*, *TSQ*, *Feminist Studies*, *Yale French Studies*, and *Small Axe*.

Karen Tongson is associate professor of English, gender and sexuality studies, and American studies and ethnicity at the University of Southern California. She is the author of *Relocations: Queer Suburban Imaginaries* (New York University Press, 2011) and the forthcoming *Why Karen Carpenter Matters* (ForeEdge). She also has two books in progress: "Empty Orchestra: Karaoke, Queer Performance, Queer Theory" (Duke University Press) and "NORMPORN: Queer TV Spectatorship after the 'New Normalcy.'" Postmillennial Pop, the award-winning book series she coedits with Henry Jenkins at NYU Press, has published over fifteen titles. You can also hear Karen talk about pop culture, the arts, and entertainment on the weekly Pop Rocket Podcast, hosted by Guy Branum.

Salvador Vidal-Ortiz is an associate professor of sociology at American University in Washington, DC. He has coedited two books in English, *The Sexuality of Migration: Border Crossings and Mexican Immigrant Men* (New York University Press, 2009) and *Queer Brown Voices: Personal Narratives of Latina/o LGBT Activism* (University of Texas Press, 2015), and coauthored *Race and Sexuality* (Polity Press, 2018). In Spanish, he coedited *Travar el Saber*, or "Trans-ing Knowledge," based on narratives of trans and *travesti* people completing their high school degrees and attending college in Argentina (*Universidad Nacional de La Plata*, 2018). He continues work on his *Santería* manuscript, tentatively titled "An Instrument of the Orishas: Racialized Sexual Minorities in Santería."

Rachel Walerstein is a doctoral candidate (ABD) at the University of Iowa in the Department of English. Her research interests are in masculinity studies, queer theory, affect studies, and nineteenth- and twentieth-century American literature. She is currently at work on her dissertation, "Masculine Gestures: On Imitation and Initiation in Modernism."

Mary Zaborskis is a postdoctoral fellow in the Humanities Center at the University of Pittsburgh. Her current book project explores productions of queer childhood in nineteenth- and twentieth-century boarding schools established for racialized, criminalized, and disabled children. Her work has appeared in *GLQ*, *WSQ*, and *Journal of Homosexuality*, and she is a contributing editor at *Public Books*.

DOI 10.1215/10642684-7275731

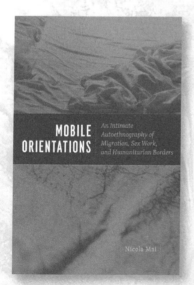
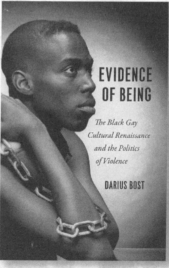

Looking for new ideas for teaching twenty-first-century literature?

Approaches to Bechdel's *Fun Home*

Edited by Judith Kegan Gardiner
Afterword by Alison Bechdel

"A valuable, thoughtful, and broadly engaged set of essays that will inform the teaching of *Fun Home* across a number of levels: late high school, undergraduate, and graduate."

—Jane Tolmie
Queen's University

Alison Bechdel's *Fun Home: A Family Tragicomic* has quickly joined the ranks of celebrated literary graphic novels. Set in part at a family-run funeral home, the book explores Alison's complicated relationship with her father, a closeted gay man. Amid the tensions of her home life, Alison discovers her own lesbian sexuality and her talent for drawing.

Approaches to Teaching
Bechdel's

Fun Home

Edited by Judith Kegan Gardiner

AFTERWORD BY *Alison Bechdel*

November 2018 • 204 pp.
Cloth $40.00 $32.00 with promo code
Paper $24.00 $19.20 with promo code
Also available in e-book formats.

Modern
Language
Association | **MLA**

bookorders@mla.org ■ www.mla.org/books ■ phone orders 646 576-5161

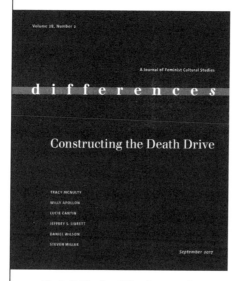

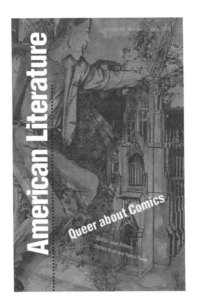